£2-00

GW01454334

HAWKESEYE

HAWKESEYE

The Early Life of Christopher Hawkes

DIANA BONAKIS WEBSTER

ALAN SUTTON

First published in the United Kingdom in 1991 by
Alan Sutton Publishing Ltd · Far Thrupp · Stroud · Gloucestershire

First published in the United States of America in 1991 by
Alan Sutton Publishing Inc. · Wolfeboro Falls · NH 03896–0848

Copyright © Diana Bonakis Webster 1991

All rights reserved. No part of this publication may be reproduced,
stored in a retrieval system, or transmitted, in any form, or by any
means, electronic, mechanical, photocopying, recording or otherwise,
without the prior permission of the publishers and copyright holders.

British Library Cataloguing in Publication Data

Webster, Diana Bonakis
Hawkeseye: the early life of Christopher Hawkes.
1. Archaeology. Hawkes, C.F.C. (Charles Francis Christopher)
I. Title
930.1092

ISBN 0-86299-882-6

Library of Congress Cataloging in Publication Data

Webster, Diana Bonakis.
   Hawkeseye: the early life of Christopher Hawkes / Diana Bonakis
Webster.
   Includes bibliographical references.
   1. Hawkes, C.F.C. (Charles Francis Christopher), 1905–
2. Archaeologists–Great Britain–Biography. 3. Archaeology–Great
Britain–History–20th century. 4. Archaeology–Europe–History–20th
century. I. Title.
CC115.H39W33   1991
941.082′092–dc20
[B]   90–24585
                                                                CIP

Typeset in 11/12 Melior.
Typesetting and origination by
Alan Sutton Publishing Limited.
Printed in Great Britain by
The Bath Press.

To and for Christopher

Christopher Hawkes
November 1987.

Pencil drawing of Christopher Hawkes by Diana Bonakis Webster

CONTENTS

LIST OF ILLUSTRATIONS

Jacket and frontispiece:
Pencil drawing of Christopher Hawkes by Diana Bonakis Webster,
November 1987

PLATES

FIGURES

ACKNOWLEDGEMENTS

First of all I must thank the subject of this book. Christopher's remarkable memory and infinite patience with thousands of questions made it not only possible, but immensely enjoyable for me to record his early life.

My thanks are also due to his wife Sonia, whose idea it was in the first place that I should write the book, for allowing me the house keys and full access to the marvellous archive from which I was able to select the illustrations and take home letters and documents to read; and for her most generous contribution towards the cost of copying the photographs.

I am grateful, too, for Jacquetta's kindness, and for her help and advice with those chapters which concern her and her father; and Jacquetta and Christopher's son Nicolas for answering my questions with such tact and candour.

To Christopher's cousin, Mrs Joan Lampen, I owe the beautiful photograph of Aunt Helen, and my thanks for her hospitality and help with the early years at Backwell; and I would like to thank Mrs Ruth van Heyningen for the photograph of the portrait of Sir Frederick Gowland Hopkins (Pl. 56) which was given to her late husband by Sir Frederick. This photograph is reproduced by kind permission of the President and Council of the Royal Society. The fine photographs of Wheeler (Pl.29), O.G.S. Crawford (Pl. 20), J.P. Williams Freeman (Pl. 31) and Heywood Sumner (Pl. 32) are reproduced by courtesy of the Oxford University Institute of Archaeology, which holds the Crawford collection. I would also like to thank Miss Tessa Dunning for the photograph of her father (Pl. 43); Professor Stuart Piggott for the portrait of Gerhard Bersu by Irwin Scollar (Pl. 53); Mr John Hopkins, formerly Librarian of the Society of Antiquaries of London, for allowing me to make copies of sections of the group photograph taken during the International Prehistoric Congress in 1932 for the Society of Antiquaries (Pls. 49–51); and Mr Paolo Scremin for his skill in creating publishable photographs from a series of tiny and often badly faded prints.

I am indebted to the following for permission to quote passages from published works:

Barrie & Jenkins Ltd for *Portrait of Barrie* by Cynthia Asquith; the author and Chatto & Windus for *A Quest of Love* by Jacquetta Hawkes; Harper Collins Ltd for *Edward VII Prince and King* by Giles St Aubyn;

Mr Charles Daniels for the two extracts from *Handbook of the Roman Wall* by J. Collingwood Bruce, 13th edition, edited and enlarged by Charles M. Daniels (Harold Hill & Son, Newcastle upon Tyne, 1978); Faber & Faber for *Gallipoli, the Fading Vision* by John North, first published in 1936, reprinted in 1966; the author for *Prehistorian: A Biography of V. Gordon Childe* by Sally Green, published by Moonraker Press; Hamish Hamilton Ltd for the paragraph taken from p. 302 of *George: An Early Autobiography* by Emlyn Williams (1961); Harvard University Press, Cambridge, Mass., for *Memories 1898–1939* by C.M. Bowra, copyright © 1966; the author's estate for *Over the Bridge* by Richard Church, published by William Heinemann; Methuen & Co. for *The Prehistoric Foundations of Europe* by C.F.C. Hawkes; John Murray for *Another Part of the Wood* by Kenneth Clark; Oxford University Press for *New College, Oxford, and its Buildings* by A.H. Smith, *Rendall of Winchester: The Life and Witness of a Teacher* by J.d'E. Firth, and *OUDS: The Centenary History of the Oxford University Dramatic Society* by Humphrey Carpenter; Alan Sutton Publishing for *My Life in Archaeology* by C.W. Phillips. The extracts taken from *Memories* by Julian Huxley, and *J.R.R. Tolkien: A Biography* by Humphrey Carpenter © 1977 are reproduced by kind permission of Unwin Hyman Ltd and Houghton Mifflin Co. I am indebted to the author for permission to quote from *Man on Earth* by Jacquetta Hawkes, published by the Cresset Press, and *Mortimer Wheeler: An Adventurer in Archaeology* by Jacquetta Hawkes, published by Weidenfeld & Nicolson, to whom I am also grateful for permission to reproduce passages from *Said and Done* by O.G.S. Crawford (1955). The two extracts from *Gallipoli* by John Masefield, published by William Heinemann, are reproduced by kind permission of the Society of Authors as literary representative of the estate of John Masefield; and I am indebted to Michael Wheeler QC for his permission to quote from *Still Digging* by Mortimer Wheeler, published by Michael Joseph.

My thanks are also due to the following for advice and help: Lady Daphne Grierson for correcting a section of Chapter 8; Professor Maurice Hugh-Jones for his invaluable recollections of Winchester and for many happy hours of amusing conversation; Professor Sheppard Frere for his great kindness, hospitality and advice; Dr Eric Stone for talking to me at Keble College; Professor Martin Aitken and Mrs Joan Aitken for their hospitality and for talking to me about Oxford; Miss Beatrice de Cardi for giving me valuable information and copies of documents; Dr Howard Kilbride-Jones for his memories of Gordon Childe; Mr Leslie Grinsell for his early memories of Christopher; the late Sir Foliot Sandford for the excerpt from the unpublished papers of G.L. Cheesman; Lady Antonia Fraser for her hospitality and advice, and for helping me to visit Christopher's old home in Campden Hill Square; and Mr and Mrs George Thomas, whose home it now is, for allowing me to wander all over the house, taking measurements and photographs; Mr Robert Medley, for his childhood memories of the Square; the late Mr John Brailsford for talking to me about Tom Kendrick; Dr Miranda Green and Dr Stephen Green, Dr Martin Henig, Miss Jocelyn Morris, Dr Thomas Blagg and Dr Roger White and Mrs Margaret Brown, who all provided valuable information for the book, and Dr Roger Tomlin for suggesting its title.

Finally I would like to thank Miss Deborah Loven for helping with research and for nobly correcting proofs, and my husband Dr Graham Webster, whose encouragement and support throughout have been incalculable.

DBW
Chesterton, September 1990

1 Prologue

It is beginning to get dark. Cracked paving slabs, lustrous with rain, reflect the traffic as it edges its way home at half-past four. White painted railings, minus a couple of spikes, enclose a small paved garden. Beneath a white door, with its simple fanlight, are two steep stone steps, discreetly disadvantaging the visitor. Those confident of entry may stand squarely at the top. Others, less so, will hover at a distance on the tiled path uneasily regarding the flower bed, now jammed like a bus queue with an inordinate display of early crocus.

Eventually the door opens. One sees first a pair of grey-blue eyes of the most unnerving and luminous intensity. Even their colour provides some measure of disagreement, since on his passport they are described as grey-green, and he himself denies that they are blue. But that is how they seem. Christopher Hawkes is rather short-sighted. He has worn glasses from the age of six, and latterly his vision has been further

19 and 20 Walton Street, Oxford. Photograph by Sonia Hawkes

impaired by cataracts; yet he gives the distinct impression of seeing all things with inerrant clarity.

His build is slight. At eighty-two, now hampered by arthritis – his stick is always with him – if he feels impatience with a lack of mobility, it seldom shows. His colouring betrays a partly Spanish ancestry (from his maternal grandmother); dark skin and once dark hair, now white, and a nose which is characteristically Moorish. He has an engagingly crooked smile; laughs readily, and possesses an acute sense of the ridiculous. Fiercely intelligent and quick-witted, he can at times be impatient, particularly with incompetence. Impulsive, argumentative, stubborn, and, infuriatingly, usually right; he runs on the basic principle of attack being by far the surest method of defence. Swift-tempered: as with a cat playing, one senses when it's prudent to withdraw. This animal has claws! He doesn't trust easily, and is inclined to be secretive, especially about his health, often bearing considerable discomfort without complaint. He is intensely loyal, sometimes talks too much, but his often disconcertingly feminine intuition makes him serenely comforting to anyone distressed. For all the sharper aspects of his character, he is a compassionate and gentle man.

On 14 January 1932, a young assistant keeper in the Department of British and Medieval Antiquities in the British Museum was elected Fellow of the Society of Antiquaries of London. The election was reported, by post, in the usual manner, to all the fellows; and one of them, the Borough Librarian of Wigan, who was a keen amateur genealogist, wrote him a letter. The librarian's name was Arthur J. Hawkes. In congratulating a presumed kinsman, he informed him that the Hawkes family came originally from Warwickshire. They were known to be farming at Stoneleigh during the reign of Charles II, at which time a branch took lands in Ireland.

Both Christopher's father, Charles Pascoe Hawkes, and his uncle Frank had done some research into the origins of the family. A correspondence, in 1912, with the Clerk of the Peace in Marlborough, yielded a copy of the tables of descent of a certain John Hawkes, who was living at Ogbourne St Andrew in Wiltshire in the early part of the seventeenth century. His son and grandson both bore the name of Samuel. It was a friend of Charles Pascoe (Christopher's father) who shared an interest in such matters who had discovered an old iron fireback which had been made from a memorial plate to one Samuel Hawkes of Birmingham in the eighteenth century. He followed it up, thereby producing this Wiltshire connection, which in turn led back to Birmingham in the name of Sara Hawkes, who was living there between 1755 and 1820. Not long after this, there were two brothers, William and Timothy Hawkes, who became joint masters of the Eagle Iron Foundry in Birmingham. William, who was born in about 1800, was described by the labour champion G.J. Holyoake, who was employed at the foundry,

Charles Samuel Hawkes

Frances West Richards

as a brutal and tyrannical man; an ugly-faced redhead who was the terror of his workmen.[1]

In June 1824 William opened a barrow at Oldbury, near Atherstone, which he dug with the young M.H. Bloxham,[2] who published it in Charles Roach Smith's *Collectanea Antiqua*.[3] The finds, which included Bronze Age pots and urns, and a bronze knife-dagger, passed with Bloxham's collection to the County Museum at Warwick, where they still are.

After an early marriage to a cousin, who died very soon after, Charles Samuel (Christopher's paternal grandfather) had a violent quarrel with his family, and went off to South America, where he established a successful engineering business, building railways in Brazil and the Argentine. He went into partnership with Charles Shaw (the company being named Shaw and Hawkes), but the relationship between the two must have been rather stormy. After Charles Samuel died in January 1898, his eldest son, Frank, received a letter from Shaw:

> I must report my condolence to you, and sorrow on the death of your father. I much regret that I was not informed of his illness; as had I known of it, I should have gone to see him. His sudden estrangement with myself and my family has been incomprehensible. I know of no cause or reason consequent on this. I know little of you, in fact. . . .

But he signs the letter with affection, and clearly the rift was not of his making.

Despite a fiery temperament Charles Samuel must have been a shrewd and skilful businessman, for he made a considerable fortune.

In the late 1860s he returned from Rio, and presumably was reunited with his family. He maintained his connections with the iron foundry, while still running the business, with a manager, in South America. He made one final visit to Rio in September 1876. Whittle, the manager, had died suddenly, and Charles Samuel had to take over the running of the company until a replacement could be sent out from England. This must have been Charles Neate, whom Christopher remembered as a boy (before 1914) once visiting his father, who introduced him to the handsome grey-bearded old gentleman.

In a letter to his wife Charles Samuel observed that 'the whole place is much altered since I was there and very much improved and embellished'.

When he returned from Rio, near the end of the 1860s, after his first long stay there, he met and married Frances, the daughter of a Birmingham businessman, J.P. Richards. Frances, or Fannie as she was always called, was a very pretty blonde girl 'of an excitable and impulsive temperament'.[4] She was much more sensitive and practical than her sisters, especially Harriet, who seems to have been a bit of a handful, judging by the letter, of which only the middle part survives, which the latter wrote during a visit to Oxford in 1868: She was staying with her brother Wilfred, who was in his second year at Exeter College:

> ... Wilfred and two other men came for us at 11 o'clock with a four-in-hand, and drove us down to Blenheim and Woodstock. There was such a jolly fellow, an Irishman, Larry Doonan of Worcester [College], and I flirted to my heart's content. I gave him some forget-me-nots, which he put into his prayer book in Worcester Chapel, and he says he shall keep them till we meet again.
>
> Wednesday we got up early, and while we were sitting at the breakfast table, looking at our tea, which no one seemed inclined to drink, Wilfred came dashing upstairs, and quickly began to remove the cups away on to the sideboard, brought out the brandy and asked for soda water. ...

Harriet's father, who was with her on this occasion, wrote a long letter to Fannie, giving her a fuller description of events:

> The party arrived in time for the 'Boat Show' and on the same night they went to the ball at Christ Church, at which, of course, Florence (another daughter) and Harriet were in the highest state of feminine excitement.[5]

The following day Wilfred gave a luncheon party in his rooms at Exeter. His father continues:

> The rooms were decorated with paintings, Persian rugs and objects de vertu, contributed by all his college friends. The tables were all decked out, and the Rector gave the use of the service of College plate. Every guest had a sprig of hot-house flowers laid upon the table-napkin. The whole thing was absolutely perfect. All night long the rooms were open to all; and when I arrived at 9 o'clock on the Monday morning, I found the Banqueting Hall deserted, with the doors wide open to the Quad and bottles, glasses, flowers and empty wine jugs scattered in a state of confusion. In the bedroom your poor brother was lying over his bed, undressed and unconscious, looking a complete wreck.

Frances also made several visits to Oxford, keeping poor Charles Samuel in a state of constant anxiety for her safety:

> I hope you enjoyed your excursion yesterday, but I am haunted with continual apprehension about these boating voyages on the river; and I hope you will refrain from them, at least until I can come and take care of you. Accidents so often occur. ...

They were married in 1868. Shortly after the wedding he was preparing the house he had bought, St Alban's House, in Edgbaston, with great concern that everything should be entirely pleasing to her:

> The prospect of a few days in London at this season used to fill me with pleasurable anticipation; but I find now that I can feel no enjoyment without you. It is in the most attractive scenes that I most miss the bright little face. Therefore the opera, the Row and other pleasing sights will be wasted upon me this time.

Their first child, Francis Samuel (Frank) was born two years later on 23 January 1870, quickly followed by two girls, Mabel Cecilia (Cissie) and Mary Elizabeth, who was always known as May from her birthday on May Day 1874.

Two years later Fannie received a letter from her mother, who was staying at Ventnor in the Isle of Wight, where the family had a house:

> I dreaded your hearing the sad news, lest it might do you injury, and I thank God that you have borne it tolerably. NOW you understand my short, cold-seeming, uninteresting letters! I did not dare to tell you of my own darling's suffering. . . .

Wilfred had died of consumption.

> I have been looking at his sweet face; and it seems to me that much of his early beauty has returned. So pure, so delicate. His beautiful dark eyebrows, his eyes closed in dying. There was no sign of pain. He was exhausted. The persistent cough wore him out; I never saw a consumptive patient until now.
>
> Think of us on Monday morning, Florence and I; we shall see him laid in the beautiful Carisbrooke cemetery. . . .

Poor Wilfred had been a model patient; never allowing his infirmity to destroy what his mother called his 'perfect gentlemanliness in all his habits'. Throughout the distressing final stages of his illness he maintained a dignity which seems to have affected his whole family.

It was in the September of that year that Charles Samuel had to go again to South America.

Both Fannie and her husband were highly strung and emotional. He was a poor sleeper, and clearly suffered from anxiety, as well as an increasing number of ailments. Fannie had a heart condition, probably angina, given her descriptions of her 'little heart attacks' and the constant and excruciating pain she had to endure.

By the late 1870s her beautiful handwriting had begun to deteriorate, although she still managed a weekly letter to her beloved Frankie, who was then at Shrewsbury School. Many of these letters are preserved, though only a few of his replies have survived.

Another son was born to them on 3 April 1877, Charles Pascoe,

Christopher's father. A little over a year later another boy was born. They named him Gilbert, but he was never baptized as the other children had been, for he died almost immediately.

Around this time Charles Samuel appears to have encountered financial difficulties, on top of the distress that they both felt with the death of the little boy. From the Imperial Hotel in Malvern, where he must have been staying on business, he wrote:

> You cannot imagine, my love, how distressed I feel at causing you so much trouble and disturbance: but it is because of my love for you and the other darlings that I am so racked with anxiety and care; and coming at a time when other troubles are hard to bear my mind is rather disorganised. I hope, if it please Providence, for this cloud to pass over, to make amends in our future life, though it will be in a humbler position.

The letter does not relate what mishap had befallen them, but one can infer another family argument, possibly over money. They sold the house in Edgbaston, and moved to Beckenham, where they named the house Stoneleigh on account of Charles Samuel's beginnings. Three more daughters were born to them, in Beckenham: Dorothy Ada in 1879, Katherine (Katie) in 1881, and Eleanor Louise (Lola) two years later. The children had a nurse named Fanny Wright, who lived to a great age, and was remembered by Christopher as a jolly old lady, in fearsome whalebone corsets that creaked, when taking tea in the nursery with his contrastingly young and pretty nanny Rosa Giles, in about 1910, when he was five years old.

Charles Samuel took his eldest son with him on several trips to the Continent, from where they would both send amusing letters to Fannie. In 1881 they went to Bordeaux, Poitiers, Tours, Orleans and Paris; and there were other trips, often to watering places in Germany in the forlorn pursuit of better health.

Charles Pascoe, in later life always known by his initials, was a rather weak child. Being so pale and thin, he caused his mother considerable anxiety; unlike the girls, who were all robust and high spirited, as indeed was Frankie. In one of her letters to him she described an incident that had occurred while C.P. was at the Abbey School in Beckenham:

> Poor Charles had a frightful wound just half an inch above his eye. One boy was throwing a wicket across the playground to another boy. Charlie did not notice it; and the point came with dreadful force against his head, and tore the flesh right off. One inch lower and it would have burst the eyeball. As it was, the bleeding was ghastly. He was taken to Dr Carpenter at once, and bandaged up; but it made him very, very poorly for several days after. He was so brave throughout the whole affair.

Although he was only nine years old at the time, this incident displays a characteristic forbearance and courage which was typical of C.P. His dogged good spirits in adversity, inherited by his son Christopher, were most notably demonstrated during the last world war. By then his health was already beginning to fail, but he served long hours as air raid warden for his home district in Kensington. There is a reference to 'a brave man, Colonel Hawkes' in the memoirs of Charles Morgan, who lived next door at 16 Campden Hill Square.[6]

After leaving the Abbey School at Beckenham, presumably around 1889, when he was twelve years old, Charles Pascoe went to Dulwich College. There are no letters or documents surviving from this period, but Richard Church[7] in his autobiography[8] describes the village as it was in the year of Christopher's birth, and one may presume that it had not changed dramatically during the sixteen years. Richard Church went to Dulwich Hamlet School, which was in the centre of the village. 'All the surrounding houses had large gardens, with hollyhocks and mulberry trees embraced by roses.' The whole village with its many ancient trees 'had the character of being abandoned at the bottom of a canyon, green in summer and brown in winter'.

The college was founded at the beginning of the seventeenth century by Edward Alleyn, who married the daughter of John Donne. In the terms of his will Alleyn had forbidden the cutting down of trees on the estate, so that at the turn of this century the village still retained its woodland atmosphere, and a 'sense of order and dignity that characterised and controlled the lush beauty of Dulwich village and its surrounding slopes'.[9]

With its 'queer terra-cotta buildings'[10] the college seemed very grand to a small boy peering through the railings at the boys playing rugby football: 'They had the appearance of mortals of a different incarnation; for we knew that they would go to Oxford or Cambridge, and in 1905 that distinction was almost a biological one.'[11]

Throughout 1887 Fannie's health continued to decline. She was treated by a physician from St Thomas's Hospital, but he could do little for her, and on 13 December she died. There is a pathetic little black edged letter written by one of her daughters, which includes a copy of Longfellow's 'Footsteps of Angels' and the following verse:

> Though ye see me not among you,
> Though I breathe not with your breath,
> The bond is still between us,
> And love outliveth death.

At the early age of seventeen, Charles Pascoe went up to Trinity College, Cambridge, in 1894. In an essay published much later he wrote:

My Cambridge days began on a glorious Autumn afternoon, when, a man at last, and captain of my soul and of a fancy waistcoat calculated to impress all beholders with the fact that its wearer was no longer a schoolboy; I leapt from my hansom at Trinity Gate. . . .[12]

He was met by a college servant or 'gyp' called Pottinger, who was tall and athletic, 'with a pale pompous face and little eyes which regarded one with a taciturn dignity beneath an incongruous top hat.'[13] Pottinger, it seems, had a problem:

> Drink was his secret sin. Indeed Pottinger was seldom sober, although the fact never seemed to interfere with the efficient discharge of his duties. He had the gift of being able to maintain a slightly pretentious perpendicular in any circumstances, and his voice was loyal to him, for he seldom spoke. No outward sign was visible of his inward and spirituous disgrace; and it was only when he was waiting at lunch or dinner that his careful corking of the decanters, and the stately futility of his efforts to fit glass stoppers into the necks of empty wine bottles exposed his hidden failings to the hitherto incredulous observer.[14]

C.P. had no 'gyp' of his own. After a term at 19 Trinity Street, he took rooms at 10 St John's Street (almost opposite Trinity Great Gate), which he shared with two friends, Harry Tanqueray and Tom Ingram, for the rest of his time at Cambridge. His skill with a pen was very quickly recognized, and he was soon contributing sketches and cartoons to the *Granta*, the undergraduate magazine. At the end of his first term he received an invitation to a dinner at the Reform Club, where he was splendidly placed between the two famous cartoonists Bernard Partridge[15]

Mr Punch. Drawing by C.P. Hawkes

and George du Maurier.[16] Although his ecstasy at being in such illustrious company almost rendered him speechless, both men were very kind. Partridge drew for him a sketch of George Bernard Shaw on his menu card which he kept to the end of his life. At the same dinner he was introduced to Sir John Tenniel[17] (who looked, he said, something like a retired cavalry officer), and at his suggestion C.P. submitted some drawings of 'the Sage of Bouverie Street' (Mr Punch) in various guises; which, after some corrections by Tenniel, appeared in *Punch* the following year (1896).

Throughout his life C.P. continued with his drawings, publishing a large number of them in various periodicals, and filling a great many albums with delightful pictures of his family and friends.

Not everyone, however, appreciated his impish humour. A cartoon published in the *Granta* in 1896 of the well-known history don at King's, Oscar Browning,[18] caused great offence. Although Browning was said to welcome caricatures as a tribute to his fame and popularity, he was curiously sensitive on certain personal points, and clearly he felt the young man had gone too far. He was depicted as a sort of leering Turkish or Balkan brigand, with his rotund figure emphasized by the fantastic uniform. After a year of cordiality, during which C.P. had enjoyed many of the social gatherings which were a regular Sunday

Oscar Browning ('O.B.') in Uniform. Drawing by C.P. Hawkes

evening feature during term, Browning cut him, and refused to speak to him again. It was not until many years later, when C.P. happened upon him, then an old man, in a London street, that Browning tendered a renewal of their early friendship.

Browning was something of a sybarite. His fine rooms in college were luxuriously furnished; and his hospitality was generous if somewhat unorthodox. There was always a spectacular array of unfamiliar food and drink; and as there were caskets of cigarettes on occasional tables all round the rooms, the air was constantly thick with smoke. In one corner of the room a perpetually hissing samovar ensured refreshment to those who did not wish to avail themselves of the inexhaustible supply of strong drink. Although many of the undergraduates mocked him for his vanity, Oscar Browning was a vital figure in the university life of his day.

Charles's tutor was A.W. Verrall,[19] who was regarded as something of an eccentric, with his hesitating, high-pitched voice, wispy beard and lanky figure. As a scholar he was stimulating, although he was considered by some to be not quite sound. He was shy and uneasy in the company of juniors; but at home his conversations on literature and great writers were both interesting and inspiring, and C.P. liked and respected him.

For the history tripos C.P. went to Lord Acton's lectures.[20] These occasions were always very well attended, for he was an immensely colourful character, a courtier and a cosmopolite who had met most of the prominent personalities in international affairs. 'It was as though one were listening to an ex-ambassador rather than a University professor,' C.P. wrote, 'with his trim frock coat, tiny varnished boots and slightly exotic beard, which did much to further the illusion.'

C.P.'s other recreation was considerably more energetic than drawing. He used to hunt with the Trinity Foot Beagles. There are photographs of him with a group of friends, resplendent in stiff straw boaters, sporting jackets (which were dark green), white knee-breeches and top boots. They were accompanied by a houseman wearing a velvet hunting cap. C.P. wrote: 'In matters of dress men were, on the whole, much more punctilious [than they were in 1922 when he published his essay]. Slovenliness was seldom tolerated further than the Norfolk jacket.'[21]

Oscar Browning, as a staunch humanitarian, greatly disapproved of hunting. He thought beagling was 'a concession to barbarism',[22] and this fact may well have contributed to Charles's fall from favour, since he would have doubly offended with his joint pursuits.

Several members of the Trinity Foot Beagles came from families in Northumberland, and during the long vacations the hounds were packed into a railway van and taken north to enjoy the wilder hunting of the open moorland. C.P. went with them, thus beginning a connection with the county which later brought him to join the Northumberland Fusiliers.

In 1898 C.P.'s father died. Charles Samuel had been ailing for some time, so that his death on 22 January came as no surprise. Among the many letters that his sons received came one from a friend of Frank's, Joe Ruston, who lived in Lincoln: 'I always remember with pleasure how hospitable and kind he was to any of your friends; and I think there can be nothing nicer for any man than to leave a pleasant memory with his friends.'

Charles decided to abandon his intention to take a fourth year after the part 2 history tripos, reading law. Frank was eager to marry, and C.P. elected to leave Cambridge, thus releasing much needed funds for his brother's impending marriage. We have a rather sad final glimpse of his life at Cambridge:

> Pottinger did me the honour of raising his hat in dignified valedictory salute on the last Wednesday morning of my final term. But it was Peat, another college servant, who supervised my going down. On the platform of Cambridge station his last words to me were these: 'Goodbye, Sir; you may take it from me that there's no such fun in front of you as what you're leaving 'ere!' And he was right.[23]

Scholars on a Bus. Drawing by C.P. Hawkes, 1896

The London that C.P. first knew, in the autumn of 1897, was, for him, a thoroughly enjoyable place to be in. 'On £400 a year', he says, 'the oyster of London's social world was open and generous!'[24] It still retained an essential character of its own. There were no big hotels outside of Northumberland Avenue, and entertaining on the grand scale was still confined to the town mansions: 'Shawled milk-women paraded the West End streets with cans suspended from shoulder yokes; and the scarlet jackets of shoe-blacks and scavenger boys brightened the street corners. . . .'[25]

The 'Piccadilly goat' had disappeared since it was immortalized by E.T. Reed[26] in *Punch* in 1890, but C.P. could remember once having seen 'the horned and bearded mystery, reputed to be of Patriarchal age, strolling sedately about the western portion of Piccadilly'.[27] This creature used to frequent the area steps of clubs and mansions, tapping with its horns on area doors to elicit offerings from kindly kitchen staff. It may well have been one of the goats that were kept in London earlier in the nineteenth century. If a fire broke out the goats had a calming effect on the panic-stricken horses, which allowed them to be led to safety.

C.P.'s first London home was a flat in Albert Hall Mansions; a massive red brick and white stone building in Kensington Gore, directly beside the Albert Hall. He lived there with his two elder sisters, Cissie and May, for three years until in 1900 he joined the chambers of Sir Hubert Stephen and Frank Mellors. He shared residential chambers next door at No. 5, with Frank Mellors's nephew, Gilbert.

There were three Stephen brothers: Harry, who later became an Indian judge, Hubert, and the brilliant J.K.S.,[28] who was a Fellow of King's College and personal tutor to Prince Albert Victor: his career was

The Earl of Birkenhead. Drawing by C.P. Hawkes

tragically cut short by a mental condition which had already begun to show itself while he was still at Cambridge. There are many stories about him and his capricious behaviour. He had a nasty habit of playfully peppering with revolver bullets any print or picture that might evoke his admiration in a friend's house. He often went about in stockinged feet, as he developed a curious aversion to boots and shoes; and he seldom carried money with him: a fact which often rendered him something of a liability to his companions on his frequent visits to the Café Royal. Hubert Stephen lived in De Vere Gardens in Kensington, where C.P. was to live briefly, after his marriage in 1904.

Although C.P. was aware that the most valuable period of a young barrister's practice is 'that which passes in the rough and tumble of the County Courts',[29] he found that work was not easily forthcoming on circuit, and he decided to devote himself to practice in London, in the Probate, Divorce and Admiralty Division, and to law reporting for *The Times*. In an essay published in 1925, he eloquently describes the duties of a court usher:

> Jurors are particularly his care. He hangs their hats and umbrellas upon the pegs like votive garments on a temple wall, and empanels their owners with the sombre gravity of a Familiar of the Holy Office: closing the jury box doors with a solemn bang, which is at once an admonition to impartiality and a consecration of their services.[30]

At the outbreak of the Boer War in 1899 C.P. joined what was known as the Provisional Battalion, which consisted of a pool of young officers who were trained at Shorncliffe Camp above the cliffs near Folkestone. These young officers were kept in reserve, without regimental commissions, in case they were needed in South Africa, but C.P. was never called.

In 1901, 'driven perhaps like most of my contemporaries by Dr Johnson's dictum that "every man thinks meanly of himself for not being a soldier" ', C.P. began importuning his friends and 'haunting the War Office in the hope of obtaining a commission'.[31]

His application to the Duke of Northumberland, whom he knew from his beagling visits to the north, secured him a commission in the County Militia, which was soon to become the 3rd Battalion of the Northumberland Fusiliers.

In those days militia commissions were issued by the sovereign on the recommendations of the Lord-Lieutenant of the county; and the Northumberland Militia had long been associated with the ducal house of Percy. The system then embodied the old constitutional principle that every citizen who was physically fit was bound, if called upon, to qualify himself for home defence, although in practice the ranks had largely been filled by voluntary enlistment. C.P. wrote:

> Before the South African War, incredible though it may seem, the

British Army, in training and organization, was essentially unprepared for active service.

Picture yourself a Company commander, lying on the reverse slope of a hill, with his men kneeling or sprawling in close formation on the summit. He has no map or field glasses, but a big flask and a bigger sandwich case; and the leaves of a motoring paper protrude from the mouth of his haversack. His colour-sergeant, somewhere on the right flank of the Company, rises, slopes arms smartly and marches along the skyline until he reaches his captain. He advances arms and salutes. He says, 'Beg pardon, Sir, the enemy are in sight on our right front.' To which the captain, without shifting his position, replies, 'All right, poop off at 'em!' and the N.C.O. departs to supervise the execution of that order. A pause. The subaltern next appears: his sword is drawn, and he salutes with it, producing an engaging heliographic effect visible for miles. Away marches the subaltern, while his still recumbent senior seeks distraction in his sandwich case and flask.

It was obvious that, in peace time at any rate, soldiering was an agreeable caste-profession, conferring an undoubted social cachet, and with daily work which could easily be accomplished between breakfast and lunch. The company and junior officers saw little of their men, except on parade; and the men spent most of their time either in the

Henry, 7th Duke of Northumberland. Drawing by C.P. Hawkes

Eleanor   Victoria   Cobb   aged
about eighteen.

canteen or in neighbouring public houses. They were ill-paid, they were
bored. So they drank, for there was nothing else to do. As for 'general
staff', there was no general staff.

In the South African War, however, there began the renaissance of the
British army. Apart from the complete reorganization of staff duties, the
cardinal changes were in training for the field. The officer became a
responsible instructor in every practical subject, in close contact with
the men who would follow him in action. Their welfare and conditions
were vastly improved, with the introduction of recreation and field
sports, for it was realized that boredom was one of the chief causes of
military crime.

In 1905 Haldane[32] was made war minister. He was a successful and
highly pacific Chancery Silk, whose knowledge of military matters was
negligible. However, he did have one great advantage. He was brilliant
at weighing up all the available evidence, and he was able to give
immediate and positive conclusions. It was his organization of the
Expeditionary Force which undoubtedly constituted the prime factor in
its success in the early years of the First World War. After the first battle
of Ypres, there was little of it left, so the fresh recruiting, and
'Kitchener's Army' battalions, took its place on a far bigger scale.

During the long vacations C.P. made a number of trips to the
Continent and to North Africa; and it was on one of these, in 1902 or
1903 that he met two sisters, Eleanor and Victoria Cobb, who were used
to travelling for holidays in Europe with their chaperon, a French lady

Charles Davison Cobb

named Mlle Antoinette Danton, or Maddie as she was affectionately called. Christopher said that the story his mother had told him was that the three of them were disembarking in the Canaries, when a polite young gentleman, a fellow-passenger (who must have been gazing at them during the voyage), came up and volunteered to help them with their luggage. He gained the approval of Mlle Danton, who encouraged him to see more of her two charges. Maddie had been their girlhood teacher, and was, at the time, a woman in her late thirties. Apart from the fact that as a girl of thirteen she had been in the siege of Paris in 1870, and by 1905 had no surviving relatives, little is known of her background. She was greatly attached to the two young women.

Eleanor Victoria Cobb was born on 18 March 1874. Her forebears were Kentish farmers who had turned to brewing in the eighteenth century; and with the presence of the fleet off shore in the Downs,[33] they did so well with their brewery at Margate that still early in the nineteenth century Frederick Cobb[34] was able to make the socially vital transition from trade to the professions. He became a doctor. He was interested in diet and nutrition, in what would now be called preventive medicine, and would take containers of milk puddings with him on his visits to poorer households.

He married Eleanor, the daughter of a wealthy brewer who had moved from Scotland, Henry Crawford Davison. They lived in some grandeur in a large and impressive house called Pierrepoint, at Frensham in Surrey. The youngest of their children, Charles Davison Cobb, was Christopher's grandfather. He was born on 6 October 1843. At the age of thirty he married a Spaniard, Victoria Duarte, whose father Don Demetrio was in business importing goods from Spain, notably sherry.

Aunt Vickie in the 1890s

Charles Davison, whose eldest brother Frederick became the manager of Sandeman's and moved over to the Portuguese side, joined the London office of the port shippers Cockburn and Smithes, eventually becoming a partner and its manager at offices in Mark Lane in the east of the city.

On 18 March 1874 Charles and Victoria's first child was born: a daughter, Eleanor. The following year Victoria died bearing her second daughter, who was named Victoria after her. The two little girls were cared for by their mother's sister Rosario (who was known to everyone as Aunt Rosie), until their father remarried in June 1877. His new wife came from a Manchester family: Clara Marriott had very blue eyes and blonde hair; and she was to bear Charles Davison six children.[35] In winter they lived in South Kensington, where they had a house in Cromwell Road; and in the summer they lived in Surrey, at Dye House, Thursley, which is near Hindhead. When the youngest child Hester was only seven years old the news of her father's sudden death broke the tranquillity of their childhood. He had been staying with friends at a country house in Scotland, and, having won a hard game of tennis, had leapt exuberantly over the net and caught his foot in it. He fell on his chin and broke his neck.

The two half-Spanish daughters, one already twenty-one, the other

Ellie in her wedding dress in 1904

twenty, were left with a considerable fortune[36] which enabled them to travel. They did this extensively, taking their beloved Maddie with them as their chaperon. So it was that as their boat put in at Las Palmas on one voyage they became acquainted with the young barrister, Charles Pascoe Hawkes. He and Eleanor were married in April 1904.

2 Childhood, 1905–12

After their marriage Charles Pascoe and Eleanor went to live in Kensington, at 35 De Vere Gardens, and it was there on 5 June the following year that their son was born, and named Charles Francis Christopher.

Within a matter of months, by the spring of 1906, the family were established on Campden Hill, the 'most westerly of London's seven unnoticed hills',[1] at 17 Campden Hill Square, which was to remain the family home until the end of the Second World War.

C.P.'s elder brother Frank, who was a solicitor, had married Helen Cashmore in 1897, at the Church of St Michael and all the Angels at Flax Bourton[2] in Somerset. At first the couple lived in London, not far from Campden Hill; but when it was discovered that they would always be childless, Helen persuaded her husband to take a practice in Bristol so that she might enjoy the company of her sisters, to whom she was very close. All but one of them were living, still unmarried, at their old home at Barrow Gurney. They took a house, Combe House, at Backwell, some seven miles west of Bristol; and in November 1905, when Christopher was just six months old, the first entry was made in a vellum-bound visitors' book.

This has survived, although a trifle battered, to give an eloquent account of a seemingly endless stream of visitors, and an often hilarious pageant of events which took place from that autumn till 1914, and after the war until the summer of 1920, when they moved to Hampshire. 'The Combe House Chronicle', as the book was called, bulges with photographs, drawings and newspaper cuttings; and of course there are C.P.'s marvellous cartoons. His drawing of the house itself, with the church behind, occupies the title page. It shows a pleasantly solid Georgian building, with five of the seven visible sash-windows wide open and welcoming, through an all-enveloping creeper that hugs the walls on every side from guttering to ground.

Christopher remembers the main rooms of the house being spacious and rather grand, although the rest of it was older and more 'cottagey'. In the drawing-room there was a grand piano; and what was even more appealing for a small boy, there was also a pianola, with a good collection of rolls. He developed a passion for one of them: the overture to Rossini's opera, *William Tell*; and he would steal in to play it over and over again, when the rest of the family was either out of earshot or out of the house altogether. But both Frank and Helen were extremely

Cover Drawing by C.P. Hawkes for 'The Combe House Chronicle', the visitors' book kept by Helen and Frank Hawkes

kind and tolerant, and for the most part his musical persistence went unchecked.

When he was a little older Christopher's extraordinary memory had supplied him with a fund of songs of which he was immensely proud. He would lustily deliver a selection of them after he had been put to bed, until his poor father would have to come upstairs to his room to shut him up. These bedtime recitals only became possible after the night nursery was partitioned to give him a bedroom of his own. His sister, Penelope, slept in the other part where Rosa also had her bed. Like many highly intelligent children Christopher demanded constant attention; and as Frank and Helen had no children, he was the first youngster in the whole family circle, and was perhaps indulged rather more than was good for him. Although one must add, in fairness, that C.P. and Ellie would certainly have disagreed with this. Christopher remembers more than once being laid firmly across his father's knee, and being given several smacks on the bottom with a slipper, in spite of Rosa's pleading for him to be spared.

Motoring was a novel and exciting feature in the lives of many of the visitors to Backwell. Helen's mother noted sheepishly in the visitor's book in January 1906, 'Sorry we made a "dimple" in the car . . .', and she was followed by another visiting enthusiast, John Brooke-Little:

> Better than beer, than tea, than gin,
> Better than whisky far,
> Better than all the joys of sin
> I love my motor-car![3]

In the same month (August) Amy Brooke-Little, his wife, paid tribute to Helen's efforts in the garden:

> The artist like a fairy works
> with wand of magic powers,
> In barren rocks she shows there lurks
> A paradise of flowers.

In 1909 C.P. took his family to France; and it is of Berneval-sur-Mer, a watering-place on the coast of Normandy, near Dieppe, that Christopher has his earliest memory:

There is a colour picture in my mind, very distant, but sharp in the colours. I can see the in-shore part of a sandy beach, and along the edge of it there are what I suppose must be dunes. And there are poppies growing, scarlet poppies, and I'd never seen poppies before!

He also remembers on board ship between Newhaven and Dieppe, Maddie saying to him: 'Look, the big, big sea. . . . *C'est la mer!*' He was brought up to speak French and English side by side, which suited a natural aptitude for languages which served him well in later life.

In April, and again in June the following year, the family were once more at Backwell; and in the summer they went north, taking Ellie's step-sister Madge with them. C.P.'s battalion was in training in Alnwick Park, and they stayed nearby at Alnmouth, the small seaside resort by the mouth of the Aln.

Madge had a bathing dress which made a distinct impression on the three-year old boy: 'It was dark navy blue, with long trousers and a kind of skirted tunic, with white piping round the edges; and with it she wore a bright orange rubber bathing-cap.' Aunt Madge lived to within a year of her 100th birthday, and Christopher confirmed with her on a visit just three months before her death, in 1983, that she had indeed worn such a garment. She was very surprised that he had remembered it. It was Madge who said with a smile, recalling those days, 'You were a *tempery* little boy, you know!'

When it rained and they were unable to go to the beach either his mother or Madge would read to him. One day, in order to show off to the landlady, he took a copy of Beatrix Potter's *Peter Rabbit*, which he already knew by heart, and pretended to read it, turning the pages at the appropriate moments, to the utter astonishment of the good lady, who gasped, 'How *can* he? He can't *read* . . . he must have lived before!' Very soon afterwards he could really read.

Life at Campden Hill Square must have been exceedingly pleasant in those years before the First World War. After it C.P. wrote many descriptions of life in London, giving an evocative and often beautiful glimpse of a world which he knew by then to be vanishing. Here is one such, of a summer evening in Campden Hill Square:

> In the star-strewn sky sombre and thickening clouds, driven by puffs of sultry wind, drift menacingly across the moon, like moods across the face of a woman on the verge of tears; and the air, tainted with the stifling exhalations of a London summer, is moist and oppressive with the threat of thunder. The square is still awake, as if reluctant to face the prospect of unrest through hours of sweltering darkness; and in the owl-light the architectural meanness of the drab brick houses is softened to a romantic indistinctness. Most of the lower windows are wide open, and here and there lounging figures, male and female, are sharply silhouetted against the bright orange of lighted interiors, from which ring out occasional crackles of talk and distant laughter. . . .
>
> The hours and the company grow smaller and smaller, until with a regretful yawn, the host turns out the lights, and leaves the drawing-room at last, smoke-wreathed and empty, in the chill, tired silence that precedes the dawn.[4]

Eleanor's sister Vickie came eventually to live at 16 Holland Street, and C.P. describes the house:

Christopher with his mother in August 1905

On the slopes of Campden Hill there stands a little street of small William and Mary houses, contemporaries of the neighbouring Palace; and perpetuating with the same suggestion that fragrant early 18th century atmosphere with which the relics of old Kensington still seem imbued. It leads out from a road of more pretentious modern residences, and seems after a distance of some fifty yards or so, to have lost heart as a thoroughfare; and with an old-maidish timidity to have shrunk to a mere passageway between two high walls of ancient rosy brick, overhung with spreading greenery. These are the garden walls of two of the old houses, which, encircled by their lawns and shrubberies, dotted with groups of elms and chestnut trees, make Campden Hill still rural, and soften to a distant droning the raucous clamour of the two great arteries of traffic which are its northern and southern boundaries. A tiny garden, set with bright-hued flowers, and intersected by an uneven red-brick path, separates the little house from the street. The neat front door, seldom seen open, and the six prim windows, the lowest barred, seem, however dull the day, always to reflect a demurely smiling sunshine. . . .[5]

As Christopher remembers it, the garden at 17 Campden Hill Square had a gravel path with a border of flowers on either side, edged next to the path with London Pride. At the far end of the garden was a circular lawn, and in the middle of this was a lead figure of a naked boy holding on his head a leaden basket in which flowers were planted. Copying a joke from his father, Christopher took to calling it 'the little stupid' (see the illustration on p. 230).

The nurseries were up on the third floor of the house, with the servants' bedrooms above them. The big room at the front was the night nursery; the day nursery, smaller, was at the back. The floor was covered with a kind of dark green felt; on top of this, pinned with brass headed tacks, was a drugget. Being a white hard-wearing linen or cotton cloth, it could be taken up and sent to the laundry, and so was ideal for children to play on.

In the wall of an inner corner of the room was the toy cupboard. All toys had to be put away tidily at bedtime. There were several bent-wood chairs, painted black, with yellow rush-matting seats, and a child's high chair. Hanging in the window was a birdcage with a canary in it, which sang most beautifully whenever the sun fell upon it. Beneath the cage stood a substantial wooden table, and in the corner, beside it, was a basket chair with a flowered cotton cover and cushions, where Nanny Giles would sit sewing or knitting. Rosa was a very pretty dark-haired young woman who came from Lambourn in Berkshire. She once took Christopher to see her family there, but he doesn't remember the visit. She wore long cotton dresses, with a white apron and a tight white belt, and, except in the warmer weather, she wore starched white collars. When they went for walks she wore a dark blue bonnet and cape, and she had a lovely big floppy straw hat in summer. She would take him on

The Hawkes family in the garden of Campden Hill Square in the winter of 1910

the southern slope of Campden Hill where the roads were very quiet; there was scarcely any traffic.

When he was four years old, in the September of 1909, Christopher was sent with Rosa to stay with his step-grandmother Clara at her house on Farnecombe Hill, near Godalming. His mother was nearing the end of her second pregnancy, and on 1 October a daughter was born. They called her Eleanor Frances Penelope. As with Christopher, it was the third name that was chosen, the first two being, in both cases, family names.

Grandmother Cobb (the former Clara Marriott, widow of Charles Davison Cobb) had very piercingly blue eyes, and, by that time, snow white hair. She wore the formal long-skirted Edwardian costume, and Christopher has one vivid memory of her then:

My father had instructed me carefully before going there that Grandmother was an old lady, and little boys should help old ladies whenever they can. She and I must have come out on to the landing at just the same moment, so I said to her; 'May I help you downstairs, Grandmother?' She stared at me, so I went on, 'Little boys should HELP old ladies . . . ' Manfully suppressing her laughter she allowed herself to be solemnly escorted downstairs, with me holding her

Aunt Helen, before the First World War

hand. We were met at the bottom by her two youngest daughters, Madge and Hester, who had been in the morning room; on being told what had happened they burst into peals of laughter, which I was very puzzled about, and didn't understand at all.

Clara wrote to his mother describing the occasion in great detail, and it was from her that Christopher later came to put words to what was otherwise a purely visual memory.

In 1910 the family spent a holiday at Lee on the North Devon coast. Rosa, of course, went with them, and she took both children (Penelope, ten months old, was of course in the pram) for walks along the magical Devon lanes, where there were fuschias growing wild along the banks. They rented a house which had once been a mill, overlooking the bay, with the little mill-stream running beside it. The land rose up behind the house, becoming a steep cliff further round the bay.

Frank was there; and being a sturdy, muscular man, he was a strong swimmer. With Christopher clinging excitedly on his back, he would swim right out into the bay. That was wonderful! And on one occasion they saw the cormorant that used to perch on the rocks actually dive into the sea and emerge triumphant, a wriggling fish clamped firmly in its bill.

They were joined at Backwell that autumn by Aunt Lola, who was the youngest of the Hawkes sisters. Lola had a young man with her, Daniel Corbett, who was an army medical officer. She had first met him on a trip to India with her sister Katie. They were to be married two years later. During this visit the whole family was called upon to support Frank, whose interest in his solicitor's practice in Bristol was being increasingly eroded by his devotion to local politics. One of C.P.'s

The Family Work for 'the Cause'!
Drawing by C.P. Hawkes

cartoons shows them canvassing in force, 'assisted' by an engaging little dog whose name was Rags.

In that same year, on 6 May, King Edward VII died of bronchial pneumonia. His body remained in the bedroom at Buckingham Palace, where he had died, for over a week, because neither the new king, George, nor his mother could decide upon a date for the funeral. However, on 14 May his remains were placed in an oak coffin in the throne room, draped in the royal standard, with the crown, sceptre and orb at head and foot. After three days it was transferred to Westminster Hall, where the king lay in state until 20 May. His coffin was then borne on a gun-carriage drawn by eight black horses on a circuitous procession through the streets of London, to Paddington station, where it was met by the royal train for the final part of the journey to the royal mausoleum at Frogmore.[6]

It had been a stormy night, but already by 1 a.m. the streets were crowded with people. Christopher was taken by his parents to watch the procession from the east side of Oxford and Cambridge Terrace, close to Paddington, where large wooden stands had been set up on either side of the road.

The gun-carriage was followed by King George, in admiral's uniform, walking alone. After him, Alexandra had instructed that her husband's charger, Kildare, should be led, with his top-boots strapped reversed into the stirrups. But the most poignant and lasting impression on the five-year-old Christopher, as indeed for many thousands of other spectators, was not so much the magnificence of a solemn state occasion, but the pathetic sight of Edward's little white fox-terrier, Caesar, being led by a groom behind his master's body.

For the coronation of the new king on 22 June 1911, C.P.'s battalion provided a detachment under his command to take part in lining the route of the procession to Westminster Abbey. None of these detachments brought up from the country can have been bigger than a single platoon. Christopher was taken to the camp in Regent's Park, and he remembers that the number of Northumberland Fusiliers was certainly small. They were allotted a section of Parliament Street to line. The weather was brilliantly sunny according to C.P.,[7] but Christopher wasn't taken to see this procession. He saw instead a film that was made of it, which was shown afterwards in London, at the Scala Theatre, off the Tottenham Court Road. At the head of the procession was a naval detachment from the Gunnery School at Whale Island, Portsmouth, led by C.P.'s cousin, Captain A.V. Campbell, who was also Christopher's godfather. Alick Campbell was short and slight in build; and the sight of this small, serious-faced man with his drawn sword, cocked hat and gold-braided uniform, at the head of rank upon rank of immensely tall sailors, is one which Christopher has never forgotten. Alick, who was later promoted Rear-Admiral and finally Vice-Admiral, was a very popular officer. He was the elder son of Rosario Duarte (Aunt Rosie), who had looked after Ellie and Vickie when their mother, her sister,

Working for the Cause. Drawing
by C.P. Hawkes

died. She had married 'Uncle Lewis' Campbell, and there were three
children: a daughter, Rose Isabel, Alick, and Noel. Alick remained
unmarried until after his retirement, when he settled down very happily
with the widow of a fellow naval officer. Noel, who had always loved
horses, had been commissioned in the 11th Hussars. He did marry.
When his regiment was posted to India, his wife Muriel refused to go
with him, and he had to obtain a transfer to another regiment in order to
please her. The idea of 'little Noel' as a heavy dragoon was clearly
absurd and not unnaturally it produced a great deal of amusement in his
family. C.P. was rather shocked by Muriel's behaviour.

That summer C.P. went on a course at the School of Musketry at
Hythe, in Kent. He rented an old farmhouse at Pedlinge, a village which
lies about a mile and a half to the west of Hythe, on the Ashford road.
Ellie and the children, with Nanny Giles, were joined by Christopher's
adored Aunt Vickie. There were picnics in the bracken and heather, and
walks in the woods, when Vickie entertained the children with her
imaginative tales of a little creature whose name was 'Puchi'. What sort
of creature it was Christopher never really found out; but Vickie would
suddenly point to the overhanging branch of a tree, exclaiming, 'Look,
look, there he is!' Try as he did, the little boy never managed to catch a
glimpse of him.

C.P. would set off each morning on his bicycle down the hill from
Pedlinge. It was one of the hottest summers for many years, and his return
at tea-time up that steep hill gave Christopher a vivid memory of his
father's perspiring face as he got off his bicycle outside the farmhouse.

Their customary autumn visit to Backwell was followed, in the last week of September by Christopher's first term at a day-school, the Norland Place School in Holland Park Avenue.[8] To begin with he was escorted by Rosa, but it was soon found that a troop of his friends led by a doctor's daughter, Isobel Keppel-Barrett, could be joined on its way to the school down Holland Park Avenue. Isobel was older than the others and responsible enough to take charge of them. School started at 9.15 a.m., with prayers in the gym, and it finished at 4 p.m. The boys' uniform was dark blue, with a sky-blue jersey in winter and a white shirt in summer, a dark and light blue striped tie, black stockings, a dark blue cap with light blue ribbon sewn on to it in radials, and a blazer to match, which bore the initials NPS (Norland Place School) on the breast pocket.

In his second year (1912–13) he was taught history, for which he was already developing a remarkable aptitude, by a jolly 'elderly' lady, Miss Helen Newman, who was clearly not as 'elderly' as she seemed to him. It was presently announced that she was engaged to be married to a Dr Needham, who in fact lived two or three doors away from the Hawkeses' house in Campden Hill Square. Very shortly after the marriage the good doctor was knighted. Sir Frederick, as it turned out, was one of the leading mental specialists in the country, so their jolly Miss Newman became the rather grand, though no less jolly, Lady Needham. Before

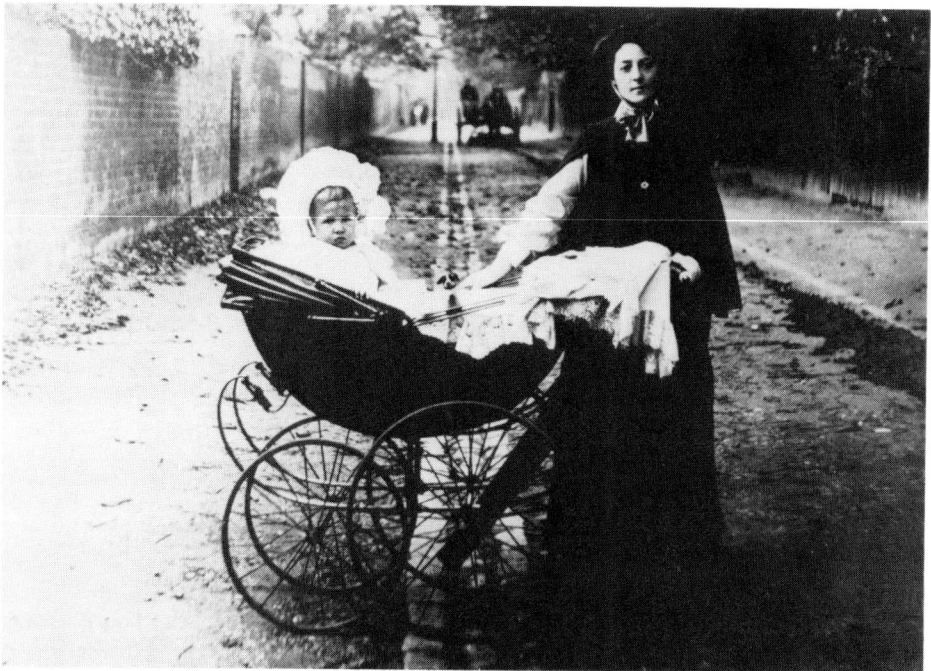

Christopher with his Nannie, Rosa Giles, in Bedford Walk, near Campden Hill Square. Photograph taken by an itinerant photographer

this, in the summer of 1912, the then Miss Newman had to write a letter to Christopher's mother. He had consistently achieved the highest marks in all subjects but one:

> I am very sorry to have to tell you that Christopher did not speak the truth when he told you that Miss English said he was the best in the class at arithmetic. I found this out because in talking to Miss English I said how very pleased I was she thought he was getting on. She was very much astonished to hear what he had told you. What she *really* said to him was that he was the *worst* in the class, and must try to do better, and be more attentive. We have just spoken to Christopher, and he owned up at once that he had not spoken the truth but had invented it. We had a very serious talk with him about it. I am so thankful we have found out, and he has not smugly prospered!! I am only sorry to grieve you; but do not worry too much, this kind of thing is not rare with small people. I told him he *does* know the difference between right and wrong, even though he is a little boy. Of course the worst of the punishment for him is having to tell you, and bring this letter home.

They were also taught Scripture, by Miss Flavell, who was known as 'Flavie' by the children. She used those splendidly evocative pictorial scrolls to illustrate the stories from the Bible. There was Joseph with his 'coat of many colours', Moses as a baby in the bulrushes being found by the Pharaoh's daughter, the prophet Elijah fed by ravens in the famine, and another of him denouncing the prophets of Baal on Mount Carmel.

Even before he went to school Christopher's mother had given him weekly sessions on the Bible. They would sit facing one another on either side of the dining-room table, which would be covered with a green baize cloth to protect its polished oak surface, and she would read to him from some rather battered little books which she had been given as a child. One of them, on the sayings of Jesus Christ, was the somewhat oddly named *Peep of Day*. This book was very popular in its time: it was reprinted several times. Christopher enjoyed these sessions. He was stirred by the imagery and heroic language of the Bible, and it was this, together with the influence of his parents and his aunt and uncle (for both Helen and Frank were extremely godly), that lay behind the advance in Christian devotion begun in his last years at Winchester, and continued afterwards at Oxford. Although the consequent attitude of mind has remained with him, the enquiring nature of his intellect gradually turned him away from accepting many of the fundamental tenets of Christian belief. He sees himself now as a 'a reverent agnostic'.

In April 1912 the family went to Backwell for the wedding, on the last day of the month, of the twenty-six-year-old Lola, youngest of the Hawkes sisters, to Dan Corbett, who was by then a captain in the Royal Army Medical Corps. Christopher and Penelope attended the bride, who was given away by Frank. A report of the wedding in the local

The Wedding Reception at Backwell. Drawing by C.P. Hawkes after the marriage of his sister Lola to Daniel Corbett in 1912

newspaper was afterwards pasted into the visitors' book, together with a delightful drawing by C.P. of the couple leaving Backwell after the reception:

> Great interest was evoked at Backwell on Tuesday by a very pretty wedding with which were associated several pleasing and unusual features. The bridegroom was Captain D.M. Corbett, RAMC, younger son of the late Mr D.F. Corbett, FRCSL, of Dublin; [the bride was] Miss Lola Hawkes, youngest daughter of the late Mr C.S. Hawkes of Rio de Janeiro and Beckenham, Kent. The service was fully choral, and the church was tastefully adorned with white flowers, palms and other plants in pots. . . . The bride wore a dress of ivory Ninon broché, trimmed with pearl and silver embroidery with a court train of Limerick lace, lined with silver tissue. She wore a Brussels net veil over a wreath of myrtle leaves and orange blossoms. She carried a sheaf of lilies tied with silver ribbon; and this, together with a diamond ring, was the gift of the bridegroom. She was attended by her nephew and niece, Master Christopher and Miss Penelope Hawkes. They wore picture costumes of white, with touches of green and silver; the little bridesmaid carried a silver basket filled with apple blossoms, and wore a pearl necklet, the gift of the bridegroom, as was the pearl pin worn by the page. On either side of the approach to the church were 31 little girls attending the village school. They were dressed in white; wore wreaths of apple blossoms, and carried white wands with white satin streamers. An arch of apple blossoms was erected over the church gate. . . .

It must have been an exciting day for the children, and a most exhausting one for those adults who had organized the elaborate festivities. Combe House was full. Aunt May and her husband Maurice Fenwick were staying, besides C.P., Ellie, and both children, with Nanny Giles, and of course Lola herself.

There was another wedding that year. Ellie's step-sister Audrey married a tall handsome journalist named R.C.W.(Raymond) Bush. The wedding took place at the country church at Brasted, near Westerham in Kent, in the beautiful Darent Valley – that magical countryside so unforgettably observed by Samuel Palmer in his Shoreham paintings.

The occasion was chiefly memorable for the fact that poor Penelope, bridesmaid again, and naturally overawed by the proceedings, knelt on a tin-tack. It was sticking up from the newly-laid red carpet in the aisle. The child heroically stayed on it throughout the ceremony, only slowly melting into tears after the couple had gone into the vestry to sign the register. Something of the Hawkes temperament must have sustained the three-year-old through the miserable pain: it was marvellous self-control in one so young.

That summer the family went to Switzerland for a holiday; but it was inauspiciously begun. When they arrived at Dover harbour to take the boat to Calais, and had come to the gangway, Ellie saw that there were sailors roping down the chairs on deck. At once she refused to go on board. 'There's going to be a storm,' she said, and insisted on their trudging all the way back with their luggage. And she was right. From the comfort and safety of the Lord Warden Hotel that evening they were able to watch the boats tossing on the raging water. Happily, by the following morning the wind had abated enough for them to get across to France. Neither Christopher nor his father suffered at sea, but poor Ellie was a terrible sailor: 'sick at the sight of Charing Cross', her husband once said.

Their first stop was Paris, where they hired an open carriage – coachman in customary white top hat – so that the children would enjoy their first view of the city in the sunshine, before they caught the night train from the Gare de Lyon, which was to take them over the Jura to Lausanne. Not having booked a sleeper, they spent a rather uncomfortable night; but the excitement of the journey more than compensated the children, who woke to see the valleys of the Jura with their browsing cows.

When the train stopped at Lausanne, Christopher was allowed out on to the platform to stretch his legs. Unknown to them, the train had to be joined up with another, from Lyon; and Christopher had not gone far when it was suddenly drawn out – backwards. Very soon the small boy was the centre of attention: not least because he spoke in understandable French. Meanwhile, the trains, now coupled together, were shunted back to the platform. Nanny Giles leapt down and came swooping along the platform like a navy-blue seagull, with her cape flying, to fetch him. All well; but there was worse to come.

The train continued to Montreux where they had to change to the electric railway that would take them over the mountains to Château d'Oex, where they were to stay at the Hotel Beau Séjour. Having been strictly forbidden to go anywhere near the lift in the hotel, the temptation proved too much on one occasion, and Christopher summoned the lift, stepped inside, clanging the wrought-iron gates shut behind him, and up he went. When he reached the floor where their rooms were he stopped the lift and drew the first gate across, pausing a moment before opening the one on the landing. As ill-luck would have it, at that precise instant a young lady summoned the lift from the ground floor. Down it went, leaving the terrified* small boy clinging to the outer gate, now immovably shut. His piercing cry gave the unfortunate girl such a fright that she collapsed in a faint. It was some little while before Christopher's mother appeared; but as soon as she discovered what had happened, she fetched the proprietor. All he could do was to send the lift back again, up to the floor where the boy was

---

*Christopher altered my word 'terrified' here to 'seriously alarmed'. The reader is left to decide which word is the more appropriate under the circumstances.

trapped. He assured Ellie that there would be room enough between the two gates not to squash him. Christopher felt the lift's gate grazing his back, but there was just enough space for him between the two gates until they were level and could both be opened.

Characteristically, though he was ashamed of having disobeyed orders, this incident did not give him a life-long fear of lifts as perhaps it might have done. His irrepressibly high spirits seemed to carry him scarcely damaged through any such experiences.

While they were staying at Château d'Oex they went on several sightseeing expeditions. One was to the beautiful little medieval walled town of Gruyère, famous for its cheese. The market-place still had the ancient corn-measures, built of great slabs of granite, hollowed out into rows of cavities for measuring the grain, and narrowed into slanting channels for its release through the side, with the old wooden stoppers hung on chains at each outlet. Eager, as usual, for an amusing photo-graph, C.P. lifted his small son into one of these measures and began taking pictures. A few people gathered round, no doubt intrigued by the antics of these English visitors. When C.P. tried to lift his picture's subject out of the granite cavity, the boy had got both his legs firmly wedged into the outlet channel, and he couldn't be shifted. After a good deal of pushing and shoving, accompanied, one may guess, by enthu-siastic advice from the natives, he was safely extracted; but he was stuck for quite a time, and he behaved with commendable self-possession throughout the rather undignified incident. He does now admit that he secretly half enjoyed it, as might be expected in a seven-year-old who was, in any case, often found to be a bit of a 'handful'.

Before they left for home they went to visit an old gentleman who lived in a hotel at Vévèy, close to Montreux. C.P. had been given an introduction by a friend in London who had urged him to take the opportunity of introducing Christopher to this man, who by virtue of his birth alone had achieved a toe-hold on the ladder of European history. His father had been a midshipman at Trafalgar, and second officer on HMS *Bellerophon* when she took Napoleon into exile on St Helena in 1815. This, however, meant little to the boy, who now remembers mainly that the man seemed very old indeed, and not really all that interesting. But Christopher did become aware of the essential conti-nuity of history quite early. What first kindled this awareness was being given a beautifully illustrated copy of Kipling's *Puck of Pook's Hill*, which he read eagerly.

3 Childhood, 1912–14

During the last two summers before the First World War Campden Hill Square would often resound with the merry crack of leather-covered wood against willow. J.M. Barrie, the novelist and creator of Peter Pan, lived nearby, and he was a great cricket enthusiast.[1] He was also, not surprisingly, wonderful with children. Every week during the school holidays he would organize cricket matches in the middle of the Square's garden, where its grassy slope is not quite so steep. All the boys who lived in the Square, and were old enough, were taught to play. Christopher, at eight (almost the same age as Barrie's youngest adopted son Nicholas), was allowed to join in.[2]

Barrie was fifty-three at the time, although he looked younger. He was small and dark and intensely shy, with a droopy moustache and rather short legs. C.P. had in fact exhibited a drawing of him at the Baillie Gallery in December 1912, but sadly this portrait is now lost. Cynthia

Sylvia Llewellyn-Davies. Pencil drawing by C.P. Hawkes

Asquith, who was Barrie's secretary for the last twenty years of his life, and to whom he left the copyright of all his books and plays except *Peter Pan*[3] recalled: 'I was struck almost painfully by his sad, sunken eyes, huge domed forehead, and the mournful – almost hoarse – voice.'[4]

As a child, Christopher was unaware of that 'deep-hoarded sadness'[5] that others saw in Barrie's disquietingly blue eyes. The 'strange sombre dark little man'[6] was blissfully at ease with young children. On one occasion, when the cricket was interrupted by a passing grown-up, Barrie simply hid behind a tree until the intruder had moved away. He suffered all his life from bouts of the most crushing and impenetrable depression; yet he could be gloriously funny. To his many devoted friends 'knowing Barrie was always like snakes and ladders. After progressing a long way, you have to go right back to the starting point and begin all over again.' On a bad day he would look 'Ineffably weary, his face all dark shadows . . . he might have had ink instead of blood in his veins.'[7] He was very dark skinned, and described himself somewhat ruefully as 'rather sallow'. His almost black hair remained so throughout his life, a fact which caused him considerable distress, as he thought that people would presume that he dyed it.

J.M. Barrie. Photograph by W. and D. Downey

There is a description of one of his impromptu cricket matches, not in Campden Hill Square, but at Stanway in Gloucestershire, the home of Cynthia Asquith's father, Lord Wemyss:

> Barrie had not been many hours at Stanway before he produced some stumps. These, with several little boys dancing round him, he pitched on the lawn quite close to the house. Then, flinging off his coat, he began to bowl left-handed balls at the boys . . . to small children he would bowl the gentlest, most enticing daisy-cutters: 'The reason I bowl so slowly', he once explained, 'is that if I don't like the ball, I can catch it up and bring it back.'[8]

He always wore dark suits, made by a good tailor, but the effect was usually ruined by his lifelong habit of cramming his pockets with 'useful and necessary' items. A pipe smoker, he used to burn holes in all his clothes by dropping tobacco sparks. Christopher said he never saw Barrie without his bowler hat, which he wore even when he was playing cricket. Apart from a faint memory that his voice was very Scottish, he doesn't remember more about it, but Cynthia Asquith gives a deliciously vivid impression:

> I loved his burry voice, with its subtle Scottish lilt. He pronounces certain words strangely. 'I had a haddock this morning,' he declares now and again. At first I thought he meant he'd had fish for breakfast, and I didn't know how to look suitably interested. Not until the third time did it dawn on me that he was telling me he'd had a headache![9]

The Square was also ideal for another weekend pursuit. C.P. was very keen on Baden-Powell's ideas, and he took Christopher to Gamages, where he bought scout uniforms for him and a group of his friends: Barton Worthington, Charlie Davies, Robert Medley,[10] George Michelopoulo, and Humphrey Slade. They all shared a small tent, and although regulations forbade the building of fires in the Square, they used to light one on a pile of bricks, which didn't damage the grass, and they were able to brew up cocoa in a billy can, which was great fun.

All the boys were too young to join the organized scout troops, which were intended for eleven-year-olds at least; but C.P. thought it a splendid idea, and having given them Baden-Powell's book, *Scouting for Boys*, they were left to work things out for themselves. The book was full of information: how to pitch a tent, how to build a fire, and the six different kinds of knots that could be tied with a rope. They had staves, which were long wooden poles marked off in feet and inches, with a small round hole drilled through it at eye-level; which, according to Baden-Powell, could be looked through, enabling one to see better. The patrol leader (guess who . . .) had a pennant on his staff, with a hawk cut out of a piece of red flannel, stitched onto a triangle of calico. They

Christopher as a Boy Scout. Drawing of Christopher by C.P. Hawkes

Baden-Powell. Drawing by C.P. Hawkes

would march into the Square with George beating a side drum, behind the leader of the Hawk Patrol.

Their summer holiday in 1913 was spent at another seaside resort in Normandy, Étretat, where there were good sandy beaches for paddling and swimming. Along the edge of the sand there was a great strip of water-worn pebbles; and beyond these stood two rows of wooden bathing huts. There was strict segregation of the sexes, of course: Christopher shared a hut with his father, and they were attended by a 'Dame' called Marie, who could be summoned to bring a metal pannikin of hot water after a bathe, so that they could wash the sand off, especially from between the toes – a thoroughly civilized and comfortable idea. But the holiday had begun badly. When they arrived at the Hotel de Normandie where they had arranged to stay, Ellie went upstairs to inspect the rooms. She was always exceedingly (and quite rightly) fussy about cleanliness; and to their dismay this time she found them unsatisfactory. She firmly told the proprietor's young wife that they were cancelling their booking at once. The poor woman burst into tears, imploring them to stay: it would ruin their reputation if it became known that their rooms had been found *désagréables*. But Ellie was adamant. It simply would not do. They moved to the very much grander Hotel Hautville, where they remained without further mishap for the rest of the holiday.

Christopher made friends with an American boy who was about the same age as he was; and one day he asked Christopher if he knew how babies came. He didn't. Being both innocent and incurious in such matters, the idea of childbirth terrified him, and he fled before the boy could tell him very much.

September found them once again at Backwell and this visit was marked by one of C.P.'s cartoons in the visitors' book of the four of them playing cards. C.P., who was partnering his wife (a notoriously hazardous exercise for any husband in a card game) played a wrong card. Ellie jumped up in utter exasperation, exclaiming 'To think that I married an *idiot!*' They stayed at Combe House until the middle of September, when Ellie took the children back to London. C.P. joined his battalion for the big army manoeuvres which were to take place across the south-eastern Midlands from Buckingham to Northampton. For the first time in a large-scale exercise there were naval officers attached to the different divisional staffs; among them was his cousin Alick Campbell. There was also a special French military mission, headed by a general with a number of senior officers, one of whom, Commandant Souvestre, shared a billet with C.P. at an Aylesbury inn. C.P. wrote:

Manoeuvres on so large a scale in an area so accessible attracted many thousands of spectators . . . and the military police had their hands full. At any moment round the corner of some lane one encountered groups of well-known people.

The Grande Finale took place at Sharman's Hill near Charwelton, in

Not a Family Tragedy – Merely a Game of Cards as Played at Backwell. Drawing by C.P. Hawkes in the Backwell visitors' book of C.P., Ellie and their hosts, Helen and Frank

September 11th — 21st. 1913.

front of the King, the Prince of Wales and the Duke of Connaught, with his son Prince Arthur . . . as well as Lords Roberts and Methuen and Generals Grierson and Rawlinson.[11]

In July 1914 Churchill had ordered a test mobilization of the fleet to take place in the English Channel. This mobilization had nothing to do with the European crisis. The fleet was anchored off Spithead, the strait between Portsmouth Harbour and the Isle of Wight. The Commanding Officers of all the ships were allowed to invite guests, and Alick Campbell, then in command of HMS *Vengeance*, invited his cousin to bring his son Christopher, 'so that the boy might see a sight that he should remember all his life.' It was; and he has – vividly.

They went by train from Waterloo station to Portsmouth, where they were met at the harbour by a petty officer, who escorted them to a launch which was to take them out to where the battleship lay at anchor. Alick welcomed them aboard, and they were entertained in the captain's cabin: sherry and cake, and lemonade for the little boy. After refreshment they boarded the launch once again, and they were taken up and down the magnificent lines of ships. As well as seventy battleships, there were light cruisers, destroyers and submarines. It was wonderfully exciting. A few days after this, on 19 July, the fleet was to pass in front of the royal yacht, which was anchored at Spithead, while King George V took the salute. Four days later the ships were ready to disperse, and at the time Churchill saw no reason to halt this process of dispersal and demobilization, since he shared Asquith's view that Britain could keep out of the European war. The reservists who had taken part in the test mobilization were already on their way home. The fleets which were then at Portland were to be dispersed on 27 July.

Winston Churchill. Drawing by
C.P. Hawkes, 1913

However, on 25 July Churchill discussed the crisis at length with the First Sea Lord, Prince Louis of Battenberg,[12] before leaving London to join his family at Cromer. He spoke again to the prince the following day, but it was a bad line, and they had some difficulty conducting Admiralty business on the telephone. Churchill believed that he had specifically asked Prince Louis not to let the fleet disperse. The prince recalled the conversation differently: according to his own recollection he had carefully re-read all the telegrams and Admiralty orders before he sent the order, entirely on his own initiative, to the Commander of the Home Fleets, Sir George Callaghan, telling him not to disperse the fleet.[13] In any event, the presence of this enormous fleet at the outbreak of hostilities must have acted as a powerful deterrent to the German navy.

The Hawkes family were intending to spend their summer holiday on the Normandy coast; and in order to avoid a repetition of the unfortunate episode at Étretat, C.P. set out alone for Quiberville at the beginning of August to make the necessary arrangements in advance. He had just booked rooms at a hotel in the square, opposite the *Mairie*, when he was startled to meet the town drummer, already beating the *Point-of-War* to summon the reservists. He returned home at once. Next day, 4 August, war was declared.

Frank, at forty-four, was considered to be too old for active service, so he and Helen made their contribution to the war effort by taking in 'refugees'. Ellie and the children were staying with them already, and on the day war broke out Ellie wrote in the visitors' book:

> See the refugees arrive
> Here they come as bees to hive!
> Ellie, Kit,[14] Penelope,
> Lola and her 'Dinkie Wee' . . .

Lola and her seven-month-old son, Brian, were the other 'refugees'. Her husband Dan, as a doctor in the RAMC, had been sent to France.

The house in Campden Hill Square was let: first to a distant cousin and great friend, Lily Cancellor (who was the wife of the Metropolitan Magistrate, Harry Cancellor), and then to a couple from Newcastle named Finch, whose own house whether by accident or design was called 'The Perch'.

The 1st Battalion of the Northumberland Fusiliers was at Portsmouth; and as it formed part of the striking force, it had to be brought up to war strength by reservists and special reservists. More than half the other ranks of the 3rd Battalion were transferred to the 1st, and were sent

Christopher aged about eight

immediately to France. Throughout the war the Special Reserve continued its work of drafting and training, and as C.P. later wrote:

> It is not too much to say that the British Expeditionary Force during the early months of the war would have been wiped out if it had not been for the unfailing response of the Special Reserve.
> One of our most distressing functions was the reception and classification of many thousands of men temporarily unfit from disease and wounds, and their dispersal to the various hospitals and camps: so that both before and after compulsory service, the hundreds of recruits in training were at all times in constant contact with casualties from every theatre of war.[15]

The authorities were anxious to ensure that all the public services should be kept running smoothly. There was a widespread fear of spies, and it was thought that the enemy would attempt to sabotage all the means of communication. A military guard was placed on Newcastle Central Station, under C.P.'s command. A sentry was on duty at all

C.P. Hawkes at East Boldon during the First World War

times, and all the trains were carefully checked for bombs. The men slept in the waiting room, which must have been a pretty bleak experience. However, by the autumn a hutted camp had been built at East Boldon, a village between Sunderland and Gateshead, seven miles from the Tyne Bridge, and the battalion was moved there, along with the other battalions in the brigade. C.P. rented a house in the village (the first of four houses they were to live in over the next four years), and the family were able to join him.

Stratford House was on the eastern edge of the village; it was in fact half of a large red-brick house; the other part, called 'Avondale', was occupied by a businessman, John Wallace Taylor, and his wife and two daughters. Mary, the older one, was a bosomy blonde, much admired by the young officers; her younger sister Florence was equally cheerful, but more modest, and smaller, with rosy cheeks.

The second house, Hill Lodge, was outside the village, on a hill, as the name suggests. Lawn Cottage, their third house here, was right on the village street; the lawn itself was very small, but the house was older than the others, built of brown brick, and quite attractive. The last house was called Fairfield: grey brick, with a slate roof. It had a kitchen-garden at the front, and there was a lawn with borders, and small trees and shrubs, with a low hedge separating them from the fields beyond. It stood in a row of detached houses along a lane on the south-west of the village, opposite part of the camp; from where the rousing strains of the battalion band rehearsing inside its hut would often drift pleasingly across the grass. Christopher can still whistle some of the marches he heard, and he even remembers the name of the bandmaster, which was Cooper.

Earlier in 1914 Christopher had started riding lessons. He went with a riding master to the narrow stretch of tan on the northern side of Hyde Park, along Bayswater Road, where it was quiet. During the war, when they were at Boldon, he was able to resume his riding lessons, which he enjoyed. As his confidence grew he was taken by the riding master on a pony called Silvertop, so called because of its pale blonde mane, out on to the Town Moor, an extensive tract of unspoilt grassland that is still ideal for riding.

His confidence in the saddle only once led him astray. While staying with his friend Neil Johnson-Ferguson[16] in Dumfriesshire, he attempted to mount a pony when there was no one there to hold its head. It bucked, throwing him instantly. When he got up he found that his left wrist simply swivelled to and fro, out of control. Neil, showing great presence of mind, took him straight to the local doctor. It was a perfect example of Colles's fracture.[17] The doctor laid his arm on the table and said something like, 'Grit your teeth' or 'Hold your breath'. With a single blow he snapped the bones back into position. It was a moment of anguish, but the doctor set it, assuring him that it would be alright. It was, although he didn't set it quite straight, which has left Christopher with a slightly protruding bone just above his wrist. He continued to ride occasionally up until the early thirties, though never with the dedication which he devoted to his other interests.

In December 1914 one of Backwell's regular visitors, Amy Brooke-Little, wrote a letter to Helen about Christopher at the Norland Place School, which he had just left:

I lunched today with Miss Tisdall, one of the Heads of Christopher's school. When he first went there she didn't think him as wonderful as you and Mr H. and I do, and thought we wanted sitting on. Today I said, 'What do you think of C.H. on further acquaintance?' 'Oh' she said, 'He's *brilliant* – there's nothing that child can't do. He acted in a French play the other day, and not only acted well and spoke with a lovely accent, but he took the principal part and ran the whole play. His business was to flit about from flower to flower (other children) talking to them, and he was a wonder. Afterwards the French teacher said sadly, 'And to think that before long we shall lose that boy. I would teach him always, for nothing; always, until he is a man if I could keep him, just for the pleasure of listening to him.'

One day Miss Tisdall and another teacher were in a room divided from another by a curtain or a folding door, and they heard someone teaching a child about sound. 'You see, sound can be modulated by different pipes – even the same pipe can make different sounds by means of stops. You know what stops are? Well, by manipulating them you get different sounds. I dare say you've heard a soldier's bugle call . . . etc.' They peeped in, and there was Christopher holding forth to an infant who understood not a word, but was gazing up at him in open-mouthed wonder. Miss T. says he must be a great advocate, or something in which his great gift of language is used. . . .

4 Sandroyd, 1914–18

According to the Edwardian prospectus Sandroyd School 'stood in its own grounds of thirty-seven acres, on the highest point of the surrounding country; open to the South and West, and sheltered on the North and East by Claremont pine-woods', between Cobham and Oxshott in Surrey, seventeen miles from London.

Term began in the last week of September; and Christopher was taken by his mother, from Backwell, where they had been since the outbreak of war. Ellie wrote:

> We got up to London early yesterday and Christopher had his hair cut and shampooed and returned to V's (Aunt Vickie's) to change before going with me to Harrods to lunch with Maddie. Christopher was delighted with everything, especially the hard straw hat with brilliant purple ribbon. He wore his brown suit and looked awfully neat and smart. His spirits were such that he could not desist from singing lusty songs at the hairdresser's – and his remarks sent the man into fits. After a good lunch we returned to V's to pack, a hasty tea, and then Penel[ope] and I took him on to Waterloo, where I found Mr French, a Master, and introduced Christopher. He told him to get into the saloon and secure a seat, which he promptly did, after wild hugs to Pen, Me and Vickie, who had now joined us. He looked so fit and strong – several boys were tearful, but not he! Though he looked rather serious once he was in the saloon. But the train soon went off and I was left lamenting – an awful void he has left. But I feel confident about him; he spoke so sensibly about it all. . . .

The nearest railway station to the school was Oxshott, which was only half a mile away; but there was no road – only a footpath through the woods – so Christopher's first approach was from Cobham, some two and a half miles to the south.

'It was a very well-behaved school,' he said. It was certainly expensive. The fees in 1914 were 50 gns. a term. But C.P. had his full pay, first as a captain, then as a major; and with the income they received from the Duarte money they were able to ensure that their son was both humanely and imaginatively taught. And they chose well.

Sandroyd had two headmasters: Charles Plumpton Wilson, who had been at Marlborough and C.P.'s old college, Trinity, Cambridge; and W.M. Hornby, who was known as 'Uncle Bill' (who had been educated

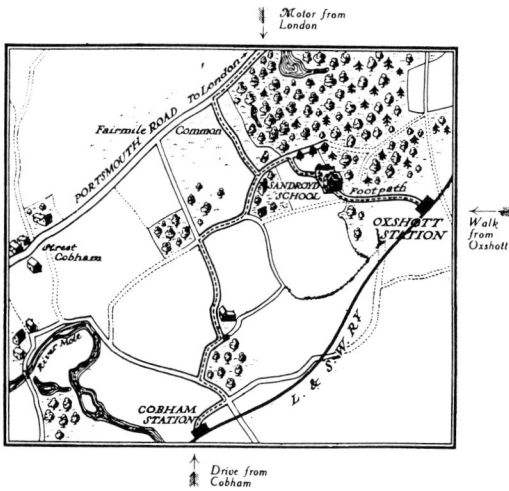

Sandroyd School

at Harrow and New College, Oxford). Hornby was a wealthy man; the brother of Charles Harry St John Hornby, the painter and connoisseur, who was a partner in W.H. Smith and Son, which was the first big chain of stationers to be established throughout the whole country.[1]

The boys' ages ranged from eight to fourteen, and there were seven forms – the lowest being the 7th. Christopher began in the 6th with Mr Shortt, who was a delightful character. He *was* short. A quietly-spoken, middle-aged bachelor,[2] who wore Norfolk tweed jackets and smoked a pipe, he was a brilliant teacher and head of mathematics for the whole school. It was largely due to his careful tuition that Christopher was able to overcome the one weakness that could have prevented him from getting his scholarship to Winchester.

In his first report at the end of the autumn term, Hornby noted that

Christopher was rather 'excitable and slap-dash', and he could at times be careless; though Shortt observed, 'with his ability and a little more ambition he could be top'. By the end of the spring term, 1915, he was top – in Latin, history and French. He began to learn Greek, but again, 'although picking up the language well', he was 'apt to be careless'. His undoubted abilities were hampered to some extent by his capricious and impatient temperament. 'He has a good deal of originality,' wrote Wilson, 'thinks quickly – but is apt to sacrifice care to pace', and, he added, 'just at present I do not take up his written work with any feeling of security. It may be a treat, or much the reverse.'

The school colour was a vivid purple. The uniform was grey: a flannel jacket and shorts, grey stockings with two purple stripes at the turn-over, and a grey jersey in winter. The tie and belt were purple, as was the cap; it had a monogram of the school's initials, SS, which was repeated on the belt fastening. In the first winter he was there, the boys had to wear an Eton suit on Sundays, though this was very quickly dropped because of the war. Christopher's suit was eventually given by his mother to the London Museum's costume collection, where, presumably, it still is.

For a preparatory school of the time Sandroyd was really very comfortable. Discipline was strict, but there was no bullying, and, as far as Christopher can remember, none of the boys suffered the miseries that many have had to endure at school. They were not allowed hampers apparently, but the food was good – very good, considering there was a war on – and there was always plenty of it. There were the inevitable cold baths, of course; but they had hot water every morning to wash in, which was brought to the dormitories by a manservant. The first of these was called by his Christian name, which was Sidney. The second, a rather more cheerful man, was called Hoare. A bell would be rung to wake them, and they they would chorus acknowledgement for the water: 'Good morning, Sidney!' or 'Good Morning, Hoare!'

They had regular hot baths, showers after games, and swimming all the year round in the 40 ft pool, which was kept at a constant temperature of 70 degrees. The general standard of health and hygiene seems to have been remarkably high. The sanatorium was a separate house some distance from the school. Christopher only once had to go there, and that was due to a risk of infection with whooping cough; if he had it, it was scarcely noticeable. He was always a robust and healthy child, and the life at Sandroyd suited him.

Though he was never very good at games, he was good enough to enjoy the exercise. There was a four acre cricket field, and several soccer grounds, as well as a nine-hole golf course. He was taught to play golf by Mr Shortt, whom he grew to like very much.

Boxing was encouraged (though not for Christopher: 'spectacles, you see . . .'), and there was an unwritten rule that if two boys had an apparently unhealable quarrel, they should be made to fight it out with boxing gloves. He had one such encounter with Michael Ramsey, later

Mlle Antoinette Danton (Maddie)

Archbishop of Canterbury, who was the nephew of one of the headmasters (his mother was Mr Wilson's sister).[3] Christopher took a photograph of him in another confrontation, this time without gloves, in which his opponent was another future clergyman, Roger Wilson, another nephew of Mr Wilson.[4] A healthy combative spirit was obviously no impediment to high office in the Church.

During the first winter of the war, Maddie remained in London, but she was very lonely. Her beloved family was scattered. The house on Campden Hill was let; no one knew for how long. Ellie had taken Penelope with her to join C.P. at Boldon, not long after Christopher began his first term at Sandroyd. By the spring of 1915 she had decided to leave her flat in Earl's Court, and find somewhere to live in Cobham. She took lodgings with a policeman and his wife, who had no children and so were able to let her have two quite comfortable rooms.

Every Sunday during term-time she would walk to the school to attend the morning service in the chapel. Christopher was found to have a clear alto voice, and had learned to read music at sight, so he enjoyed singing in the choir, although he disliked the chaplain, a rather humourless Canadian. After the service was over, around noon, he would walk with Maddie back to her rooms in Cobham, where the policeman's wife would have left a cold lunch for them. They would spend the afternoon reading and speaking French together. She was an excellent teacher, and these sessions were immensely profitable for him.

Then she would give him dictation and tea and cakes, all of which he enjoyed, before walking him back to school in time for evensong at five o'clock. He was fond of Maddie. She was always so elegant and immaculately dressed. It was only in retrospect that he came to understand how poignantly she must have loved him.

Early in 1915 Frank could no longer tolerate his inactivity in the war effort, and he persuaded his brother-in-law, Graham Snow, who had been brought from retirement to command the 11th Devonshire Regiment, stationed at Exeter, to get him a commission.[5] He was very soon sent, attached to the Manchester Regiment, to join the Expeditionary Force at Gallipoli. Helen wrote to him on 21 May, her birthday. The letter reached him just over a month later:

> . . . I wonder if you really have been in the fighting line yet – how I wish letters took less time to come. Last Thursday, the 17th, I was really very depressed and miserable all day, and wondered so much if you were having an extra bad time. You must let me know. It seems as though after all the years we have been together there ought to be a sort of bond of sympathy which would tell me when you are in trouble. . . . Ellie said that they had a Zeppelin there last week – and she was terrified. The lights went out; Charles [C.P.] was on night manoeuvres, and Ellie had to get Pen and all the servants out. It dropped several bombs, but was really heading for Newcastle. It did some damage at Jarrow. . . .'

The British and French attack on the Dardanelles began on 19 February, and merely served to revitalize the dispirited Turkish army. Their defences on the peninsula were strengthened, so that when the first landings took place on Sunday 25 April, at half-past four in the morning, losses were heavy, and very little was achieved. Two beach-heads were established, one at Cape Helles at the southern tip of the peninsula, the other fifteen miles to the north at Anzac Cove, which was named after the Australian and New Zealand Corps which had landed there. In the summer it was decided to extend the attack, and on 7 August further landings were made at Suvla Bay, which lies about five miles to the north of Anzac Cove:

> The plan was to capture a range of hills in the middle of the peninsula, which was thought to be only lightly defended. These hills commanded the straits; and if they could be captured, the Turks who were on the peninsula would be cut off, and the Fleet would be able to sail up the Straits into the Sea of Marmara, and thus to Constantinople.[6]

Ellie's step-brother Fred[7] had joined the Artists' Rifles as a private, and he was also sent to the Dardanelles, writing to his sister first from

Cairo in September 1915, and then again in May the following year. This letter is so vivid that it is worth quoting in full:

With B.M.E.F. at Gallipoli
November 16th and 17th 1915

Dearest Ell,
So many thanks for your letter which I was delighted to get. We have now been here between seven and eight weeks, and life is – well, it's hard. One week firing line, one week Reserve, and there is not much to choose between the two, except that in the Reserve you get more sleep and shells. It makes me smile when I read in the papers about troops in France going into billets and eating Belgian butter. Our only billets are open dug-outs full of flies and dust, and mud for a change, when it rains. As for butter – I'd sell my soul for a tin of the rankest. Rations is what we get, and no bread or fresh meat at that when the sea is rough. And as most of us are sick with bowel complaints you can imagine what merry parties we form at our recherché little meals. Not that the commissariat is to blame: considering the difficulties, they do wonderfully. But there is no accommodation for proper cooking or washing up, and the flies and dust are awful. So it is next to impossible to get clean decent food. Other units like the Hampshires and Worcesters have comforts sent them by their county associations. We Londons have nothing. What the devil should a cosmopolitan plutocrat from Park Lane care about a French polisher from Hoxton? Another thing is the wicked postage. I received a little parcel of almonds and raisins the other day, from England, but the postage was 1/–. I do think somebody at home might take up this question of postage. We do get a tiny pinch of tobacco once a week from Lady Hamilton's Fund. The other day there was a windfall. One of us received a package containing a tiny veal and ham paté, a cake, some dried soup, and some acid drops; I tell you truly that we and four officers of my company sat round these things with tears in our eyes from pure joy. Everybody from home writes, pressing papers and warm clothes upon us. Personally I don't want the damned lying papers; I get the *New Age* and *New Statesman* pretty regularly, and there is some truth and a good deal of intelligence in them at any rate: as for clothes, we can get tommies things – coarse, but warm enough, and everybody dresses like a tommy. But we do want *food*. One comfort here is the climate, which is glorious now; sunny, yet fresh and invigorating. The country is beautiful; wild and hilly; and just behind us are the lovely mountains of Imbros.

Next Day
A horrible night of wind and storm. Today I am pinched with lumbago and neuralgia, as well as the perpetual stomach trouble. Also I have just made the pleasing discovery, which we all make sooner or later – that I am lousy. This in conjunction with depressing thoughts

about the hideous disorder in which I left my affairs at home – a long story which I will tell you one day, if I ever get out of this horrid situation – has brought my spirits down very low.

Ell, will you send me some food? A cake? Perhaps a tin of sausages? I am too tired to write more now. Love to Charles and the children. Write to me again; and write news, gossip about your new servant. Anything.

Your loving brother,
Fred

P.S. Things should be in tins and strongly packed.

In sharp contrast to this letter, there is a description of the landscape of the peninsula by the poet John Masefield, who published a heroic and idealized account of the campaign of 1916, without, of course, having access to official records:

The Gallipoli peninsula, viewed from the sea is singularly beautiful. It rises and falls in gentle and stately hills between four hundred and eleven hundred feet high, the highest being at about the centre. In its colour (after the brief spring) in its gentle beauty, and the grace and austerity of its line, it resembles those parts of Cornwall to the North of Padstow. . . .[8]

He adds that 'in the brief spring the open ground is covered with flowers'. The poet sees the nobility of human suffering, and the pathos:

On the body of a dead Turkish officer was a letter written the night before [5 May 1916] to his wife. A tender letter, filled mostly with personal matters, but in it was the phrase: 'These British are the finest fighters in the world. We have chosen the wrong friends.'[9]

But it must have been very far from heroic and noble. John North observed that a man had three foes to fight: 'the enemy, lack of water, and dysentery, [which] was so rife in all ranks that, as one commentator remarked, a man might go into battle holding his rifle in one hand, and his trousers up with the other'.[10] Both Frank and Ellie's step-brother fell victim to this debilitating complaint; Frank was very badly affected and was sent back to England. Fred remained throughout the campaign. It was not until 9 January 1916 that the last battalions boarded the ships at Cape Helles. 'In the attempt to achieve this five-mile advance the Allies flung nearly half a million men on the Peninsula, and sustained over a quarter of a million casualties. At the end of eight months they were not in occupation of a single position of the least tactical importance; and the survivors were hazardously withdrawn.'[11]

The boys at Sandroyd School were very much aware of what was going on in the various theatres of war. They read the newspapers, which were delivered daily to the school library; and, when they were finished with, Christopher and his friend Hal Elliott used to cut out photographs and reports of battles, which they pasted into a book. They called this their 'War Book', and in it Christopher also drew cartoons of imaginary German soldiers in their spiked *Pickelhaube* helmets, and, copying those he had seen in *Punch*, he drew the Kaiser, and his son 'Little Willie', the Crown Prince. Their patriotism was channelled more into rendering the enemy as an object of ridicule, than in expressing a positive hatred. But sometimes they were more acutely touched by the suffering of war. One of the young masters, R.S. Knowles, who had taught Christopher in the 5th form, returned from the Front to visit the school. His appearance horrified the boys. Bandaged and half-blinded, with a patch across one eye, he was scarcely recognizable as the debonair young man who had taught them only a matter of months before. He died not long afterwards. His much younger step-brother, Kenneth, presently came as a pupil to the school.[12] Three years Christopher's junior, he was to follow him to both Winchester and New College; but it was not until many years later, when they were both again at Oxford, that they really got to know each other well.

Hal Elliott was one of Christopher's closest friends at Sandroyd. He was a very good-natured boy, with a grinning, freckled face, the son of a country clergyman at Winslade, near Basingstoke. They shared many interests; despite the fact that Hal was very athletic and good at games, their friendship only faded at last at Oxford, when their various activities meant that they saw less and less of each other, although always remaining on very friendly terms. At Sandroyd, besides the 'War Book', they invented their own imaginary countries, Hawkonia and Elliottia; each with a royal court, armed forces, and an elaborate constitution. Ramsey had his own – Ramsonia – which copied the Roman republic.

The fertility of Christopher's imagination is beautifully demonstrated in this letter to his mother from Sandroyd, dated 28 October 1917:

I must tell you about the Hawkonian Colonies: Ram Gug I., Stopan, Tillotonia, Brankian and Pipin Island. This last is the convict station, covered with sugar and tobacco plantations. They are on the Equator. The criminals work on the plantations and great hulking overseers come round with beefy whips and lam into the miserable convicts. Meanwhile, the Emperor keeps up terrific state – two slaves stand behind his throne with fans made of peacock feathers; an executioner with axe and block, is always in readiness. Dancing girls with tambourines leap about; and all the great men of the Realm come and prostrate themselves; Halberdiers stand round at attention. Silver trumpets in the background. Two little braziers full of incense make a nice smell, and a table covered with pineapples, wines, nectarines etc., is ready for use behind the throne. . . .

Hal failed to get a scholarship to Winchester the first time, but he was young enough to try again, this time successfully, the following year; and he joined Christopher in the autumn of 1919.

At the middle of the autumn term in 1915 'it was decided to knock off Christopher's English for the rest of the term, to let him have extra time for maths'. This idea proved to be a good one. By the end of December Hornby reported 'a great improvement in maths, which shows that the extra tuition is bearing fruit'. By the following summer he was firmly established at the top of the top forms in all subjects except this one, which still held him back, despite his efforts. But the report continued encouragingly, 'he has a remarkably quick brain, and his memory is retentive. He learns without apparent effort.'

During the school holidays Christopher's already awakened interest in history began to develop along more positive lines. Both he and his mother had bicycles, and they went off together several times into Northumberland, staying either at Hexham or Chollerford.

The most exciting discovery for him, of course, was Hadrian's Wall. They visited the fort at Chesters, which 'guards the west side of the bridge across the Tyne. It's name, Cilurnum, means 'the cauldron pool', which is not inappropriate to the North Tyne at Chesters.'[13] It is a tremendously impressive site, covering almost six acres, with its 5 ft thick defensive wall, and ditches beyond it. About a mile from the fort there is a turret, opposite High Brunton House,[14] on to which Christopher was able to climb, although it was in the grounds of a private house. It turned out that the owners of the house, the Waddilove family, were known to C.P.; Captain George Waddilove was a Fusilier contemporary of his.

Then there was Corbridge (Corstopitum), where the last excavations in 1909 were still open – in spite of weeds the massive foundations of the granaries or store-buildings could be seen. The first season's work, in 1906, was carried out by Leonard Woolley[15] under the direction of Haverfield.[16] This was followed by three further season's work by W.H. Knowles (who drew all the plans), and R.H. Forster, who were joined in the final season by several others, among whom were G.L. Cheesman, who was soon to perish at Gallipoli,[17] and J.P. Bushe-Fox, who was later to become a great friend of Christopher's.[18]

These visits fired his already active imagination. At Corbridge the outline of streets and buildings was visible, and in his mind he filled them with people. He began to want to know how they had lived.

It was possible to visit Durham in a day, by train, from Boldon; and this they did, on more than one occasion. In 1916, when visiting the cathedral, they awaited a verger, who could open locked doors for parties, once enough people had gathered together. Close to Bede's tomb in the Galilee Chapel, when they saw the door open slowly, 'there entered a white-bearded cleric' wearing a black skull-cap and cassock. He shuffled towards the tomb, and after fixing his gaze one by one on those present ('all women but for me . . .') he proceeded to address him at considerable length, on 'Bede the monk of Jarrow – the father of English history'.[19]

This elderly cleric was Canon Greenwell, whose book on British barrows, which was published in 1877, is still one of the best known on the subject.[20] He was ninety-six when Christopher saw him, and he still had two more years to live, keeping active right up to his death in 1918.

Christopher and his mother also visited Jarrow and Monkwearmouth; and they once went on a longer trip to Bamburgh, where they stayed at The Lord Crewe Arms. They saw the much restored but splendidly romantic castle which had been the home of Sir William Armstrong, the inventor and steel magnate, who had bought the castle soon after the turn of the century.[21]

In early January 1918 Christopher's French lessons took on an enchantingly new dimension. Ellie had found a French girl (presumably through an agency) who could teach him for a fortnight before he went back to Sandroyd. Marguerite had come to England to earn some money teaching, just as Maddie had done, while her fiancé was in hospital at Hyères in the south of France. He had been wounded, and the poor girl was missing him dreadfully. Every day she wrote to him, and Christopher, posting the letters, remembers the young man's name: Sous-Lieutenant Henri Barry de Limé, Hopital du Mont des Oiseaux. Christopher wrote eight letters to his mother during the time he was in Hexham.

'I don't think Marguerite is altogether happy here,' he observed shortly after their arrival; 'it isn't the life but the being here . . .' But they soon began to settle down and a note of contentment started to creep into his letters. They were very well fed: 'eggs every day for breakfast, and bacon too, and one day we had roast chicken for lunch'. 'There are three other men staying here, one is a lance corporal in some regiment. It is so funny to see hardly any soldiers, and also to hear no bugle calls.'

And there were expeditions:

The day before yesterday we went to Carlisle. There are tremendous bastions and whole complete long stretches of old city wall along the street. We were shown over the castle by a corporal of the Boldon (?Border) Regiment with the South African (Victoria) Medal. His history was rather comic.

'Yes,' he said. 'That's the tower where Mary Queen of Scots was imprisoned by Bloody Mary for fifteen years. Mary Queen of Scots, you know – her who was 'hexecuted' at Fotheringhay Castle in Herefordshire in 1649. . . .'

They also visited the museum, which was 'full of Roman altars. There are about twenty, and on at least twelve one can read the inscription perfectly. One was about an Emperor with seven or eight names: IMP. CAES. M. AUR. ANTONINUS. P. PERTINAX. D. or something like that;

and there is also the blade of a tremendous Viking battle-axe. I bet it has gone through a good many skulls in its time. . . .'

It was very cold. The large pond just outside the town was frozen over. When they went for walks Marguerite wore a cap of short grey fur, and a jacket to match, which Christopher remembers her letting him stroke. She had grey-blue eyes and fair hair. They played chess together in the evenings, and she would talk to him confidingly. His last letter to Ellie ended with the words, 'Nothing much to report except utter contentment. . . .' He knew that what he felt for her with all his eleven years' eagerness was something special, though he didn't know what to call it. And that fur had such a beautiful smell.

That summer, with just a year till he would face examination for a Winchester scholarship, there was still some anxiety over Christopher's progress in maths. Although he had worked very hard and had in fact caught up quite well, Shortt believed that he would gain from more concentrated coaching. After consultation with his parents it was arranged, with Wilson's approval, that Shortt should travel to Boldon soon after the end of the summer term, and stay with the family for a fortnight to work with Christopher.

Shortt was a sociable man; he brought sheet music with him, and he would sit at the piano singing songs, which he got Christopher to learn. (Typically, he can still remember the words of many of them.) Shortt must have enjoyed the conversations with C.P. in the evenings too, after dinner. In one of them he told the sad tale of how he came to be a maths teacher. His father had been a skipper in the Merchant Navy, and it was his great ambition that his son would rise to be a captain in the Royal Navy, but being away at sea so much, he never was able to get the boy properly prepared for the Dartmouth entrance exam. He was given a geometry paper – on Euclid – and, hopelessly misunderstanding the questions he translated them all into Latin. He was thrown out. His poor father was mortified; and Shortt resolved from that moment to become a teacher of maths himself, so that he could at least ensure that no boy in his charge should ever have to suffer such a humiliating fate as he himself had. This determination certainly did help Christopher.

The Winchester examination was held in June 1918. He went with three other boys, Ramsey, Wilson, and his friend Hal Elliott, under the genial supervision of Mr Hornby; staying at a boarding-house at 35 Southgate Street.[22] Christopher wrote to his mother on 11 June 1918:

We arrived yesterday at about a quarter past four, and after a good tea, sallied forth with Mr Hornby to 'sniff round'. We went as far as St Cross, and going through the Meads spoke to many old Sandroydian Wykehamists.

This morning we began at nine with Latin translation – not a bad paper, the second piece easy. This went on till 10.30 a.m. and at 11 First Maths began. I was flabbergasted with the easiness of the paper. This afternoon (I write at 1.45) at 2.45 we do Latin Prose till 4 o'clock;

4.30 to 5 history, 5.15 to 6 geography. I wish I had a longer time for the last two.

I am number 52 on the exam list. We do the papers sitting on chairs like those in Hyde Park, at trestle tables; they give you five nibs, blotch and ink gratis. I have my fountain pen, four nibs of my own and two pen holders. We are very comfy here – jolly good meals . . .

As well as the two maths papers, the second of which was the nasty one, they had Latin and Greek prose, French, history and geography, Scripture, and general papers. There was also an 'optional extra' – a set of Latin verses – which he did; and finally each candidate was interviewed by the headmaster, and other members of his staff.

The results came that Saturday, with cricket being played, and Christopher fielding. Wilson was umpiring. The head parlourmaid came out in her long black skirt, white cap and apron. She had a telegram in her hand. They all knew what it was. Wilson tore open the orange envelope with a flourish, announcing the results at the top of his voice: 'Hawkes . . . First!' There was a roar of applause. Christopher was naturally gratified, but he was also rather abashed by this unexpected outburst. Wilson went on; 'And not only that – he's actually held a catch without dropping it!' And he had; although he never was much of a cricketer.

The half-term report revealed that his Latin papers had been 'far more brilliant than accurate', but that they had 'impressed the Winchester examiners to award him the highest honour a young boy can win'. Wilson also noted that 'he bore the great honour with a becoming modesty'.

At the end of each term the long corridor leading to the library was narrowed by a row of iron-bound boxes. As well as the regulation trunks of clothing, linen and equipment, each boy had to bring with him what was known as a 'play-box'. These were unvarnished wooden boxes with blackened iron corners and fittings, in which games and books, and all the indispensable items without which no boy could contemplate the passing of a term, were transported to and from the school. They had to be unpacked on arrival, and their contents stored away until the last two days of term, when they would reappear, like static carriages outside the gate, to be repacked for the journey home.

On Christopher's final evening at Sandroyd, when all the packing had been done, and the time of the train each boy was to catch had been carefully chalked on the top of his box, the order came for those boys who were leaving the school to put on dressing-gowns and slippers, and report to the headmaster's study. The high-spirited holiday mood that reigned in the dormitories was momentarily hushed by this unexpected summons. The dozen or more, including Christopher, to whom it applied, hurried along the passage, wondering what it was all about. They knocked on Mr Wilson's door and were admitted. The headmaster beamed at them from his armchair; clearly this wasn't a ticking-off.

'Sit down, sit down!' he said cheerily, 'I want to talk to you boys about something.'

Nobody moved.

'Some of you have sisters. Some of you may remember, when you were smaller – much smaller – having baths with your sisters; and I expect you will have noticed that there is a difference between you in your "private parts". Now why is this, do you think?' Without waiting for a reply from the now distinctly embarrassed row of dressing-gowns, he launched into a most comprehensive and practical explanation of the sex act.

'It's a perfectly natural thing,' he said, 'Something which gives great pleasure, and there's nothing whatever to be alarmed about. But there is a perversion of this act; and it's about this perversion that I want to give you a warning. There are, you must understand, some boys who have . . . well, who have prettier faces than others. . . .' He then proceeded to give them a rather less full, though sufficiently graphic account of those undesirable practices to which they could be exposed, especially in the public school environment into which most of them would be going next term. It was all done without the slightest trace of solemnity; and Wilson's amiable and enlightened attitude gave Christopher, at least, a protectively disinterested view, which remained undamaged throughout his years at Winchester.

Armed with all this newly-acquired knowledge, and a perfectly justifiable sense of achievement after his spectacular examination results, Christopher arrived at Boldon for the start of the summer holidays in an exuberant state of mind. He was positively bursting with self-confidence.

They used to bicycle on fine afternoons (though there were few of these that summer – it rained almost constantly from the middle of June, right through till the autumn), to the seaside. The nearest beach was at the small coastal village of Whitburn, some three miles due east of Boldon. Having done a lot of swimming at school, Christopher very much enjoyed pitting his strength against the sea. One afternoon he took his nine-year-old sister, who could swim, although obviously not as well as he could, on to some rocks which jutted out like a shelf below the steep cliffs. They didn't realize how quickly the tide came in. Within minutes the water was swirling around them. Had it not been for the watchfulness and prompt action of two local fishermen, who had seen them heading for the rocks, and had climbed down to carry them to safety, they would almost certainly have drowned.

5 Winchester, 1918–24

I had no garden, but was allowed to construct a bower of white roses behind the wall in Outer Court, which every summer since has shed light on a dark and dishonoured corner.[1]

This beautiful passage was written by Montague John Rendall towards the end of his life.[2] In looking back to the time of his appointment as second master at Winchester in 1903 he reveals a great deal more of his

The cloisters at Winchester College. Drawing by Diana Bonakis, 1988

character than a simple love of gardening. When Christopher went to Winchester in the autumn of 1918 Monty Rendall had been its headmaster for seven years. Everything about him was impressive. 'He was a tall, handsome man with what can only be described as a magnificent presence, large romantic eyes, and a flourishing moustache.'[3] In both dress and bearing he was wonderfully eccentric. His total lack of inhibition made him an unforgettable target for mimicry; yet nothing ever seemed to diminish his natural authority. 'His speech was a kind of stressed incantation, as of a poet reading his own works, and was punctuated by unpredictable snorts.'[4] His flamboyant love of the more lofty aspects of the English language – every letter he wrote, every report, was a conscious work of art – together with an almost theatrical delivery – produced the one weakness in his otherwise outstandingly robust constitution. He frequently suffered from a sore throat. Characteristically, Monty's bower of white roses and his 'dark and dishonoured corner' were rather less poetic than he makes them sound. The building alongside what became the second master's little rose garden was the old brewery, which had only fallen into disuse shortly before the outbreak of the First World War. It still contained the old brewing equipment, all covered with cobwebs and dust. The stables beside it 'sheltered not horses but bicycles' and there was a little workshop there, where a manservant used to mend punctures, and carry out minor repairs. The actual corner Monty refers to was 'an old boot-hole known allusively as *Edom* (over Edom will I cast out my shoe)'.[5] The block was not finally cleared until 1933, when the brewery,

Monty Rendall. Drawing by Christopher

together with the former slaughter-house and wood-store adjoining it, was skilfully converted into a library.

Early in 1911 the then headmaster, Dr Hubert Murray Burge, was ordained Bishop of Southwark;[6] and as second master Monty was expected to take up the post. He wrote:

> I had no ambition to be Headmaster of Winchester: I did not expect it, and I did not ardently desire it; mainly because knowing my own limitations, I wished to see an abler man in the Informator's [head-master's] chair.[7]

But he did in fact want to be headmaster very much indeed, and this letter merely serves to illustrate the curious conflict in him between humility and ambition. He was duly elected in May that year.

The garden of what is now the headmaster's house was acquired for the warden during the sixteenth century. It had a beautifully smooth lawn bordered by tulips; and there were magnificent holm-oaks and plane trees. Across the warden's stream there was a fine view of the college. Monty savoured his surroundings with an almost lyrical fervour. 'His love of beauty in nature and art and literature was almost

The seventy scholars of Winchester College in 1920

more Greek than English.'[8] So when he moved into the headmaster's house, which, 'though dignified, could hardly be called an attractive residence',[9] there was much to be done. There was a splendid study, with an elaborately carved Jacobean chimney-piece, but the drawing-room had to be completely remodelled. The north window was made into an oriel, and it was enlarged, to give a better view of the cathedral. In the foreground there was a high and rather bleak brick wall. This was converted into a series of handsome railings, with tall pillars between, and behind them he planted hollyhocks in a long herbaceous border up against the old cathedral precinct wall. This was a great improvement on what had been a rather dingy street. Although the new terrace outside the study was laughingly known as 'Monte Fiasco', this was an injustice; as J.d'E. Firth, Randall's biographer, rightly says: '*Moberly Court*, hitherto mean and bare, was thereby given dignity.'[10]

Monty was an erratic but sometimes inspired collector. With his considerable salary[11] and a good eye for pictures and furniture, he filled the house with a highly individual collection of seemingly disparate objects which somehow became united by the sheer force of his personality.

There was a side of Monty's character that was perhaps rather less admirable. He could be capricious; and preferring, as he did, the black sheep of the flock, as Kenneth Clark observed, he tended to have favourites. He was also quite shamefully inconsiderate at times, especially towards those younger members of his staff who had families. He himself never even contemplated marriage. Indeed, the 'only woman who really counted in his whole life was his mother';[12] and from an early age her suffocating and obsessive love for him had merely served to reinforce his natural preference for solitude.

After his retirement in 1924 he set off on a tour of what was then the British Empire, and he was continually out of the country until the spring of 1926, travelling on behalf of the Rhodes trustees. On his return he moved to Butley Priory in Suffolk, an Augustinian foundation dating from the late twelfth century, although the earliest standing remains are those of the fourteenth-century gatehouse, which is virtually intact. It had been converted into a dwelling in the early part of the eighteenth century, and from the Victorian period up until the first years of the twentieth century it was the vicarage of the parish.

Butley was not a 'cosy' place to live. Many visitors complained of the intense cold in winter, which Monty never seemed to notice. He lovingly restored the buildings, and created a walled garden, which, typically, he named 'Paradise'. When a stray bomb fell close to the house during the last war, making an enormous crater, he cheerfully described the shattered glass and showers of sandy soil that covered everything in sight, rejoicing in his lucky escape; and the crater was ingeniously transformed into a sunken garden. He refused to be depressed by the troubles and infirmities that began to creep up on him. 'He was still riding his bicycle at the age of eighty-five, as strenuously as

M.J. Rendall

ever and even more perilously; for by this time he could not dismount, and could only come to rest by running into something or somebody. In the end his machine had to be hidden away.'[13] Monty would never admit defeat.

Although he was unrestrainedly optimistic, many people were aware of an underlying melancholy and 'a sense of strain, which communicated itself to all those who were in his presence. He was not a man with whom it was readily possible to take one's ease and let the conversation run where it would.'[14] He had no deep friendships, although there must have been many among his numerous acquaintances who regarded him with real affection. Kenneth Clark, whose time at Winchester was far from happy, must have been one. In the 1950s he was able to buy a few pieces of the Jesse window which had been taken from the chapel in 1821, when it was thought to be deteriorating. It was sent for restoration to a firm called Betton and Evans, who persuaded the fellows to let them make a new set. The originals were sold into private chapels and collections; some even crossed the Atlantic; and there are three of the original saints in the Victoria and Albert Museum in London. However, Clark managed to return a few pieces which he had bought from a private chapel at Ettington in Warwickshire. 'I have never written a cheque with greater emotion,' he recalled.[15] The glass was carefully cleaned and installed in the window of an annexe, built by Butterfield, to Thorburn's chantry. Lord Clark, who could hardly be called a retiring, or even a particularly modest sort of man, wanted the window to be associated with one name only, that of Monty Rendall. His gift was anonymous.

Up until 1917 Winchester was largely unaffected by the war. They did not suffer air raids, or even the threat of them; and there was no real shortage of food. The cooks managed to produce reasonably satisfying meatless meals, and although the price of sugar and sweets or 'suction' as they were called, rose dramatically, 'the outside observer would not have noticed many variations from normal school life'.[16] However, by the winter of 1917/18 the food shortage had become acute, and with it came the inevitable lowering of resistance and morale. The disastrous epidemic of influenza that killed so many who had been weakened by the years of war swept through the college, though with less devastating results than in many institutions. Christopher suffered from it, though not at all badly; apart from a mild attack of measles the following spring, it was his only prolonged visit to the school sanatorium. There were minor injuries, of course; and those which he sustained while playing Winchester football[17] were to have long-term consequences. His left knee-cap was displaced on several occasions, damaging the cartilage behind it. Each time it happened the doctor managed to put it back, and he was bandaged up. He was rather proud of this bandage: it was a kind of 'battle scar', and professional footballers wore knee-bandages. The last time it happened, however, in November 1922, the doctor failed to get the knee-cap properly back in place, although he thought he had.

There was no further trouble for almost forty years, but it was the cause of the arthritis which started in 1960, and has eventually become bad enough to lame him.

Throughout the summer of 1918 it rained almost continually. There was a terrible harvest and the farmers were desperately short of labour because of the war. Winchester, along with other public schools, was called upon to provide men to work in the fields (the word 'boy' was never used).[18] They were paid threepence an hour, working mornings or afternoons on alternate weeks.[19] They also went to a 'harvest camp' at a place called Burrator, on Dartmoor.

Christopher's arrival at Winchester, towards the end of September, was in glorious autumn sunshine. He and Ellie travelled down by train from Boldon, arriving in the middle of the week, with a few days in hand to look round the place before the start of term, which was always on a Friday. The three school terms at Winchester are known as Short Half, which is the autumn term, Common Time, the spring term, and Cloister Time, the summer term. This last name was derived from the use of cloisters for teaching on days when the weather was too hot to work inside; a practice which was almost universal in medieval times; and it is safe to assume that the college cloisters were built with this in mind.[20]

When he had come to Winchester for the scholarship exams that June, with Mr Hornby, as has been mentioned, they had stayed at 35 Southgate Street. This was the Chernocke Private Hotel, a stately town mansion, next door to the Hampshire Club. It was run by a Mr Ludford, who was a very dignified, rather self-important man, not unlike the Cambridge 'gyp' described by C.P. He was always immaculately dressed with a starched collar and perfectly fitting dark suit. After the reforms of the college in the 1860s Chernocke House had become the first of the new houses to be established ('A House'). There were ten houses in all, denoted by the letters A to K, omitting J. By the early part of this century Chernocke House was found to be inadequate, and a new house was built in Kingsgate Park. The old one was bought by Mr Ludford, who had been house butler, and he ran it very successfully as a private hotel. Ellie and Christopher stayed here for two days looking round the town, as well as at the college and cathedral. It was all very exciting. But by the last afternoon Ellie had become unexpectedly irritable and short-tempered. Christopher, who was eager to begin this new life, couldn't understand what was the matter with her ('Mummy, why *are* you so cross . . . ?'), but he was sensitive enough to realize after a while that his mother was actually making a brave attempt to disguise her feelings. Although he had already been to a boarding school, this was different. It really *was* the end of his childhood – after all a boy was a man from the age of thirteen at Winchester – and she must have felt the severing of those links acutely. As he left her at Outer Gate he could see that she was fighting back her tears, and like most young men he was more than a little relieved that she was sparing him an embarrassing outburst of maternal affection.

A 'new man' in Winchester College is given a fortnight's grace in which to learn his 'notions' under the direction of a 'one-year man' (Lester Simpson Gray[21] in Christopher's case). This not only meant learning all the rules and customs, but also the names for each of them. During this two weeks he could not be beaten. At the end of this time the prefects would hold an oral exam (or examinā, as it was called), where many words were shortened (to gymnā, confirmā, and so on), to make quite sure that he 'knew his notions'. A great many of these 'notions' applied to clothing: all the house colours had to be learnt,[22] and what could be worn and when. After the more serious questions (which were all conducted with good humour, and often ended in gales of laughter), there was what was called 'dressing a man up'. Here an imaginary man would be given articles of clothing which denoted his position and standing in college; and more and more preposterous ideas would be suggested by the 'inferiors', as well as the prefects in each of the upstairs chambers for the occasion. At the end of the ceremony the 'new man' was officially 'in sweat'. That was precisely what it was. Known as 'fagging' at Eton it meant a great deal of running around, doing chores for prefects, washing up tea things, polishing, sweeping, and in winter, lighting the fires in chambers, which could be a thankless job with newspaper and faggots of sticks which were often damp. But the system was not unfair, and there was very little resentment since everyone had to endure it; and in the college at least there was no intimidation or real abuse of privilege.

> First we waited about twenty minutes in the rain. Then Prefects having arrived we first had to run up the hill till one of us saw the top of 'Clump' (i.e. the clump of trees on the top) when we all fell on our faces at his shout of 'feathers!' We were then blindfolded in the middle of the Clump and made to walk out of it, which was easy enough. Then we were put in the middle of Labyrinth, a maze cut in the turf, and made to 'toll' (run) out. Then we had to 'toll' down a short but very steep slope, fall on our knees at the bottom, and kiss Domum cross, which is cut in the turf at the bottom, also to put a stone in it at the same time. We had to walk across the first Hatch on the river; it is about 3 inches wide . . .[23]

Up until the end of the First World War there were initiation ceremonies, which were not unlike those of a primitive tribe;[24] though by the time Christopher was there many of these had been discontinued. They always included a visit to St Catharine's Hill or 'Hills' as it was called. There were a number of other trials of strength, and a man was not recognized as a true Wykehamist until he had been beaten twice; though this requirement was fairly quickly satisfied with all the possibilities of error that were open to the novice during the two years that followed his first two weeks in college.

For a public school of its time Winchester was really quite small. There were seventy scholars in college,[25] and in each of the ten houses there were about thirty-eight men; so that in the whole school there were not much more than 450 men. There were five or six prefects in each house, and the head of the whole school was always a college man, prefect of hall. The other college officers were two prefects of chapel, a prefect of library, and a prefect of school, which was not the whole establishment, but the fine late seventeenth-century building which was almost certainly designed by Wren. This building was then used for lectures, concerts and examinations, but for its first 180 years it was the school, where all the teaching was carried out. Classrooms were known as 'Div rooms' and going to class was 'up to books'.

In college the main centre of life was around the beautiful Chamber Court, which is a quadrangle of about 115 ft square, with the original massive, iron-studded oak doors:

> In the evenings after lock-up, Prefects and Inferiors alike can honour the old custom of 'tolling Chamber Court' – that is, pacing with a friend as 'socius' round and round the paved walk that encloses the central oblong of cobbles.
>
> It is difficult to convey the mysterious sense on immanent life by which Chamber Court seems to be possessed. It may be vivid in the flooding of summer sunshine, or quiet and almost brooding under the moon; but an intense awareness of the unending successions of vitality that they have witnessed seems to dwell in its friendly stones, and makes one feel, as elsewhere Ruskin felt, that they have become steeped in that vitality themselves.[26]

All the main rooms on the ground and first floors were known as 'chambers'. Originally the men had both worked and slept downstairs, with the upper floor given to the headmaster, the second master, the warden and the ten fellows. The chambers were numbered from I to VI, with the addition of Thule Chamber, where Christopher spent his last eight terms. Along the walls of each chamber there were open cubicles which were known as 'toys', where the men worked when they were not in class. Evening preparation was 'toy-time' and the work itself was called 'mugging', a term which has escaped into general use. Each piece of composition work was a 'task'. The 'toys' were very solidly constructed of oak, with a desk top and a seat below it; with at one side a bookcase, above a cupboard with sliding doors.

By the time Christopher went to Winchester any brutality in the enforcement of discipline, at least in college (it was not so in some of the houses) had disappeared. Kenneth Clark was far from happy and even Leonard Cheesman, in college, while he was not apparently damaged by his experiences, certainly found Monty 'unsympathetic'. A boy called Herdman was beaten with quite appalling ferocity; and Christopher did have his share of the ground-ash during his first two years:

The Prefect of Hall would say, 'may I have the shop?' which was the vulgar term for the Chamber, and everyone had to clear out. He would then conduct a formal cross-examination. 'Have you any excuse?' If there was none he would say, 'I'm afraid I must ask you to stand round.' This meant leaning up against the central post of the Chamber, with your arms clasped round it, and your face pressed up against it. Your gown was removed, but the black broad-cloth waistcoat didn't have a silk back – it was made of the same material back and front and this had to be kept on. Then you were beaten across the shoulders with what was called a ground-ash. It was an extremely uncomfortable experience.

In about 1921 it came to be felt that beating across the shoulders was too dangerous, and the matter was taken up with the headmaster. It was suggested that it would be a great deal safer to beat on the bottom; which although still painful and undignified, was a lot less injurious in the long run. Monty's objection to this change, which he quickly withdrew was afterwards related by the prefect of hall with predictable results. 'Ah,' he said solemnly, 'some of us are differently built . . . you might strike a boy across the testicles. . . .' Clearly the headmaster's imagination knew no bounds.

Beatings with a ground-ash were finally abolished in 1926, after an accident when the sufferer imprudently looked round during the proceedings and received a splinter near his eye.[27] A.T.P. Williams was by then headmaster, having taken over from Monty on his retirement in 1924. He introduced the cane, which became known as the 'Little Willie' because of him. But in fact during Christopher's last three years he remembers very few beatings taking place; and as prefect of school himself, he never beat anyone.

Christopher's first close friend was one of the War Scholars, Michael Zvegintzov. He was the son of a Czarist colonel who had been killed in the war, in the offensive led by General Brusilov.[28] His widow had escaped from the Bolsheviks during the time of Kerensky's brief premiership in 1917,[29] and had brought her two children to London. Christopher told his mother about it in a letter dated 27 October 1918:

Zvegintzov is my great friend. A tall Russian, excitable but friendly; talks French well, of course, and is keen on everything that I am. His father is believed to be dead after the Terror; and he, his sister and his mother had a most exciting, interesting and terrible escape to England. They had arranged to start for Archangel on the night of the Bolshevik *coup d'état*, of which they knew nothing, until two hours before their time of departure. The Bolsheviks were on the other side of the Neva. The Government shut the bridges (all swing); they had to wait for their car. It finally came, and the chauffeur said that the Bolsheviks had quietened down, and that the Government had re-opened the bridges. At that moment they received a telephone message to say that the Bolsheviks had begun again and that the bridges were still open. Quickly they entered the car, with all the lights out in pitchy darkness; they drove through side streets (the Bolsheviks had cut off all the lights) to the station. They got into the train and waited two hours. Finally they started. At Vologda they had to change to get to Archangel. The other train was not there. They waited. Finally about two hours later the train appeared, and with it a message that a large force of Bolsheviks, in trains, were coming up as quickly as they could from the direction of Siberia to seize Vologda. Their train wouldn't or couldn't start. Longer and longer they waited, knowing that every minute the Bolsheviks were drawing northwards. Twenty minutes later the Bolsheviks seized Vologda. At Archangel they waited three days. In the harbour was *The Vindictive*, who escorted them half way home. After a fearful stormy voyage, in which they were nearly wrecked, they arrived at Newcastle. . . .'

Another branch of the family also managed to escape the Revolution, and Christopher got to know them quite well during the holidays, as his mother liked both the Madame Zvegintzovs, especially Michael's mother, whom she often invited to Campden Hill Square. Michael's sister Mary was a very clever girl; after going to Oxford she married the brilliant son of Sir William Holdsworth,[30] but he died tragically in an accident, so she returned to academic life, eventually becoming head of one of the Durham colleges, where Christopher stayed with her on at least one occasion. Michael was some years older than she was, an almost exact contemporary of Christopher's. He was a most amusing and delightful character with black stubbly hair and a blue chin. In spite of the powerful influence of Winchester ('a great absorber of men, she quietly converts those who would dramatically convert her'),[31] he never became Anglicized in the way that his sister did. He married Diana Lucas, a girl whom Christopher had met briefly at Oxford, and they lived in Hammersmith, in a house that had gardens which went down to the river. Every year they gave a party for the Oxford vs. Cambridge boat race, which Christopher usually went to, keeping in touch with the family for many years. Dimitri, one of the four children of the other Zvegintzov family, who were in fact cousins of Michael and Mary, was a near contemporary of theirs and he also became a friend of Christopher's.

Serge Orloff-Davidoff, who arrived at Winchester a year later, was entirely different in both looks and temperament from his compatriot. The Orloffs, or Orlov as it was sometimes spelt, were an old Russian patrician family which had risen to eminence during the eighteenth century. One of its members, Gregory, who was born in 1743, became the favourite of Catherine II; and it was he who planned the murder of Peter III in 1762, although it was his brother Alexis who carried out the deed. The legitimate line of the family became extinct, but Feodor, another brother, left four illegitimate sons, one of whom distinguished himself in the French wars in Turkey, and represented his country at the London Conference in 1832. He became head of the secret police in 1844, and was a favourite of Emperor Nicholas I.[32]

Serge's father was a count, an extremely benevolent but rather disgustingly corpulent man, whose visits to Winchester were something of an embarrassment to his elegant auburn-haired son. Like Christopher he had been brought up to speak French from earliest childhood, but it was through the school choir that Christopher first really got to know him. Serge had a typical Russian bass voice, while Christopher had become a light baritone, able, if necessary, to sing tenor. Serge could also speak German, which was a help to Christopher when he began to learn the language. They had a similar sense of humour, and they soon became friends. Serge was best man at Christopher's wedding in 1933.

Both Serge and Dimitri Zvegintzov joined the British army during the last war. Dimitri survived to meet Christopher again quite by chance when they were both living at Dorchester-on-Thames in the early 1960s, although he and his family moved away within a year, and Christopher lost touch with him again. Serge, who had served right through the war, died in a road accident, while still in uniform, in occupied Germany in 1945. He was forty years old.

The autumn of 1918 was miserably cold and wet, following one of the worst summers on record. But there were a few fine days in early October and on one of these the prefects, who were leaning against the doorways in Chamber Court, enjoying the brief afternoon sunshine, were astonished to see the figure of a still quite small boy in a top hat and Eton suit, walking nervously into Chamber Court from Middle Gate. One of the junior prefects, Victor Bates, was instantly reminded of *Tom Brown's Schooldays*,[33] and he began to shout the name which was at once gleefully taken up in a resounding chant. The poor boy was terrified. His late arrival, caused by a quarantine for some infection, was quite bad enough; but this dramatic response to his attire – the result of his parents' failure to discover what clothes he should wear – was too much. C.E. Stevens was to retain that nickname throughout his life; but the initial mockery was very soon replaced by an amused respect, for this Tom Brown was in every sense a singular man.[34] Christopher enjoyed his waywardness and sudden flashes of inspiration, and a friendship grew up between them which was only to be broken by Stevens's death.

The day in college began at 6.30 a.m., with the peal of a bell from the fifteenth-century tower adjoining the chapel. 'First Peal' was rung by the under-porter, whose name was Rawlins. However, there was a tradition which must have started some time in the 1860s, that the junior porter should bear the name of an Old Testament prophet, and by the time Christopher was there, they had got as far as Joel.

The first junior in the chamber had to get up first, take a hasty cold bath and dress himself, calling out at five minute intervals as he did so, to give the senior men warning: the older you were, the longer you could stay in bed. This rule applied at the other end of the day as well – the youngest went to bed first, and a prefect could virtually go to bed when he liked. It was not uncommon for a senior man to do what was called an 'all-nighters', especially when he was working for an examination. Christopher's habit of working right through the evening and on into the small hours was established during his last years at Winchester. In later years, when the necessity for rising with the lark was removed, his owl-like characteristics became more and more pronounced. Now, in old age, his day begins with breakfast around noon, with dinner perhaps at midnight.

When you were dressed in the morning, you went up into the dining hall for a mug of tea or cocoa and a biscuit, before the first session, which was known as 'morning lines'. This teaching period, from 7.30 a.m. till chapel at 8.15 a.m., was abolished during Christopher's time: the day beginning with chapel, after which it was up into hall again for breakfast. 'Not as good as Sandroyd', but the rationing had a lot to do with that, and things did gradually improve. Each man's trencher of beech-wood had a 'share' or slice of bread, and to begin with at any rate, margarine, or the merest scraping of butter. 'And you had to provide your own jam and marmalade.' There was also 'honeysugar', which was a rather sticky by-product of the breweries, not unlike a kind of pale molasses, which has long since vanished. Occasionally there were eggs; and in the winter, porridge.

Lunch always consisted of two courses: the first, except during the immediate aftermath of the war, was meat (usually mutton, but sometimes beef) with vegetables; and there was a pudding, of the baked jam-roll or rice- or barley-pudding variety. There was often cheese as well. By the time Christopher was there they had china plates and bowls, besides the traditional beech-wood trenchers; but it was not long since they had only the trenchers. This meant that anything sloppy had to be carefully walled in with mashed potato, to prevent any seepage of gravy. Earlier still they had to mop up the trenchers carefully after the first course, turn them over, and then eat the pudding off the other side. When there were boiled eggs for breakfast a hole had to be cut in a hunk of bread to hold the egg while its top was removed.

Life in 1918, though relatively hard, was a great deal easier than it had been at the end of the last century. When asked what it was really like to be at Winchester, Christopher remarked that there was no surface anywhere that wasn't hard. Benches, stools and chairs were all solid oak, and the beds were hard too. It was perpetually cold in winter ('everyone had chilblains') and there were the inevitable cold baths as well. In no sense was it a privileged or pampered existence.

The dining hall was one of the few warm places in winter. In the middle there was a big coke-burning stove, which had been put in during the nineteenth century. Its capacity was increased by the flue that ran along under the floor before making its escape up a chimney on the far side of the hall. Once you were seated at the long oak tables, you were not allowed to get up – not unless you were a prefect, that is. Prefects could make toast in front of the stove using three-pronged wire toasting forks with long bamboo handles. It was such an agreeable task that they regularly made toast for juniors. They could carry on enjoyable conversations while they warmed themselves in front of the fire. Christopher, as a prefect, with his unstoppable delight in talking, must have been responsible for quite a lot of burnt toast.

When the armistice was declared on 11 November 1918, Christopher was in a maths class with Mr Aris, the grey-haired, rather desiccated housemaster of 'B House' (who was known as 'The Hake' or 'The Haddock' because of his fish-like profile). It was just after 11 a.m., and he was about to set some questions when there was a commotion in the court below. Someone came rushing out shouting 'Armistice! Armistice!' at the top of his voice, and all the classes erupted simultaneously.

'Yes, yes, cheer away . . .' said Mr Aris with a terrible weariness; 'There'll be a great many troubles . . . many reconstructional troubles.' The bewildering spectacle of the elderly master with his head in his hands effectively silenced the spontaneous outburst of jubilation; but he soon recovered himself sufficiently to let them go, and the optimism of youth very quickly reasserted itself. Although going 'up town' was not allowed without leave, there was no stopping them that morning. They surged up and down the High Street, mingling with the huge crowd of townees, all cheering and waving flags.

The evening meal was normally a modest affair, just bread and butter and tea, but the school shop provided 'extra dishes' to order, sausage and mash or egg and mash (no chips in those days). It was sent up to hall between two plates, wrapped in a brown paper bag, with your name written on it. That evening Christopher ordered a really big one to celebrate.

Up until the end of the war there had been two school shops that sold cakes and ices, drinks and sweets, as well as hot meals. In Christopher's time the shop was run by a Mr and Mrs Dean, with the help of their daughter and a handy young man. The Deans served the college for nearly forty years till their retirement in the middle of the 1930s.

In spite of the shortages during those first months immediately after the armistice, there were occasional bouts of indulgence:

Last night there was a Chamber Sport (i.e. heavy meal in our 'shop'), lasting from 9.50 p.m. till 11.10 p.m. First came a large bowl of very thick mock-turtle soup – scalding hot; it took me years to swallow! Then came tinned beans in tomato sauce, in which were occasional forlorn looking pieces of sodden pork. However, a slight mishap had occurred. They were cold! And very greasy and horrible, too. We devoured them in silence. Next . . . oh joy! a vast dish containing 30 sausages, steaming hot, along with a large mountain of potato and fried onions. I had two sausages with dollops of potato and onion to match for a first helping; and 1½ sausages and more potato for a second. I couldn't manage a second helping of onion – I didn't even finish the first one it was so vast. Next came cakes (rather dry). There would have been eggs if there had been time to cook them. The meal was washed down with copious draughts of lime-juice. Then I retired to bed. I got violent indigestion which kept me awake till 12.32 a.m. . . .[35]

Christopher's first school report, that Christmas, was most encouraging.

The second master, Mr Williams, wrote: 'He has begun his year in College very well. I like his keenness and energy.' His history was particularly good; he was 'alert and businesslike, showing wide reading for his age'. The only cautionary note came from Monty. After the assurance that he had made a good start, he added 'his classics are not among the best in the exams.' However the general assessment – all subjects combined – placed him a very creditable second out of twenty-one pupils.

That Christmas was the last one the family was to spend at Boldon, as C.P.'s battalion was transferred to a camp on Salisbury Plain towards the end of the following January. The demobilization of an army is always a lengthy procedure; and with the ending of hostilities, the men were quite naturally impatient to get back to their homes and families. Bored and frustrated, they began deserting in droves, and the authorities were forced to close the camps at Boldon, and move the men to an existing one at Larkhill, some seven miles north of Salisbury – well away from the temptations of Northumberland.

During the difficult weeks before the move to Larkhill there were a number of serious desertions from the camps at Boldon:

The ordinary man's idea of demobilization was that he should, henceforth, with the least possible delay, be set free to do whatever he liked. . . . This was not understood by those who prepared the official scheme for the demobilization of armies. The result was a succession of mutinies.[36]

On one occasion C.P. arrived on his bicycle first thing in the morning to discover that a group of about thirty men had been seen some distance away on the road to Gateshead. Ever resourceful, he stopped a passing van which was heading in that direction, and, hiding himself inside, he told the driver to follow the escaping party. When they had overtaken them, he stopped the van, out of sight, and jumped out. By the time the men rounded the corner he was already striding purposefully towards them. The sudden appearance of their Commanding Officer, who certainly must have had some pretty sharp words for them, was enough to defuse a potentially nasty situation, and he was able to march them back to camp without any further trouble. Typically he said nothing about the incident. His family only heard the story some time later, from a brother officer.

The move south from Boldon to Bournemouth affected Christopher very little. The fact that 'home' had already changed four times since the outbreak of war was one of the main reasons for his uncommon lack of home-sickness when he first went to boarding school. ('I never *was* home-sick – there *wasn't* a home.')

> Even by the standard of English seaside towns, Bournemouth is a peculiarly unloveable place, an urban sprawl that owes most of its architecture to the late nineteenth and early twentieth centuries, an anaemic English equivalent of the French Riviera. Like the majority of south-coast resorts, it attracts the elderly in large numbers. They come to spend their last years in bungalows and villas, or as residents in faded hotels where they are welcomed in winter but where the weekly rates rise sharply during the summer season. They take the air along the sea-front at East Cliff or West Cliff; they patronise the public library, the Winter Gardens, and the golf course; they stroll among the conifers of Boscombe and Branksome Chine; and eventually they die. . . .[37]

Ellie came down first, soon after Christmas, to find somewhere for them to live. She managed to take a short lease on a villa called Saxonholme in Winton, a residential suburb on the northern outskirts of Bournemouth. C.P. was able to join her and Penelope at weekends, spending the rest of the week in camp at Larkhill, making the journey both ways by train. It must have been a pretty bleak few months for Ellie, away from friends and familiar surroundings; living in a place of genteel decline at the fag-end of winter, weary of the war. 'The Armistice had marked a cessation, a vacuity, and at first nothing more. The nation was overtired, underfed; just exhausted . . . The dawn of the post-war world was a very grey and chilly dawn.'[38] The atmosphere of Bournemouth in those weeks immediately after the end of the war would have had little to offer by way of amusement. Ellie was by nature both active and sociable; her occupations were all dependent on other people, unlike her husband, who was able to express himself admirably through his pen, both in drawing and writing. She wrote innumerable letters to relatives and friends, and she read voraciously, biographies mostly, seldom novels. She also read the newspapers 'with an air of disapproval' according to C.P., who was always amused by this. Without the presence, in Salisbury, of Frank and Helen, she would have been thoroughly miserable. After Frank had recovered from the severe enteric fever which had brought him back from the Dardanelles in a hospital ship, he was no longer considered fit for active service, and as a lawyer he had been appointed assistant to the Government Land Agent, Major Piggott, working for the War Department, in charge of all the properties in Wiltshire. They took a house, the Buttery, in the Cathedral Close in Salisbury; and within a few weeks they found a larger one just off the close, and Ellie was able to take over the Buttery. But the Easter holidays were spent in Bournemouth, though Christopher remembers almost nothing about the time.

The Easter term – 'Common Time' – at Winchester was also unmemorable except for an attack of measles, which seems to have been the start of a rather unsatisfactory period for him. His work suffered, and he seemed to be unable to apply his mind in the vigorous and enthusiastic way that had marked his first term in college. He was 'not yet at home in Roman History,' and his Greek was 'rather a handicap'. Monty's report ended with the percipient phrase: 'I hope he won't get worried.' He was still a very good fourth out of twenty-two. But in truth he was tired.

Emotionally and academically he had been pushed very hard to get the scholarship, and a period of adjustment was needed before he could develop any further. If his academic work was sometimes slapdash ('he has a fatal fluency in language which covers a good deal of inaccurate and ill-digested information'), his undoubted abilities and energy made him a singularly well-adjusted member of college. During the whole of 1919 and much of the following year his academic progress was not as rapid as he (or the staff) expected. Monty observed in June that year: 'I'm sure he means to do his best, but it is strange that he has for the moment lost the power of leading.' In a letter to his mother written on 2 July 1920 he wrote:

> I'm afraid 'conduct very good' is rather negative evidence – it means I haven't done anything flagrantly illegal (or if I have, I have not been caught!). Monty's remark about the 'power of leading' does not fit with what he told me the other day – that my place was just as much a matter of age as ability.

The following year his reports still showed some weaknesses, although by then he was beginning to find his feet. In some subjects, notably history and French, he was already at the top of the respective 'divisions', or classes. 'He has worked better, but even his best is rather slip-shod, and he never attains real accuracy except over things which interest him particularly. He has a certain degree of imagination, but it badly needs discipline.' Williams wrote: 'He is a curious mixture of real scholarship and slovenliness. When he gives his whole mind and energy to a piece of work, he can attain an astonishing grip of it.' But he needed to be deeply interested in a subject before he would apply to it his 'eager and inventive mind'. Obviously, he was not inspired by science: 'I think he regards time spent on this work as a time for mental relaxation.' By the time he reached the junior classical sixth, in the autumn of 1921, his work in all subjects had greatly improved, though it is only fair to say that even during the two years before when he seemed to lack 'the necessary dedication for real scholarship', his work was, by most standards, more than satisfactory. As with all gifted children, much was expected of him. Standards of judgement always rise with shining prospects of excellence.

Throughout the dreary months they were in Bournemouth C.P. was searching for a house in Amesbury, which is the nearest big village to the south-east of Larkhill. By the early summer he had found what he was looking for. Redworth House was a substantial Edwardian red-brick building in the middle of the village, which was later to become the District Council Offices. It was a very large house, and it had quite a lot of land, which included a grass tennis-court and a kitchen garden which was positively bursting with fruit. After all the shortages of the war this garden must have seemed like paradise ('it did', Christopher added). He and his sister gorged their way through the raspberry and strawberry weeks, through the plums and peaches, until the apples ripened just before the start of his second year at Winchester. They managed to cut the grass short enough to take advantage of the tennis-court, though the whole place had been allowed to run wild throughout the war, and the garden remained something of a magical wilderness.

At the end of the summer C.P. took Christopher to stay for a weekend with his sister Dorothy and her husband Owen Bayldon, at Beaulieu, where they had taken a house on the estuary. Uncle Owen was the son of a wealthy Yorkshire businessman, who had provided well enough for his family to enable them to do exactly what they wanted. Owen was a brilliant natural mechanic. In the garden of Dock House (the first of the two houses they lived in at Beaulieu) he had a shed which he had turned into a kind of mechanized den, full of power tools and bits of engines. This glorious 'play-room' was forbidden to everyone else, though Christopher used to peep in through the half-open door, to watch his uncle tinkering happily with some piece of machinery. When 'callers' appeared (which they frequently did) Owen would emerge reluctantly to greet them, usually covered in oil. He was once seen sneaking across the drive carrying his shoes in his hands to minimize the tell-tale scrunching of the gravel.

Owen Bayldon was one of the first people to have a wireless set; and in fact C.P. and Ellie were staying with them in the spring of 1912 at their house at Newton St Loe near Bath, when he picked up a distress call, giving the name and exact position of a ship in the Atlantic. He came into the room where the others were sitting talking, and said 'There's been a terrible disaster . . .'. He gave them the name and position of the vessel. It was the *Titanic*.[39]

That weekend in early September the weather was glorious. Owen had instructed them to bring their bathing-dresses, as they were all going swimming. They had a motor boat which was moored at the bottom of the garden on the east bank of the river. Christopher loved swimming, and he enjoyed the weekend immensely. It was conspicuously less agreeable for his poor father. The first bathing party they went on proved to be altogether too much for his constitution, which had obviously been weakened by the four years of war. He had to be hauled out of the water, shivering and blue with cold after not more than a few minutes. Much alarmed, his sister produced a stiff brandy to revive him; but the shock and embarrassment of this incident upset him so much that he never went swimming again. He must have hated betraying such weakness, even to his family, for his powers of self-control were keenly exercised. He was by nature a gentle and deeply emotional man, and it is a measure of his courage that he seldom allowed this vulnerability to show.

Christopher's Aunt Dorothy was C.P.'s favourite sister; nearest to him in age, she was the only one of the eight children to inherit their mother Fannie's lovely fair, coppery hair. She wasn't as pretty, but her sunny nature and the huge smile endeared her to everyone. She was once being photographed by a professional photographer, as a rather apprehensive young lady, eager to please. 'Now, smile,' he said cheerily, disappearing beneath his black cloth to take the picture. Her response elicited a sudden 'but gently, *gently*!'. As short sighted as her brother, she always wore *pince-nez*, through which she would twinkle at everyone with her laughing blue eyes. They had taken a lease on Dock House from Lord Montagu's estate, and when it expired they got his permission to build their own house a mile or so down the river. The land was called Spearbed Copse, and in keeping with the estate's policy of preserving all the old names the new house was built to Owen's design, with the help of a local architect, and duly called Spearbed Copse. It was thatched with Norfolk reed, of which Owen was immensely proud, and it had a large and beautiful garden, carved by Owen and Dorothy out of what was once just a wild piece of the New Forest. Parts of it were still wild, with masses of rhododendron bushes, and on the river bank they had a wooden landing stage that was built on stilts to take account of the high water ('tidal there, you see'), where the boat was kept tied up.

Christopher spent another pleasant day with them in the summer of 1921, as he wrote in a letter to his father, dated 13 June:

I did have a delightful time at Beaulieu on Saturday. Leaving here at 8.15 a.m. with Bobby Hamilton, we got to Southampton by 9. We put off in the dinghy from the pier to where the new motor boat was moored (they [Owen and Dorothy] had spent the night in her). Aunt Dorothy in a miraculous headgear appeared from the cabin; and in the saloon was spread a gorgeous breakfast – our second – eggs, ham and strawberries. Uncle Owen then appeared from the town with newly bought rolls to complete our happiness.

The boat – Uncle Owen's design as you know (average speed 9 knots) is replete with every modern convenience – gas, electricity and apparently unlimited locker space. We took till 12 or so to get round to Beaulieu, where soon we were sitting before a groaning board. After lunch Uncle Owen had to pore over a clutch, and we went for a jaunt in the canoe.

Tea, strawberries, company and six sets of tennis rounded off the day, with a race to Brockenhurst Station in Mrs Farrar's Rolls Royce. We enjoyed ourselves tremendously . . .

During the last war Owen served in the RAF as a wing commander, on administrative duties. He was attached to the Ministry of Aircraft Production (in which Christopher also served), in charge of the development of marine craft. This involved the design and production of small craft and inflatable dinghies, that could be carried in aircraft, for use when the crew were forced to bail out over the sea. He and Dorothy lived in London throughout the war, in a flat just across the square from South Kensington tube station. At the end of the war they returned to Beaulieu; but Owen, a life-long smoker of untipped cigarettes, was already stricken with lung cancer, and he died very soon after their return. Poor Dorothy was deeply unhappy; but her loneliness was most affectingly mitigated by the attention of an elderly friend, a retired army officer, who approached her, after a decent interval, revealing that he had loved her for years. He wouldn't, of course, ask her to marry him – that would be presumptuous – but he begged to be allowed to see her every day. She wrote to C.P. asking him what she should do. He must have encouraged her, for she agreed to see him, but never in the mornings. He was to come at three in the afternoon. This arrangement sadly didn't last very long, as she died – 'not of any particular disease', as Christopher said, 'she had just come to the end of her vitality'. She and Owen had had a wonderful life together. His ample resources provided them with every comfort, and they lived well, entertaining a wide circle of family and friends. They used to dress for dinner every night; and by the time Christopher was fifteen, his father had already had to have a dinner jacket made for him, which he first wore on one of the family visits to Beaulieu.

Owen was exceedingly generous with his money, too. He gave Christopher a motor cycle for his twenty-first birthday, which enabled him to travel considerable distances with ease, and a great deal of enjoyment, throughout his years at Oxford. He sold it in Oxford just before taking a train to London on the day before he was to begin working in the British Museum.

Apart from the riches of the garden at Amesbury, and the visit to Beaulieu, the summer of 1919 brought Christopher some far more significant experiences, that were to develop into a career, which was at that time barely recognized. At weekends with his father, and at other times on his own, he would cycle all over the surrounding countryside, exploring and learning. His sense of history was already attuned to the Romans. He was fascinated by their roads; he had seen the Wall snaking across the Northumberland landscape, and he had visited fortresses and camps. The Middle Ages were real for him too, with Durham, and the splendid churches at Hexham, Corbridge, Jarrow and Monkwearmouth. But here, on Salisbury Plain, there were traces of a much remoter past; barrows and trackways – and above all, of course, there was Stonehenge.[40]

At the beginning of his second term, towards the end of January 1919, Christopher was given a choice: he could take either four or seven hours maths teaching in a week. He opted for the seven, knowing that the extra teaching would help him, only to find to his dismay that it meant he would study no French at all. Maddie was appalled. She was by then living in rooms in St Faith's Road, not far from the college, at St Cross, where he used to visit her most Sundays. She offered to coach him again, if he could get permission, but there was a rule preventing men in the school from going into private houses. Undaunted, Christopher decided to do something about this. He waylaid the headmaster one afternoon in Moberly Court, as he was returning from one of his solitary walks. Monty was sympathetic, allowing him to slip away on one afternoon during the week, without first asking permission. 'But on no account must anyone know about this,' he insisted. He must simply vanish. This happy solution enabled him to continue with his French, which was already quite good, and of course it delighted Maddie.

Her rooms were in a house where two elderly ladies lived: Miss Perry, who seemed to own it, and her friend Miss Fowler. It was not entirely a satisfactory arrangement, as one can see from a letter that Christopher wrote to his mother on 3 February:

> I go to see her every Sunday and for walks some days during the week. . . . When I told her about Mrs Williams she was annoyed.[41] She says she has no particular need of company, although of course she would like to give lessons for the sake of the money. You see it is quite different at Winchester. At Cobham she had to have society; for there was no other amusement. But here she goes to bed early; gets up late; goes to the public Reading Room, reads all the papers and illustrated weeklies; takes books to read from the Public Library; takes her lunch out very often (for she is very much afraid of annoying her landlady), goes for a walk – and sees me often. . . .

However, in December that year he wrote:

> Maddie is enrolled in the Legion of voluntary Cathedral sweepers, and sweeps and dusts the stalls in the Chancel and replaces books, etc. every week, under the leadership of Miss Braithwaite, daughter of the Canon. . . .

These worthy ladies were somewhat unkindly referred to as the 'Cathedral Fowls'. Maddie certainly became quite a devoted church worker, and when she eventually managed to find lodgings, again with a policeman and his wife, as she had done in Cobham, she seems to have been happy in Winchester. She even told Christopher that she thought of making it her permanent home. P.C. Collier was a very kindly man, 'with a motor-bicycle and side-car' in which she was occasionally given lifts to the railway station.

'Maddie was rather like a sort of honorary aunt', Christopher said, aware of her love for him, of course; but the eyes of youthful inexperience saw only a quietly elegant lady, dressed almost always in black, who was clearly fond of him. That he was the very centre of her solitary world came to him only recently on the rediscovery of her one surviving letter to him, reading which it is hard not to feel a pang for the undoubted anguish behind the delicate restraint.

In the late autumn of 1919 C.P. was finally demobilized, and the family home was re-established at Campden Hill Square, in time for the Christmas festivities. There were the usual family gatherings with the Holland Park cousins, which had been interrupted by the four years of war, and Maddie expressed considerable fears about the state of the house after the Finch family had left it. But her anxieties were groundless, and there was no serious damage to the house or its contents.

During autumn 1921 Christopher was engaged in a number of interesting projects in addition to his schoolwork. By then he was

O.G.S. Crawford

beginning to overcome the difficulties which had beset him during his first two years: 'an excellent term in all ways' reported the headmaster. At the end of November he wrote to his mother:

On leave-out day Stevens and I spent a most enjoyable expedition on foot, following the old British road over the Downs, 13 miles to the Meon Valley, and back, via Alton, by train. We spent a long time at Chilcombe, and our archaeological ardour carried us to trespass on H.M. range. We were duly sent about our business by a warrant officer, who was superintending some work at the Butts. . . .

This 'archaeological ardour' prompted him to write a letter which was to lead eventually to a career in which all his talents could be put to use:

I wrote to Mr O.G.S. Crawford[42] a few days ago, and yesterday I received a vast envelope with an encouraging and interesting letter; two archaeological tracts of his 'with the author's compliments', and another one on loan. Also a prospectus of lectures in Southampton. Separately, by parcel post, came a roll of eleven 6 inch ordnance maps, covered with his own notes in pencil, inviting me to mark in all my discoveries and observations for him, all over them. I am marking everything I have seen . . .

Crawford's letter (dated 12 December 1921) is indeed encouraging – full of helpful suggestions:

British roads are dangerous. Most so-called 'British' roads are, in their present state, the remains of tracks (doubtless very ancient sometimes), which went on being used right down to a century or two ago. There is no means of dating hollow tracks which often began to be formed only in the Middle Ages. The winter, if fine, is the best time for field work.

Christopher set to work on the maps, and by the early part of February the following year, he had returned them to Crawford, together with some of his own plans and drawings of sites.

'Do you want the drawing of the earthwork back?' Crawford replied. 'I think it very good – you should use better paper, however – I enclose a couple of sheets for your next. . .'.

O.G.S. Crawford was then the archaeology officer for the Ordnance Survey at their headquarters in Southampton. He was a man of thirty-five when Christopher first wrote to him. The son of an Indian high court judge, he was orphaned in infancy and brought up in England by two aunts: Dora ('Auntie Do'), who was 'solid, worthy and low church', and Gertrude ('Aunt Pogga'), who was 'quiet, pietist' and equally 'low church'. Both were 'very kind hearted and good to me', he wrote in his autobiography.[43] He was educated at Marlborough, which he hated, and got an exhibition at Keble College, Oxford, where, according to his own judgement, he 'wasted his energies, and only got a Third'. During the First War he served in the front line with the Ordnance Survey – the army's map service, doing trench photography, surveying, and map-making. He finally joined the Royal Flying Corps as an observer, was captured, and spent a short period as a POW, during which time he became aware of the potential of viewing archaeological features from the air. After the war, a contact he had made with the then Director-General of the Ordnance Survey, Sir Charles Close, led to his post as archaeological officer, though he had no staff and a minimal salary.

Crawford's chief recreation was travel. 'To get the most enjoyment out of travel', he wrote, 'one should visit the wrong places at the wrong time'.[44] Curiously, he lists among some amusing dislikes, 'certain kinds of ruins; that is perhaps unusual in an archaeologist, but I can honestly say that to be shown over the ruins of a Roman Town or Villa is one of the things I try to avoid ... the same goes for Mediaeval Castles. Churches, however, are nearly always interesting'.[45] A confirmed bachelor, he adored cats:

> Unlike dogs, which will bark for hours on end, cats only become vocal when they are moved to do so by some urgent need. There are people who are irritated by these nocturnal symphonies but one only has to open a window and join in; an intervention of this kind will generally disperse the party.[46]

Crawford admitted that on the whole he 'preferred things to people', but he must have been an inspiring companion. His letters to the young enthusiast from Winchester, and there are more than a dozen of them, are full of encouragement and practical help. Christopher, also, asked his advice, and the following letter is typical of the courteous and constructive way in which Crawford responded:

> It is rather difficult to give advice about writing up your observations. In writing a paper of this kind it is generally better to take some general theme, not necessarily of much importance in itself – and bind the odd facts together — e.g. take your own observed hollow tracks, and compare the road system they reveal with that on Isaac Taylor's map, and Ogilby's survey (which I think you have access to). But I would much rather leave you to work out some system for yourself. Remember that the ultimate object is a map of the road system of a given area at a given time. The ideal is seldom, if ever attained, but if you can keep it in front of you, it helps you work, and makes it clear and consistent.[47]

The first two letters from Crawford have not survived – Christopher had first written to him the previous summer, as he tells his mother in a letter dated 2 July 1920:

... It has been grand fun, both the exploration of the ground and the poring over old volumes in the Fellows' Library. I have had two delightful letters from O.G.S. Crawford; and Stevens has had one from a man called Williams-Freeman, a field archaeologist to whom he wrote. They both seemed pleased, and regarded us as promising (though Crawford, to judge from his tone, thinks I'm a don). I have learnt a good deal about the local history of this part of Hampshire generally; and anyhow it is excellent practice for the future. ...

Alongside this growing absorption in archaeology, he was also enjoying a number of other activities. Although in one of his early letters home he wrote: 'I am not altogether delighted at the prospect of learning the piano this Half . . .',[48] he did in fact like singing very much, and he was at once taken into the chapel choir when it was discovered that he could read music at sight and had a good clear alto voice which had already been trained in the school choir at Sandroyd. His hands were never sufficiently agile, nor his fingers long enough (he could barely stretch an octave) to enable him to play the piano well enough to satisfy his highly developed musical sense. Wisely he was directed more towards a study of harmony and counterpoint, for he had already begun to write music himself, and later on he directed others in productions of his own plays and musical entertainments. There were outside events too:

We all went to *The Yeomen of the Guard* on Thursday afternoon. The orchestra was very good, but whether by accident or design, the bassoonist was placed on a small platform at the corner of the Proscenium, on a level with the stage. It was too ludicrous – as you

Bassoonist. Drawing by Christopher

know how absurd a bassoon is when in a noticeable position, or when it has an eventful part to play – in this case it had both; and I couldn't help laughing all through the overture. The man looked as if he was working an anti-aircraft gun. . . .[49]

Many of Christopher's letters of the time are illustrated with delightful little drawings and diagrams, following his father's ready wit, as he described events and people with a delicious eye for the lighter side of human frailty. In the summer of 1921 Uncle Frank and Aunt Helen came to a concert, bringing Aunt Katie with them, and her old Wykehamist husband Graham Snow:

They all came over from Empshott for the concert, and were delighted – Auntie Katie giggling immoderately all the time. Uncle Frank with a rapt grin, leaning forward and beating time with one finger. Aunt Helen whispering to him not to make himself so conspicuous, and Uncle Graham swaying as he stood on his chair, bellowing forth an enthusiastic 'Domum'.[50] I showed the Big Four all over the place. Uncle Graham was very shocked at his wife's unWykehamical and inappropriate levity. Then we all went to the Medal speaking. We saw all the mighty in their robes; heard the speeches made and the prizes given, and then we separated – they to a meal 'Up Town', I to College supper. . . .

He goes on to describe the meal: 'salmon mayonnaise, chicken, ham, new potatoes, salad, green peas, fruit salad and cream, and ices – of which I had FOUR – and gallons of splendid cider from a cask'. They returned for the concert, which ended with the singing of the school song. The irrepressible Frank was determined to enjoy himself:

'Now we'll have a family quartet,' he said, as soon as 'Domum' singing began. He started singing an al-fresco bass part, inventing as he went along. The next verse he invented a tenor part, in the rococo style. The third verse, in spite of Aunt Helen's almost tearful protests, he sang a falsetto. At first Uncle Graham and I sang a stout Wykehamical unison, but he was infectious, and very soon we started the same stunt. Aunt Helen laughed and remonstrated shamefacedly by turns. . . .[51]

Another of Christopher's interests at this time involved his skills with both pen and paintbrush, as well as a great deal of hard work. He began drawing and colouring what were known as 'Hot Rolls'. These rolls were originally lists of names to commemorate games of Winchester football (hence the use of the word 'Hot'; see note 17), and it was the senior prefect, Alfred Snell, who suggested to Christopher that he should do something more elaborate for Ken Chamber. He produced sheets of brass rubbing paper, which were stuck together to form a scroll

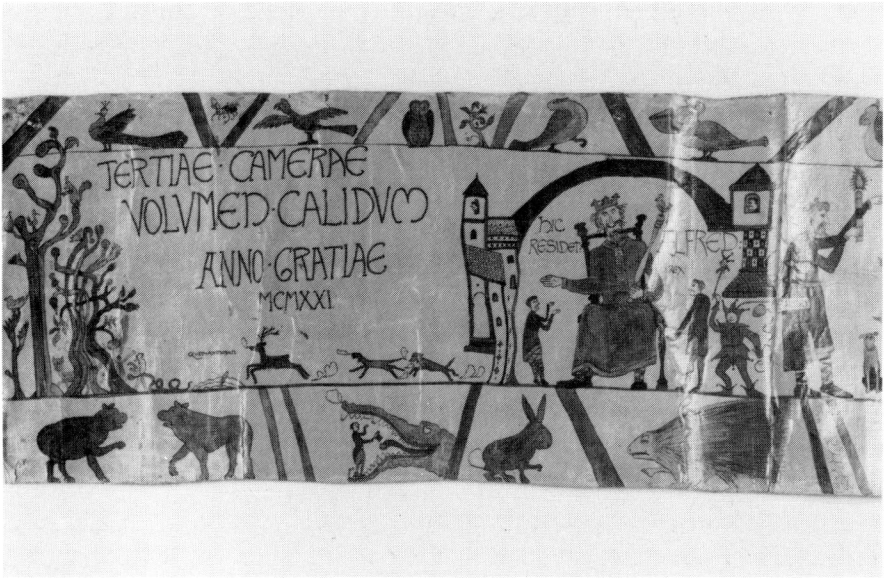

Beginning of III Chamber 'Hot Roll'

based on the Bayeux Tapestry over 15 ft long, and 1 ft or so broad. As the senior prefect of Ken Chamber, the roll was kept by Alfred Snell, who had it carefully glazed and backed with a sort of fine linen to preserve it. Christopher now has it, still remarkably fresh, wrapped in brown paper, returned to him by Alfred Snell not long before his death. Because of its size, it is difficult to reproduce, but his description of it gives a pretty good idea of what it looks like:

> ... It has a border, top and bottom, like its original, of irrelevant animals, birds and other figures. Starting in its main line with symbolic pictures of the Psalmist's heart desiring the water-brooks. It goes on to three scenes from the life of King Alfred (symbolizing Alfred Snell our Senior Prefect), sitting on his throne in a rickety palace, producing his horn candles, and burning the cakes. It then goes on to a fearsome Beaver with a pink head and hands, an orange body, purple tail and brown legs – in two attitudes (one of them devouring his dinner) for Beevor, our Junior Prefect. Tom Brown slaughtering the Rugby bully was the next scene – an attempted caricature of Monty looking on. Then three sober and sagacious Hawks, and some greedy and conceited looking Sparrows.... The Hot Roll ends with Bishop Ken, the Chamber Patron, blessing the assembled team. It took me a week ...[52]

Christopher also illuminated a list of names with humorous Christian names corresponding to their initials, including his own – Camomile

Forcemeat Cheesecake Hawkes, Archimago Snell, Jonquil Geranium Beevor, Cummerbund Elastic Stevens, Joblilly Huckleback Antigropelo Sparrow, Rumpelstiltskin Oberammergau Wilberforce, and finally a junior who was to become a great friend in later life, Karter Garter Jarta Carter Knowles.

Always keenly inventive, his tastes ranged widely; and one can appreciate the admirable way in which his enthusiasms were allowed to develop. There were a few anxious observations from time to time, from Monty as well as the second master, Mr Williams, that he was in danger of dissipating his talents in his eagerness to excel in so many different fields. But his letters reveal a strongly practical streak[52]; and in retrospect it would be difficult to imagine a better grounding for his chosen career than that which he was given at Winchester.

One of the most influential characters during his later years in college was that of the genial master of 'H House', Cyril Robinson. He was a most gifted teacher, and it was due almost entirely to him that Christopher finally overcame his early difficulties and began to work with the concentration that he had sometimes lacked. Robinson's father had lived to be a hundred, and his own life was almost as long. He was to remain a friend of Christopher's right up until his death in the early 1960s. His division was the Classical Senior Part I, and it was when Christopher was 'up to him' (taught by him) that he really began to benefit from all the teaching that he received. Robinson's methods were often brilliantly unorthodox. He appeared to be learning as he went along, taking his pupils with him on a voyage of discovery. He made them write essays on all manner of subjects, which would have to be read out and discussed by the whole class; and every week they would have to learn by heart a piece of poetry of their own choice. This was recited, without a title, and the class would then have to ask questions to find out what it was – the writer and period – thus making each individual performance a lesson for the whole class, with the added element of surprise to keep their interest fresh. Learning by rote is no longer approved of in schools, but the poems that Christopher learned have remained with him all his life; and such a background must surely bring a richness of language that can sustain much more than a purely literary expression.

Then there were Cicero's speeches. Instead of a simple reading they first went through the text (in this case the *Pro Milone*) so that they understood it properly; then Robinson arranged a performance of the trial in which they could all take part. The *Pro Milone* is a speech that was delivered in a court in Rome; it was the defence by Cicero of an eminent citizen, one Milo, who had been charged with murder. Nothing could have made the words more vivid than to perform them in this way. Not surprisingly the 'Bin' or the 'Beast', as Cyril Robinson was affectionately known, was immensely popular. The two names arose in different ways. He had joined the staff at Winchester at the same time as

Malcolm Robertson, the 'Bobber', so that they were 'Binson' and 'Bertson' to distinguish between them. The 'Beast' came about because he was at that time unmarried, living with his sister Helen, who kept house for him until he married in about 1922. He was what could be described as an agreeably ugly man, and as Helen was rather less ugly, though by no means a beauty, they were known as 'Beauty and the Beast' in typical schoolboy humour, which in this case was greatly softened by the fact that he was so nice. Increasingly he became known as the 'Bin', and it was he who ran the archaeological society, which Christopher joined as soon as he was old enough to do so. It was mostly 'church crawls' and visits to certain monuments, but with his contact with Crawford Christopher was able to broaden these activities considerably. His first publication, apart from short reports in the Wykehamist was the result of his field work at this time which was published by the Hampshire Field Club (of which Crawford was editor) in their proceedings in 1925. It was entitled 'Old Roads in Central Hants'.

On 3 April 1922 there was a performance in Ken Chamber of a play that Christopher had written and produced, in which he also took one of the leading parts. The plot was a burlesque, mostly in verse, of the sort of school story that appeared in boys' magazines. The hero (Eugene, played by Christopher) had some nice lines:

> Star of my life and apple of my eye,
> My joy, my gladness, my Felicity!
> In lowly suit before thy feet I fall,
> Those feet for which I'd gladly risk my all!
> I'm about to make what I suppose'll
> Cause you no small surprise: viz. a proposal . . .

The object of his devotion, one Rainbow Terminus, daughter of the Housemaster, Dr Terminus – both absurd characters – was played by Bogie Higginson, a friend of Christopher's, who was blessed with the largest pair of feet in college: hence the reference, which drew a huge laugh from the audience. Christopher's mother was prevailed upon to provide some of the costumes for the play, and the performance was a great success.

The love-sick Eugene continued:

> Well, well I know the gulf that separates
> Or ought to separate us, but the Fates
> My destiny with thine have interwoven.
> By Jove! My heart is blazing like an oven . . .

> I cannot check my words resistless flow:
> Whatever else may be, yet this I know
> I swear it is the truth and no mere fable –
> Thee only among women I'll be able
> To face each morning at the breakfast-table.

The plot creaks a bit by modern standards, but the undoubted wit and novelty of the language are clearly visible. The success of the play was repeated the following year with another, this time set in fifth-century Athens, called *The Nights of Alkibiades*. The typescript yields the following couplets:

> The whole delight of matrimonial union
> Consists in intellectual communion

> And love on both sides would be ineffectual
> Were we not both so vastly intellectual.

He wrote a third play, called *The Wife and Debts of King John*, which was finished at the end of February 1924; but it was never produced as there was an epidemic in the school. King John had some memorable lines:

> What horticulturalist could e'er eclipse
> The puckered rosebud of thy matchless lips?

This is simply funny; but another couplet shows very real skill with language:

> Will not my dear one pity my distress?
> Comfort and clothe me in my nakedness?

At the very end a kind of worldly cynicism creeps in, which is so much out of character for the young man who retained an unclouded innocence well into his adult life, that it is worth quoting:

> Anyhow, the mistake, when marriage fails
> Is always expiated by the males.
> No it is worse than shameful, it's absurd
> To knuckle down to Innocent the Third.
> King John has better things to do, he hopes,
> Than kissing the repulsive toes of Popes!
> And yet those toes must certainly be kissed,
> For it is worse than useless to resist.
> He'll take my crown, you bet one in a million;
> Make me a lower-middle-class civilian.
> And worse – to doom me to perpetual strife –
> Grant me no separation from my wife!

In March 1922 Christopher wrote in some excitement to his mother:

On August 13th there is an expedition to Munich, Nürnberg and Oberammergau. It is organized by Toc H (Talbot House).[53] This is an expedition for Public Schools and other boys and young men – about fifty altogether – lasting eleven or twelve days. At the present rate of exchange it costs about £12. One travels second class, and stays a week at Oberammergau. Toc H guarantee good seats for the play. If you turn it down I don't in the least mind, but I think it is a chance in a thousand. The awkward thing is that one has to decide about it now. The £12 includes everything . . .

Christopher's parents readily agreed that he should go, and he sent them the proposed timetable in June. They were to leave Victoria station for Dover on Sunday 13 August, where they would take the ferry at 4.15 p.m. That night they were to stay in Brussels, crossing the German frontier the following afternoon. After spending the night at Cologne, they would visit the cathedral, before leaving for Munich, and thence to Oberammergau. The play itself was on Sunday 20 August, beginning at 8 a.m., and ending at about 6 p.m. The cost of the ticket for the play was 12s. 6d.

He wrote to his mother from the British YMCA in Cologne on 14 August:

Arrived here about 8; departed Ostend 9.30 – Bruges, Bruxelles, Louvain, Liege, Vervier, Aix (3.30 a.m.), and so here. Good wash and a thumping breakfast at YMCA, then sally forth to see the town. The *Dom* (Cathedral) contains the finest old glass I have ever seen, and wonderful architecture – though proportions better in than outside. Streets are narrower than I expected, and dangerous from dashing trams.

Coherent cash account with all these millions is impossible. Pockets bulged with 6,700 mks – about £2 . . .

Tubby (Clayton) tries to invigorate the party when flagging at stations or anywhere, by singing – often very inappropriately. . . .[54]

The party from Winchester included Alfred Snell, Robert Hamilton, Humphrey Beevor, John Brooks, Charles Stevens, Douglas Carter and Derwas Chitty, with his younger sister, the vivacious and bubblingly enthusiastic Lal.

He wrote again on 15 August, from Wurtzburg:

We left Köln at 3.30 and had a bad and crowded journey to Mainz. It was a thundery, close day. [They went by steamer up the Rhine.] The castles were fine, but all alike. Got to Mainz at 7.30 p.m. and had a splendid meal – soup, venison, pudding and a kind of hock; then bed at the Rheingauerhof Hotel. The storm broke at 9 or so, and the rain came down in torrents, with thunder. No baths: a cold wash, then breakfast and lunch all in one at 11 (more hock). We get to Munich at 10.30. Things are very cheap, allowing for the 3,350 mks to the pound. . . .

After giving details of his return journey he continued:

> I have bought the real Bavarian Hochlender's costume – green hat and feather, red tie and horn ring, brown rough cotton jacket, and embroidered stockings, braces and stock. Also presents, and exquisite large photogravures of the play. On Thursday morning (17th August) we climbed a green hill and lay at full length. Glorious sun, flowers, grasses, trees and springs. Evening bathe (there is an establishment just outside Oberammergau). Today we climbed the Kofel; the towering rock of 1,343 m overlooking the village – a fairly stiffish one and half hour climb. Glorious afternoon. Fly drive to Ludvig II's *Schloss* at Linderhof. Amazing fountain; gaudy Louis XV salons; lovely china. A splendid drive. Tomorrow walk to Ettal (village nearby) to see the monastery. Afternoon not yet decided. Sunday, the play . . .

No text survives of the first performance of the passion-play at Oberammergau, but, according to the official publication for the 1910 play, it is first mentioned in the village chronicle in 1633. As well as the terrors of the Thirty Years War, the district was stricken with plague. In desperation the villagers made a solemn pledge to 'perform the Passion of Our Lord Jesus Christ every ten years'. The plague abated. The oldest known text was written in 1662; and an attempt was made in 1883, by some scholars in Munich, to bring that text up to date. It was fiercely resisted by the people of Oberammergau, and the text used in 1910 (and presumably in the performance that Christopher saw twelve years later) was that compiled from the old words by the village priest, J.A. Daisenberger, who was born in 1799, and died in the very year that the Munich scholars attempted to bring about the changes. Concessions were made, however: although the text remained the same, they made every effort to improve the production with elaborate costumes and music; and a new theatre was built to accommodate the increasing number of visitors. In both 1910 and 1922, Christ was played by Anton Lang.

That same summer Christopher spent a fortnight with his parents in Oxford. Once it was clear that Christopher was going to New College C.P., being a Cambridge man and knowing very little of Oxford, quite naturally wanted to see the place for himself. They took a short lease on a house in Beaumont Street (now the club house of the English Speaking Union), and they explored the college and the surrounding countryside. Christopher remembers sitting with them in the beautiful gardens of nearby Worcester College. He was struck by the fact that New College itself was exactly like a grander version of Winchester, which was of course founded by William of Wykeham as a sister establishment for his college in Oxford which was founded in 1379, three years before Winchester.

Every summer there was an OTC (Officers' Training Corps) Camp, which was run alternately at three sites for public schools. There was one at the Aldershot Command at Mychett, and the other two were part of the enormous army establishment on Salisbury Plain. The first of these was at Tidworth Pennings, the second at Tidworth Park, which lies just to the south of the main complex.

There was a joke about camp at Winchester: was going to camp compulsory on a voluntary basis, or voluntary on a compulsory basis? What it meant in effect was that you had to attend for two years out of three. It was really quite rigorous, and Christopher, being both energetic and sociable, enjoyed them very much. He attended all three camps; by the time he went to the last one, in 1924, he had been promoted to sergeant-major, which he felt had more than a little to do with his lusty singing voice. On long marches (of which there were many) it was encouraging to have someone with a fund of marching songs, some of which were sufficiently earthy to produce the odd ripple of displeasure. He was told when he was at Oxford that some of his songs were still being sung on route marches, including one which was an adaptation of the hymn tune, Redhead No. 46, 'Bright the vision that delighted was the sight of Judas's seer':

> Ponto[55] plays the ocarina
> Maurice Platnauer[56] plays the drum
> Frankie[57] plays the concertina
> On the Bobber's . . .[58]
>
> Why, I wonder, does the Jacker[59]
> Never sit down with a bump?
> It's because a Chinese lacquer
> Pattern Ornaments his . . .
>
> If you want a good musician
> I commend you Adam Carse;[60]
> His superlative position
> Rests upon a solid . . .
>
> Captain Humby[61] lets his puttees
> Hang in wreaths about his knee;
> This amid a soldier's duties
> Makes it easier to . . .
>
> Quirk,[62] since both his terminations
> Are alike devoid of hair,
> Ought to be, on railway stations
> Labelled 'This side up, with care'.

One evening after the camp was over, and the contingent was marching back to college from the railway station, they sang this 'hymn' at the tops of their voices. The headmaster (Williams had by then taken over from Monty) received a joint letter of protest from the ladies in the Cathedral Close, saying that it was blasphemous to use a tune in that way, one which was used for the worship of God. It was stopped, of course, but Wally Cowland, who was the adjutant, thought it very funny indeed, and it was he who told Christopher what had happened.

As a sergeant-major Christopher did not carry a rifle, only a swagger stick; but the OTC did learn to shoot on the rifle range of the town barracks, which was the depot of the Hampshire Regiment. On the one occasion that he was put to the test he simply took aim and fired in the general direction of the target. With his poor eyesight he couldn't even see it properly, but by sheer fluke he emerged as a crack shot, having scored over the hundred points which was the measure of a first-class shot.

There is a letter from Cyril Robinson in which he expresses his delight at Christopher's emergence from the adolescent doldrums of his early years at Winchester:

> Dear Colonel Hawkes,
> I am more than satisfied. If rather careless about details in composition etc., your son does not seem to lose the sense of accuracy in the things that perhaps matter more. He has just done the most astonishing paper on two of St Paul's Epistles, showing, after ten days work, a most profound grasp on every aspect and every theory connected with the interpretation and theology of the letters. There is no doubt that he has a first class brain, and I don't think he ever lets it go to sleep. . . .[63]

That August he embarked on a walking tour of the Auvergne with Alfred and Reg Snell. Alfred was two years older than his brother and Christopher, and he was the senior prefect in Ken Chamber. Reg was not a college man, but they had seen quite a lot of him, and all three got on very well indeed.

They took the boat from Newhaven to Dieppe, and then went by train via Paris and Clermont Ferrand, to a small wayside station in the Auvergne, from where a branch line took them to Le Puy, where they had booked rooms in a hotel. They walked all day in the hills, sometimes making longer expeditions, spending the night in a local inn. As all three of them had good singing voices – Reg was a tenor, with Christopher in the middle and Alfred a bass – they took vocal scores with them, which Christopher had written: settings of part-songs, rounds and canons, which they sang as they walked. They wrote in the visitors' register of one of those inns that they were 'Etudiants Chanteurs'; as a result they were asked by the landlady to give a performance one evening. The landlord, who had retired from the army, misheard when they announced a chanson pathetique, and thought they had said patriotique. When told of his mistake he was not too pleased. Once they were stopped, as they sang their way along a road, by gendarmes, who were astounded to learn that these three young men should have come all that way just to *walk*.

On another occasion they were crossing the infant Loire by a series of stepping-stones, when Reg lost his balance and fell in. When they got back to the hotel that evening Reg was shivering, and when he told the kindly proprietress why this was so she insisted on turning on a bath for him. Unfortunately the heating system failed to provide the comfort of a hot bath; indeed they were convinced that it had not done so for a very long time. The luckless Reg had to pretend that he had enjoyed what was in effect his second cold plunge.

Christopher's only other memory of that trip was of an incident on their return journey, when they stopped in Clermont-Ferrand to have a look at the cathedral. Having climbed to the top of the tower, they were caught in a sudden gust of wind, which blew Reg's hat off – a fine black sombrero – and deposited it quite irretrievably on one of the pinnacles of the nave.

Of Monty's many enthusiasms the one which was perhaps closest to his heart was what was known as SROGUS. Pronounced 'shrōhus,' it was the Shakespeare Reading and Orpheus Glee United Societies. The Glee part of it had had its real heyday in the late Victorian period, and from the early 1900s it was made into a separate Glee Club, of which Christopher was an enthusiastic member – first an alto, and then as a bass. But the headmaster's real passion was for Shakespeare, often with less than serious results:

> 17th October 1923. SROGUS Macbeth last night – Monty really the limit. To begin with he quite needlessly got up and went out at the beginning, and in returning, fell over the thunder – a large piece of tin sheet propped up against the wall of the passage outside, for use in the Witches scene. He did so just as someone in the play asked 'What noise is this?' (answer, Macbeth falling over the thunder). He then Spoonerized and misread all through the play; not as he once did before, 'Strets and fruts' for 'frets and struts', but almost every other conceivable thing: and he would cough at the most critical moments. He then threw a note to someone across the table, and by mistake, he threw a large gold-case pencil too. . . .

In the summer of 1923, and again in the December of that year, there were two notable ceremonies held at Winchester. The *Oratio Ad Portas* dated from 1615, when a lady of Wykehamical connections, a Mrs Letitia Williams, provided a sum of money for the delivery of three orations and a sermon on the Gunpowder Plot, which were to be given each year in college. One of the orations was the address of welcome *Ad Portas*. Christopher described the ceremony:

> When the Governing Body (The Warden and Fellows plus the Head

and Second Masters) decided that some Old Wykehamist or public character should be asked to receive this honour, and an afternoon for it was fixed, the whole school assembled in College Chamber Court, leaving open the broad paved walk that runs down the middle between the flint-set areas on either side. At the appointed hour the Headmaster's party came through Outer Court and appeared through Middle Gate. The honorand then had to step forward, and the lone figure of the Prefect of Hall, awaiting him in the middle of the paved walk, would face him and give a carefully prepared and laudatory Latin speech. Not a very long speech, to which the honorand had to reply with his own, which very few could manage in Latin, so they would start with a joke about this and then continue in English.

The first of these ceremonies at which well-known people were received was the occasion when the honorand was H.A.L. Fisher, who was at that time President of the Board of Education.[64] It was he who had introduced the Education Act of 1918, which, among other things, established state scholarships to universities, and percentage grants for teachers' salaries, as well as the school certificate. An old Wykehamist himself, he was Warden of New College during Christopher's time there.

As editor of *The Wykehamist* Christopher was introduced to Fisher after the ceremony, when he asked if he might have a copy of the Latin speech to publish. Fisher was very pleased by this, and handed it over at once. After he had left Monty took Christopher conspiratorially to one side and said that there were certain infelicities in the speech that had to be corrected before it was published. This the headmaster proceeded to do, and it duly appeared in the next issue. When Christopher reminded the Warden of New College of the occasion, during one of Mrs Fisher's social gatherings (minus the bit about Monty's corrections, of course)

Painting by Alexander J. Mavrogordato of H.A.L. Fisher being received *Ad Portas* at Winchester College in 1923

Fisher said, 'Ah yes, I remember it well. I wrote that speech on the front bench of the House of Commons.'

The other ceremony was rather more elaborate. Christopher wrote to his mother on 3 November:

> . . . In the morning he inspects the 'housing scheme' and the hospital; he lunches with the Lord Lieutenant (General Seely) at the Castle; then he is received *Ad Portas* in College, and watches Commoners XV vs. Houses XV. After that he has an informal tea in a College Chamber. He then attends a chapel service at which the new altar piece is to be unveiled; then he goes back to London. The company at the informal tea (to take place in VIth, the Prefect of Hall's Chamber) consists of the five officers, six selected commoners, the Prince, Sir Edward Grigg, Clive Wigram and three other equerries. The Warden is going to give us a rehearsal in the necessary etiquette the day before. Apparently all our trousers will have to be turned down. The Prince will wear a lounge suit. The tea lasts from 4.30 to 4.50 and is succeeded by chapel. As the latter will be up to time, and we are sure to start late, it won't be a very long job. He won't have time to get much to eat. . . .

He wrote again after the event:

> . . . As for the Prince and his visit, you read about the general lines of it in the papers. But let it be said, he was quite open about never having seen the speech he read at *Ad Portas*: also about his understanding of Latin. He was terrified of the Head Man, and said he was much embarrassed by being made to stand all by himself at *Ad Portas*, by him. 'Good God!' he said; 'I've never felt such a fool . . .'
>
> He said he thought the King's signature (made at his visit in 1911) in the book he signed was disgusting, and that he must rag him about it. He skilfully concealed his cigarette behind his back when the Head Man came in after tea to take him away, and succeeded in throwing it into the fire unnoticed. He confessed to having had so much lunch at the Castle that he could only eat one crumpet at tea.

That winter it was bitterly cold: 'Iron hard frost all day and all night here,' he wrote, 'I can only sleep by dragging my bed right up to the fire. People are buying ginger-beer bottles wholesale to use as hot-water bottles.'[65]

At the end of January the following year he began on a project that was to bring him a great deal of satisfaction, and some high praise for his performance: 'Everything is now ready for the start of steady rehearsals for *Faustus*. The producer now definitely decided on is Mr Firth.[66] A young man of great literacy and considerable dramatic feeling and experience; full of keenness and sympathy. . . .'

The committee was to consist of Firth, Beevor, Moon, Crossman and Christopher himself, with sixteen players in all for the twenty-nine parts. It was an ambitious project. Marlowe's play demands a great deal from its main characters; and Christopher's performance as Faustus earned him unstinted praise from all quarters. Written in blank verse, and probably first performed in 1588 it is the first dramatization of the medieval legend of the man who sold his soul to the Devil. Weary of the sciences to which he had devoted his life, Faustus turns in desperation to magic, summoning up Mephistopheles, with whom he makes a bargain to surrender his soul in return for twenty-four years of life, during which time he shall have whatever he wants. It has one of the most famous lines in literature in one of the scenes when he summons up Helen of Troy: 'Was this the face that launched a thousand ships . . . ?'

Mephistopheles was played by Dick Crossman,[67] with whom Christopher made great friends, although he waspishly wrote at the time, in a letter to his mother, that he seemed to be physically incapable of talking quietly. Among the cast playing the Seven Deadly Sins were William Empson,[68] John Sparrow,[69] Robert Hamilton, C. E. Stevens and Penderel Moon. Serge Orloff was also in the cast, as well as the future Sir William Hayter, the ambassador, who later became Warden of New College.

The performance was on Tuesday 18 March – Ellie's birthday, as it happened. He wrote her a very touching letter the day before:

> Very many happiest returns of your birthday. What a pity you aren't spending it here. It seems as if we are getting nearer and nearer together as I keep on growing up, and you go on being just the same. . . .

During the Easter holidays of 1924 Christopher was summoned by his Aunt Vickie to act as chaperon on a holiday she was taking at Biarritz. She was being courted by an elderly professor of Portuguese named Edgar Prestage, whom she in fact married some time in 1925. Christopher did not altogether approve of Uncle Edgar as a suitable husband for his very pretty and vivacious aunt, though he was tolerated as a nice old buffer by the family.

Christopher wrote to his mother from the Villa St Jacques in Biarritz:

> At 8 on Tuesday [8 April 1924] we started in a small and unassuming charabanc for Lourdes. Travelling by way of Bayonne, we got there between 12 and 1; after lunching at the Hôtel de la Grotte, we saw the grotto and Basilique, and took a good impression of the place before the rains came down. I didn't buy any of the Paris-made medallions, but bought at some expense, and after much thought, two big books, one of masses and one of motets by the great 15th, 16th and 17th century masters of vocal counterpoint. I doubt if they are obtainable in England – and they will certainly be a life-long pleasure and study for me.
>
> It didn't rain all the way back, and as usually happens here,

tantalizingly enough, the evening was clear and sunny, with magnificent piled-up clouds over a rain washed landscape.

On Monday we went to Bayonne in the afternoon, and deposited old Prestage in the archives; which done we pottered round the old town and the cathedral by ourselves. It is very picturesque; but the cathedral has been built of such soft and friable sandstone that some of it has weathered right away, and has had to be rebuilt in a stronger whiter stone, giving it an unpleasing patched effect. V. is wicked at pulling the old buffer's leg. She made him lead us into a booth in the fair outside Bayonne, and had us all three photographed in the way you see here (see below). The picture is one of the world's masterpieces! He was as pleased as Punch, and made out afterwards that it was all his idea.

We started for Spain by the 11.20 train, which was nearly an hour late at La Negresse, and the wind got colder; and we embarked on the Spanish electric light railway that leads to San Sebastian. Passports shown at Irun, and after an hour's journey, mostly in tunnels, we arrived to find a shrieking gale blowing along the coast, and pelting rain. It was then half past two (1.30 Spanish time), and we were cold and hungry. We made for the nearest hotel. A vast place – the Londres – where we warmed ourselves; and at a quarter to three sat down to the biggest lunch I have ever eaten. Hors-d'oeuvre, eggs and sausages in tomato sauce, mussels (we didn't actually eat these), *frites diverses*,

Professor Edgar Prestage with Aunt Vickie and Christopher at Biarritz in April 1924

which was an assortment of cutlet, steak, sweetbread, coquilles and eggs, all fried separately in breadcrumbs, and served with fried lettuces. Tender beef steak, followed by cakes and fruits, washed down with a wine that is called, I think, Rioja. That was 10 pesetas.

We had arranged to meet Prestage at Hendaye, and Aunt Vickie had given him her passport to carry, and he had forgotten he had it. So at Irun we hid in the train, and at Hendaye Spanish station we passed the official, as man and wife, with one passport – mine! meeting old P in the French station beyond. . . .'

Christopher remembers that his aunt wore a large veiled hat, which she used to cover her face, and as she was a slim and very attractive woman, the deception was a huge success.

Throughout his years at Winchester Christopher's religious feelings came to play an increasingly significant part in his emotional life. He was confirmed on 27 October 1920 by the Bishop of Winchester: 'Defend, Oh Lord, this thy child . . .' he boomed magnificently over the bowed heads, half a dozen at a time within the compass of his ample arms. Bishop Talbot, who had been the first Warden of Keble as a young man, was a tremendously impressive figure.[70] By a strange coincidence it was he, in his capacity as Bishop of Rochester, who had confirmed C.P.: there cannot be many instances of a father and son both being confirmed by the same bishop in different places.

Christopher did admit at the time that he had some difficulty in accepting many of the fundamental tenets of the Christian doctrine, especially the atonement. But his was a nature that craved the dignity and concord of faith; and perhaps there is in him still something of that primary need to obey and honour some kind of goodness, whatever it may be called. He wrote to his father in March 1923:

. . . I feel my own mental condition is sounder and more balanced now, by a good deal, than even a year ago; and I know too that my faith is much more lively, and runs much more deeply than before. I find in the latter connection that I cannot stand Theology beyond a certain point, because it interferes with mystery, the only thing one can really fervently believe in. . . .

On Whit Sunday, 8 June 1924, in his last term at Winchester, he wrote a joint letter to his parents in which he eloquently explained his feelings as he contemplated the end of his schooldays:

I do really feel now that my fluid years are more or less over, and I'm settling in to being a man – and this is testified by one thing in particular, which I want to tell you about. Perhaps it's better to begin with ancient history. I was confirmed, as you know, in the winter of 1920, and I was very earnest about it, I think I can fairly say, and was very near to God in my first Communion. But as time went on, I found the thing meant less and less to me – this was due chiefly to my own fault, but also to the fact that my Confirmation took place at what I now see to have been an unwisely chosen age, when I was in the middle of my misty developings and uncertain adventures, so to speak, of early adolescence; and the fact that the preparation I received from Monty and Williams, though admirable, was indefinite in what it taught me about the nature of the Sacrament, of the Church and other things.

Well, the Easter of '21 brought me a Communion which wasn't a success, and I dropped into accepting the accomplished fact and more or less giving up anything beyond a rather fitful religion. Later on, when I got to know Alfred Snell, and to be influenced by him, I came back to more serious prayer, and trying to take Communion more seriously. But I found I was ignorant of much that goes to make up belief, and as I wasn't very energetic about finding it out, owing to self-consciousness, and what amounts to self deception, I didn't advance very rapidly.

I knew there was a section of people who bowed to the altar and went to Eucharist at Cathedral, and were known as High Church, but I suspected the whole thing of being rather insincere; or at best a scheme for introducing illegitimate aids to emotional worship, in the shape of candles, chasubles and the like. Of course I got to know more about things. Then last Christmas I was sickened, after much preparation for Communion, as earnest, I thought, as I could make it, by a rotten Christmas service at St Clement Danes. A week or two later, I read that book of Father Knox's, and I saw what the Catholic Religion in the Church of England was, and how immeasurably high its ideals were. I thought a lot about this, bearing in mind how easy it must be, to let the same degenerate into mere ritualism, but also seeing more and more that this was vastly different from the non-committal 39 Articles, the only religion I had had laid before me at Confirmation.

I decided not deliberately to frequent 'High' Churches for the sake of their attractiveness, thinking that decisions ought to be reached by inward not outward means. At the beginning of Lent I took to receiving Communion every Sunday, and I was immeasurably strengthened and made happy thereby.

When I was abroad before Easter, both by talks with Auntie Vick (who was a convert to Roman Catholicism), and by what I saw, I realised how different and out of touch the Roman Church is. I don't think I have ever doubted the validity of Anglican orders, and Rome has never had any attractions for me. When I came back I was convinced first of the necessity of doing something serious about my rather free and easy past life, and second of the truth that lies in the Catholic (not R.C.) conception of faith, and of the church and the priesthood, as opposed to Protestantism and 'Parsonism', if you see what I mean. I consulted my great friend Humphrey Lewis, and he told me of a priest in Winchester of whom he knew. I wrote to him, and he replied splendidly. He didn't suggest it in any way, but most days this week I have been to the chapel in his church, where the sacrament is reserved, to prepare myself, and yesterday I made my confession to him. It is certainly the great thing in my life. Penance and absolution is a Sacrament; and in it, complimented by my communion today, I have found incredible peace, happiness, and strength of resolve to lead a new life.

That is practically all, except that I should assure you I haven't found any of this thought morbid, or making me miserable. I haven't felt mawkish or woolly, so to speak – in fact if I had, I should never have had the courage to confess – surely an honourable and gentlemanly action always, whether to God through his priest, or to any man in ordinary life. I don't feel changed into a new character, or anything: I feel the best of my old self has come to the top, and by God's grace I want to keep it there. I haven't been influenced or talked over by any living soul, by no priest, for I knew none till after my confession; by no friend there, for I didn't broach even the fringe of the matter to anyone till my mind was made up. Not by Maddie, because she doesn't go to confession herself (though I never talked of kindred subjects with her); and certainly not by Auntie Vick. It's absolutely my own decision.

I write all this, not from self-analysis run mad – a process I have never taken kindly to – but because I am certain that you ought to know all about it and tell me what you think. That I haven't spoken to you about it before now, I hope you will pardon. It was because discussion of religion has never formed a prominent part of the family life (for better or worse), and because I didn't really know – don't know now how either of you believe about the central facts of religion. Also I felt it was my duty to deal with my own problems alone. The priest I confessed to I had tea with today. His name is Heinz Smith and he's a cheerful widower, a keen golfer, and by no means a sloppy or pretentious person. Anything further from the idea of a 'Jesuitical' priest twisting the penitant's soul could not be imagined. . . .

In 1958 Christopher recalled in an article for Winchester's school magazine, *The Trusty Servant*:

Thule Chamber in the north-west corner of College has on one side a row of four windows (looking out to Moberly Court), and opposite them a row of seven toys, above which is a long and frieze-like strip of wall.

He continues with a description of his 'Hot Roll' in the style of the Bayeux Tapestry:

Christopher's wall-painting in Thule Chamber, Winchester College

It was pinned up in the Chamber (this was in Ken Chamber) where it was seen by the Second Master on one of his occasional evening visits. He quickly discerned among its many symbolic figures, the portrait of himself, arrayed as a Bayeux-style Norman Knight, riding an uncommonly high horse, and about to draw a long bow with two strings. He was very much amused, and at the end of the Half he brought the Bursar, Herbert Chitty, to see it. He also was consumed with mirth.

Two years after this, in Short Half, 1923, when Christopher was prefect of school, Williams and Chitty took him to one side and told him that they proposed to cover a strip of wall in Thule Chamber with a fine plaster, and that they wanted him to do a permanent painting, in oils, in the style of his original 'Hot Roll'. He began the work in Cloister Time, 1924, his final term, alongside all his academic work. 'The paint takes perfectly,' he wrote, 'but one has to use an almost empty brush otherwise tears of paint run down the wall. So it'll take ages.'
He wrote to his mother towards the end of June 1924:

... The fresco is practically abandoned for the time being; but Williams has invited me to stay with him whenever in the future I can come down and finish it.

This he was able to do during his first long vacation from Oxford a year later. His letter goes on to describe all the activities that lay before him for the remainder of his time at Winchester, and he ends as his father once ended an essay on his life as a carefree undergraduate at Cambridge, with a wistful phrase:

... So there's my last month of the happiest period of my life mapped out.

6 Oxford, 1924–5

A visitor walking for the first time from the high-walled austerity of New College Lane through the fourteenth-century gateway at its eastern end may find his first glimpse of the front quad of New College a little overbearing. It is almost intimidatingly impressive. The walls of the chapel and ante-chapel rise up on the north side, with their seven great stained-glass windows accentuating the starkness of the fellows' sets, across an immaculate expanse of turf. But let him turn to the left, through a narrow ill-lit passage, past the entrance to the ante-chapel, and before him he will see, beyond a modest archway, the first bay of the medieval cloister. Christopher's eloquent description of the sister college's cloister at Winchester as 'a place of great stillness and compelling peace' is equally fitting here, where the symmetry is broken only by the spreading branches of an ancient ilex in the north-west corner, and the less-than-perfect grass, impoverished by its roots. There is no intimidation here: only the subtle agents of mortality – the names of fellows set upon its walls.

When William of Wykeham founded his New College in 1379, there were already seven colleges in the city of Oxford.[1] The earliest foundation, that of University College, whose official title is the Great Hall of the University, was traditionally ascribed to King Alfred; but the earliest record of its endowment dates from 1249, when one William of Durham gave a sum for the maintenance of ten or more Masters of Arts.

It was seven years before the main buildings of New College, the chapel, hall, and rooms in the front quad (which used to be called the Great Quadrangle) were completed; with the cloister and bell tower added in 1400, and the warden's barn two years later. In the Middle Ages heads of colleges always lived over the gates. Except for St John's, New College is unique in that the rooms over the gate are still part of the warden's lodging.

Towards the end of the eighteenth century the chapel was restored and given a new roof, by James Wyatt,[2] who was perhaps best known for his design of Fonthill Abbey, near Shaftsbury, in Wiltshire, a short-lived masterpiece that he built for William Beckford.[3] Most of Fonthill was pulled down in 1807, after only eleven years. Wyatt's roof at New College had a comparatively short life, too: it was replaced in 1865 under the direction of Sir Gilbert Scott,[4] whose grandson, also an architect,[5] was responsible for the New Bodleian Library, which was completed in 1946.[6]

As Nikolaus Pevsner observed, the modern visitor to New College will find it difficult to connect the composition of the front quad with the fourteenth century.[7] The chambers were originally in two storeys, with the upper one approached by five staircases. Each set consisted of a large bedroom with three or four beds, and the same number of small studies opening off it. These rooms were remodelled in the early eighteenth century, retaining some of the original partitions, and some of the large rooms still have their seventeenth-century panelling, among them Christopher's in his second and third years. Further alterations were carried out at the beginning of the eighteenth century, when the windows in the front quad were replaced by sashes. The earlier sashes in the garden quad, which was remodelled in 1682 by William Bird, are in fact the earliest dateable examples of this type of window in Oxford. In 1700 a gate was put in the medieval town wall, through which the later buildings of the college are now reached. Gilbert Scott's range, begun in 1872, faces Holywell Street on the north, on land which had been acquired by Merton College in the seventeenth century, and was purchased by New College in 1871, when Scott was engaged. At that time some of the existing houses in Holywell Street were already being used for college rooms, as most undergraduates lived in lodgings, as they do now, for their final year.

In 1884, as the number of unmarried fellows living in college decreased, it was thought desirable that another married tutor should live within the college walls. A house was built at the east end, with adjoining staircases for undergraduates. This joining range, with the high Robinson Tower, was designed by Basil Champneys, whose style, though less hard and uncompromising than Scott's, is still distressingly out of character with the many older houses in Holywell Street.

When Warden Sewell died in 1903 he was succeeded by William Archibald Spooner.[8] Born in 1884, Spooner had been first an undergraduate, then Fellow and Dean of the College, teaching ancient history and philosophy. His appearance was extraordinary. He was not much more than 5 ft in height, with very white hair and, as C.M. Bowra says in his *Memories 1898–1939*, 'a cherubic face'. He was an albino, which affected his eyesight, and he used to read with a large magnifying glass. His supposedly frequent transpositions of the initial letters of words were eagerly collected. Julian Huxley states in his *Memories* that 'Kinkering Kongs their tatles tike' is the only fully authenticated spoonerism, though 'this did not deter the Oxford dons, including Fellows of his own College, from inventing a whole series of imaginary ones'.[9] He had a curious unctuous voice 'as if butter were actually melting in his mouth'.[10] His undoubted eccentricity and absent-mindedness, together with his weak eyesight, belied a sharp intelligence. He seemed to know what was going on around him in an uncanny way. It was also said that there was something saintly about him, and he was certainly exceedingly kind. Maurice Hugh-Jones, who went up to Oxford two years before Christopher, from Winchester, remembered vividly how 'The Spoo' had visited him daily in hospital, where he was gravely ill for a time after being struck on the nose by a cricket ball. The doctors had the greatest difficulty in stopping the bleeding, and there were fears for his life. Spooner not only had prayers said for him (they were also said at Winchester), but he also obtained the services of one of the top specialists in the country to try and save him. When Hugh-Jones's widowed mother protested that she was quite unable to afford the services of such an eminent physician, Spooner assured her that the college would pay. 'But don't tell him, or he'll put his fees up!'

Spooner set about restoring the warden's lodgings with great vigour, for they had about them 'an air of having been long deserted'[11] His predecessor had spent forty-three years in scholarly oblivion to discomfort and decay. The task of reconstruction was entrusted to W.D. Caroe: 'always resourceful, and sometimes brilliantly successful in his planning', his highly individual style and use of decoration was, to some eyes at least, 'not easy to admire'. [12]

Spooner's wife, 'a large and majestic woman',[13] had been brought up in a bishop's palace in the Victorian period, and she was used to entertaining on a lavish scale, assisted by her comely daughter, Rosemary. 'She considered that the Warden's Lodgings required ten resident maids and a houseboy.'[14] Accordingly an additional storey was built on the quadrangle side, to the south of the Gateway Tower for the servants, while the quarters at the east end of the barn which had been the medieval guest chamber were used by the warden and his family. The west end of the barn was skilfully converted into a cottage for the gardener, though in Christopher's time these rooms were made into two very exclusive undergraduate sets.

On Thursday 9 October 1924 Christopher arrived at New College from Winchester, where he had spent three days working on his wall-painting in Thule Chamber. The following day he was among the small group of freshmen scholars who presented themselves at the warden's lodgings to be formally admitted to the college. They were, in fact, among the last scholars to be inducted by Spooner, who was to retire during the Hilary term[15] at the age of eighty. When they entered his study a single glance at the appearance of these young men brought the warden to his feet.

'But you haven't any gowns. . . . I can't admit you without gowns!' Sheepishly they retreated, bidden to return at 4 p.m. gowned. After hastily visiting Walters in the Turl, they were duly admitted, and sent on their way with the approval of the warden, who was a very kindly and considerate man. Unfailingly generous in his hospitality, he was also a Poor Law Guardian, and he had long been an active member of the Oxford Charity Organization.

Apart from a formal tea party, given by Mrs Spooner and her daughter Rosemary, Christopher had very little to do with Spooner. During his first week, however, he had one quite lengthy conversation: 'I was summoned to my formal call on Spooner on Tuesday [14 October]. We talked on many subjects: his intellect is extraordinarily active and keen, and he talks well . . .' A few weeks later he received a note summoning him once again to the warden's lodgings. When he appeared at the appointed hour Spooner greeted him warmly and enquired what it was that he wanted to see him about. Christopher explained about the note. Having carefully gone through all the possible reasons he might have had for wishing to see Christopher, a look of concern momentarily clouded the old man's face. 'I hope there has not been any misdemeanour . . .' he began. On being assured that as far as he was aware there had been no breach of any rule, Spooner smiled sweetly, and dismissed him: 'Then it must have been purely for the pleasure of making your acquaintance. Good morning, Mr Hawkes.'

On the evening of his arrival Christopher had pencilled a brief note to his mother, dutifully reporting that all was well: 'All my things are in perfect order, except one picture-glass and three plates, broken on the journey. I am very comfortable, and getting well installed. . . .'

His rooms for the first year were in Scott's new building, the next two years he spent in rooms in the front quad, on the first floor on staircase four. These first rooms faced the town walls and the chapel, also on the first floor, on staircase three. The small bedroom which led off the study looked out over the houses in Holywell Street. The walls of the room were covered with a rather overwhelming paper: 'I am gradually, and with discretion, buying pictures – three to date – for the wallpaper has to be stifled to prevent its oppressive greenish design spoiling the room. . . .' He ordered new covers for the chairs, and bought a couple of 'chocolate-red' [i.e reddish-brown] cushions for them; and he managed to exchange an uncomfortable Victorian sofa for a basket chair. The pictures he bought were colour prints of Italian religious paintings, published by the Medici Society and nicely framed.

'Things are going splendidly,' he wrote a few days later, 'But to plunge into business at once, I lack the following:

1.   A small clock for the mantelpiece
2.   A large teapot
3.   My other bookcase
4.   Some nice lampshades
5.   An eiderdown, or some such . . .'

His parents arranged to bring all these things up to Oxford for him, and they spent a night at the Clarendon Hotel.

Christopher's college servant, or 'scout', for the first year was a rather surly elderly man named Medcroft, who was slow and ponderous; but this didn't deter Christopher from entertaining. You could order a lunch to be served in your rooms by your scout, usually not for more than four people, as the tables were small. A lunch of bread and cheese and beer was normally brought to your rooms, and dinner was always in hall (unless you dined in a restaurant), and breakfast in the junior common room. You had to get up reasonably early for that, and there was a roll-call system called 'Rollers'. Alic Smith, who was then a tutor (he later became warden of the college) used to sit in hall with a printed college list on a pin board in his hand, and you had to be there before 8.30 a.m., not every day, but a certain number of days each term. This allowed a little room for manoeuvre after late nights, though Christopher found that by half way through the term he had already used up his days' grace, and had to get up every morning.

That first term was an easy and immensely enjoyable one. Having worked so hard at his classics at Winchester, he found the work that was required took very little concentration, and he threw himself eagerly into some of the varied social activities of college life, as indeed did most of his contemporaries. After the rules and restrictions of Winchester, like all young men taking their first intoxicating draughts of freedom, he filled every minute with some pleasurable activity. He enjoyed long afternoon walks, with enormous teas at the end of them; and he played rugby – once – as did his contemporary, Emlyn Williams, who enjoyed it as little as Christopher:

> The rugger afternoon was even more of a nightmare than the rowing. Was the notoriously enervating climate already gnawing at my vitals? All I knew was that the ball was not round. The game started, and among the weaving, steaming, scrumming savages I wandered lonely as a cloud. Suddenly out of the grey afternoon, the ball came staggering towards me; I headed it. There was a howl, I made a sheepish grin, struck my forehead comically, and shrank back into anonymity.[16]

Christopher, on the other hand, who had played a great deal of Winchester football, was not so bewildered by the ferocity of the game as poor Williams was; but he didn't enjoy it, and never played again.

He joined the Bach Choir, which was under the direction of the redoubtable Hugh Allen,[17] and he sang in its performance of the Brahms Requiem in the Sheldonian Theatre on 7 December, the last Sunday of term.

He had a weekly tutorial with Henry Ludwig Henderson, or 'Henders' as he was called by the undergraduates, who was half German through his mother and had a pronounced guttural accent, which of course they used to imitate. As well as being Christopher's Mods tutor, he was Dean of the College, which meant that he was responsible for discipline. But since he was notoriously lazy and easy-going, nobody took him seriously. Provided you behaved in a reasonable manner, you could do pretty well what you liked. C.M. Bowra has described his appearance: 'He had a round face and round head, closely cropped white hair, a slight moustache, an upright carriage, and a long stride.'[18] He never published anything, and seems not to have done any original work. His lectures were thought to be competent, though not very up to date. He enjoyed going to the theatre and attending public lectures, but above all he enjoyed the company of young ladies. He used to give elaborate tea parties for them, and 'Henders and the girls' were viewed with considerable amusement. He never married, which is curious in one whose interests were so single-minded. Alic Smith once asked him about this, and his reply was revealing, and rather sad: 'It is because I like only the fluffy ones,' he said. Henders died, appropriately, on holiday in Monte Carlo, on Boxing Day, 1963.

On 13 November 1924 Christopher wrote a stern letter to his mother, which can scarcely have contributed to her peace of mind:

> You really mustn't write these frantic letters, they make things feel upsetting when really they needn't, and only increases wind-up and spoils nerves, especially your own. . . .

The trouble was over the impending visit to Oxford by his newly married Aunt Vickie. Ellie heartily disapproved of poor old Uncle Edgar and was utterly unable to understand how her sister could have embarked on such an 'unsuitable' union. Christopher liked Prestage, and was naturally irritated by what he saw as his mother's totally unreasonable behaviour. His letter continues:

> It's perfectly all right about their visit, except that V's letters have been so muddly I've only just made out when they're coming, and for how long. She refused an invitation to tea when I'd invited her for lunch, saying that it would be rather late – no word about what day or anything. Of course, now I understand times and seasons I've resigned the Sunday digging, and am having them to lunch, with steak for the Uncle, and they can stay as long as they like. Now is that all right?
>
> I wish you wouldn't write HE as if the poor man were an ogre – I've no doubt marriage is going to change him a bit, as well as her, and I dare say it's begun already: anyhow it does no good to regard him as a sort of Moloch, to be placated with constant sacrifices of steak. . . .

Though he had last minute qualms, the visit was entirely successful, and Aunt Vickie went again during the Hilary term the following year. Her conversion to Catholicism while she was working as a nurse in a military hospital in Paris during the First World War had come as a considerable shock to her strictly Anglican family. The fact that Edgar was not only a Catholic, but a very serious-minded one, must have had a lot to do with the disapproval. He was also a widower, and a great deal older than Vickie. His first wife had been Portuguese, and he had taught her language as a professor at King's College, London, until his retirement. He and Vickie had met through their joint attendance at a Catholic church in Kensington.

Early in November Christopher returned to Winchester for a couple of nights, to play football, and to do some more work on the wall painting:

> I went down on Sunday afternoon on my push-bike and stayed with 'Budge Firth'. My ride down there was not uneventful – I ran into the hedge once, after it was dark – but reasonably quick – about 5 and a quarter hours for 50–55 miles or so, with halts, which made the total time taken over the journey 6 hours and 10 minutes. . . .

Even after such a short interval, he was starting to look back on his school days with a degree of detachment:

> . . . I think College is settling in for a solid era of peace and prosperity now, with its new Second Man [Williams had by then replaced Monty Rendall as headmaster] – the old jumpiness and artificiality which used to make themselves felt, only naturally, in a cooped-up community of rather clever lads, the atmosphere of which had been badly electrified by the war, had practically gone before I left, and now I think entirely. One is beginning to look at things with a more detached eye! It makes one's back ache, standing up on those Toys, but it was best to keep hard at it, for sundry reasons. . . .

It was suggested that Christopher should sit for the Ireland Scholarship, which was held at the beginning of December: 'It will be of value to me', he wrote, 'in gaining experience for Schools, though there is little chance of my appearing on the lists.' He was right about this, though the papers – all unprepared –in classical composition, translation, essay-writing and criticism, were indeed useful to him, and he even reported to his father afterwards that some of the papers had been 'quite fun'.

Part of the work he had to do in preparation for the Ireland took him to a series of lectures by Gilbert Murray.[19] Born in Sydney, New South Wales, where his father, Sir Terrence Murray, had been President of the Legislative Council, Murray had come to England at the age of eleven. He was the cousin of W.S. Gilbert[20] after whom he was named. Educated at Merchant Taylors' and St John's College, Oxford, Gilbert Murray had a brilliant academic career, winning all the prizes, and he was only twenty-three when he was appointed Professor of Greek at Glasgow. In 1908 he returned to Oxford, where he was appointed by Lord Asquith to be Regius Professor of Greek. He had been elected a Fellow of New College in 1888, the year before his marriage to Lady Mary Howard, a daughter of the 9th Earl of Carlisle. She had been a beautiful lady in her youth, but by the time Christopher met her she had abandoned all attempts to keep up her appearance: she took no trouble with her clothes, unlike her husband, who always wore very well cut suits and stiff collars. Like Monty Rendall, he wore his tie in a gold ring.

As well as attending his lectures, Christopher was twice invited to their house on Boars Hill – once for tea, and the other occasion was for what proved to be an amusing and memorable lunch, on Saturday 21 November 1925. Lady Mary was a strict teetotaller: 'I like wine,' she once said, 'but I don't think it's so good a drink as coffee [pronounced 'Korfi'].' She had in fact helped her dynamic and overbearing mother pour the family wines down the drain, at Castle Howard.[21] She was also a vegetarian, and she had converted her husband to this persuasion at a time when it was thought extremely cranky. There was always a compromise roast for their guests, who would be asked by Murray, as Bowra recalls, 'Will you have some of the corpse, or will you try the alternative?' (*Memories*, p. 223). On this particular evening Christopher had the corpse. Half-way through the lunch the door burst open to admit the Murrays' somewhat rakish son Basil, who had driven down from London unexpectedly, at great speed, in his sports car. This intrusion rather embarrassed his father, though Christopher was amused by Basil's flamboyant appearance.

After his parents' visit in the early part of term, Christopher joined the Oxford Union, expressly to please his father (who insisted on paying a 'life compounding fee' for him). C.P. clearly had hopes that his son would turn out to be an orator, but Christopher seldom went to meetings, and he never spoke at all. He was very little stirred by politics. 'This is a convenient place to drop into,' he wrote, 'to read the papers and wash one's hands before tea. Besides all the other advantages: note paper, for instance.' (He was using the headed paper for this letter.) 'In the old days members got all their letters posted free, but this has been stopped for economy. . . .' This was not exactly what his father had had in mind.

The Michaelmas term ended on 8 December, and Christopher spent the holiday at home, with the usual round of family parties, and in the middle of January he went by train to Empshott to spend a couple of days with Frank and Helen. They took him to a performance of *The Mikado* by the Petersfield operatic society, in which Frank had the part of Ko-Ko. Christopher loved Gilbert and Sullivan, and he enjoyed the performance immensely, writing an appreciation in the visitors' book, 'somewhat after W.S.G.':

> There is beauty in the new-erected stage –
> Do you fancy certain singers were not newer?
> An opinion I'm desiring
> On a question awe-inspiring:
> Is there any pro can beat the amateur?
> Throughout this wide purlieu
> It's the universal view
> That there's nobody to touch the amateur!

The performance was conducted by the young A.C. Boult, the future Sir Adrian, who had been at Christ Church before the First War, where he had been a member of the OUDS, and had taken part in a performance, in the original Greek, of *The Frogs* by Aristophanes.[22]

By 15 January Christopher was back at Oxford after a whirlwind three days spent near Worcester with the Lupton family. Cecil (or 'Cis' as he was always called) Lupton was an old friend of C.P.'s from Cambridge days. His father had been a business man in Yorkshire, but he had retired early and bought a house called Severn Bank, at Severn Stoke, near Upton upon Severn, where he indulged his passion for fox-hunting. He had two daughters: Elizabeth, who was the same age as Christopher, and Marjorie, who was two or three years younger and exceedingly pretty.

'The journey to Worcester was a bit of a snag owing to the fog,' he wrote, 'which ruined the Southern Railway service, but not the GWR, so I missed my connection at Reading, and didn't get to Worcester until 7; but that was just not too late to throw things out for the dance. . . . I also got through 1,600 lines of Virgil on various trains!'

There were three balls: the first a private one, the second the Hunt Ball, which was held in the County Hall ('an ugly room, but vast'), and the Cricket Club Ball, which took place in the Guildhall ('a lovely old Georgian place with a perfect floor, but a bit of a crush as it just wasn't quite big enough'): 'Mr Baldwin was there, with his wife, though your expectations of Jenkyn-like butlers[23] and powdered footmen were not fulfilled. . . .'

The election of the new warden took place at 2 p.m. on 28 January 1925. Christopher had heard from the Dean of Balliol that 'Fisher was a cert – but there were curiously few rumours.' This proved to be right, and the election was a popular one, as Fisher brought his wide experience in politics as well as an impeccable academic background.

During the winter of 1916 Lloyd George was entertained by Fisher when he was at Sheffield and was so impressed with him that he invited him to become President of the Board of Education. He was already a Member of Parliament, as well as being Vice-Chancellor of Sheffield University. An Old Wykehamist himself, he had also been a Fellow of New College and tutor in Modern History; but the appointment was a remarkable one. Lloyd George was a shrewd judge of character and he recognized at once the potential of this most able man.

Fisher had a talent for coining memorable phrases: he once said of a colleague's book: 'I think it excellent, and only wish that it had been written in English.'

During his second term Christopher was delighted to be taken on by another tutor, J.D. (Jack) Denniston:

I'm getting on nicely with Denniston, the Old Wyk. don from Hertford [College] to whom the overworked Henders has farmed me out for composition. His wife [née Mary Morgan] was with me at the Norland [Place School]. They are both so nice, and are always 'at home' on Sundays if I care to go. [They lived at 5 Polstead Road in North Oxford.] He is a first rate tutor: much better than Henders . . .

Rt. Hon. H.A.L. Fisher, Warden of New College

Denniston believed that you cannot claim to know a language unless you can write it; and that the only way to a proper understanding of classical literature was through the discipline given by composition. He was a fine teacher, very slow and thorough, and he used to write innumerable postcards to both friends and colleagues asking them questions. He very much enjoyed a good argument, and when he entertained at home he would often throw in a deliberately provocative remark in order to produce a lively debate. When Gilbert Murray retired he had hoped to succeed him, but Murray was against him, and the chair was given to E.R. Dodds, who was then Professor of Greek at Birmingham. He, like Murray, was interested in psychical research, and the two men shared many beliefs and interests.

During his first term Christopher's religious leanings became more and more pronounced. He was drawn to the Anglo Catholic discipline as it offered him both the spiritual guidance and the opportunity to express his beliefs in an enjoyable way. He joined the choir at Pusey House, [24] where he had already made contact with one of the two young priests, Freddy Hood, when he had visited Oxford from Winchester on a 'leave-out' day with his friend Humphrey Lewis. They had been to see Alfred Snell, who was already at New College and was one of the cantors in the choir at Pusey House Chapel. Freddy Hood had a car which he used for his pastoral work, and he took them out for a drive in the country. He was extremely kind and friendly, but Christopher was more at ease with the other young priest, Miles Sargent, who was very forthright and energetic. He was also senior treasurer of the Oxford Motor Club; and Christopher found the healthy combination of religion and the open air much more to his taste. It was to Sargent that he made his confessions. In retrospect he admits that it became increasingly difficult to come up with anything really 'sinful', but his admissions of pride and vanity and selfishness were always sympathetically dealt with by Sargent, who must have been very well aware of the extreme innocence of this ebullient young man.

There were three resident clergymen at Pusey House. The principal was a splendid character with a long white beard, Dr Darwell Stone. He was an honorary Canon of Christ Church, and had sat on the Church Assembly at the time of the great controversy over the revision of the prayer book. He had a reputation for being obstructive and resistant to change. Christopher was told a story by the Chaplain of Christ Church, who was a young man with a wife and child. His wife was out walking one afternoon with the baby in a pram, when they met Dr Darwell Stone. Bending over the pram he solemnly asked the infant what it wanted to be when it grew up. Without pausing for a response he confided, 'I should like to be a policeman, holding up the traffic!' When the child's mother related this to her husband, he was consumed with mirth, for that was precisely what the old man had always done. 'The dear man has altogether missed his vocation,' he chuckled.

Darwell Stone used to preach occasionally: Christopher heard him once or twice, and he remembered that there was always rather a lot of coughing and nose blowing as the congregation fought back its temptation to giggle. He had a most peculiar voice, which sounded rather like bath water running away. When he retired, Freddy Hood took over his position, but this was not until after Christopher had left Oxford.

The three priests were looked after by an old retainer, whose wife did the cooking. They all had rooms of their own, but the meals were communal, with readings from devotional books. At the end of term there was usually a Retreat: a weekend of silence with daily prayers and communion. Christopher attended several of these weekends, staying in Pusey House. The buildings, which still stand in St Giles, next to the Blackfriars, are mostly Edwardian. The chapel is very large and splendid; and the library, originally built to house Pusey's own books, and subsequently added to by other incumbents, is now the official library of the Faculty of Theology. Built round a quadrangle, only the chapel and a small reading room are now retained by Pusey House. The rest of the building is occupied by St Cross College.

The organist in the chapel when Christopher was there was Jack Westrup, the organ scholar at Balliol, who afterwards became Professor of Music, first at Birmingham, and afterwards at Oxford.[25]

Christopher's financial state at this time was relatively untroubled. Though by no means affluent, he was sufficiently well off to dine out quite often and entertain his friends. He had an exhibition from Winchester of £50 a year, and the New College Scholarship was £80. On top of this his father made him an allowance of £200 a year, so that his disposable income was more than enough for his needs. Many of his contemporaries were exceedingly wealthy, and Christopher had one encounter with the 'hard drinking' fraternity during his first term:

That winter there appeared at Magdalen a chap called Humphrey Slade, who'd been a friend of mine at the Norland Place School before 1914. He asked me round for a party. It was a 'blind' – a drinking party, and I was quite unaccustomed to all this. I had no idea that Humphrey, who seemed an innocent sort of chap, was all out to get everybody roaring drunk, himself included. I got away long before the end, but I was already exceedingly drunk. I staggered out of Magdalen, up Long Wall Street, to where Myres and Hugh-Jones had digs. They plied me with strong black coffee until I was sober enough to get back to my rooms. I had an appalling hangover. Never did it again – at least not while I was at Oxford. . . .

Nowell Myres was two-and-a-half years older than Christopher (his birthday at Christmastide gave him his name) so they had very little contact at Winchester, but at Oxford that age difference became unimportant. Nowell was the son of Professor (later Sir John) Myres,[26]

Dr (later Sir John) Myres

who taught Greek history, and was one of the lecturers for Greats. When he was elected Wykeham Professor of Ancient History in 1910, he and his family lived at 101 Banbury Road. At about the time that Christopher came up to Oxford, they moved to a beautiful old house on Hinksey Hill. It had a very large garden, and Professor Myres had part of it carefully laid out for growing vegetables, which he tended with great vigour, spending most of his Sundays digging. This cultivation soon began to produce ancient pottery. Nowell, fresh from the excavation at St Catharine's Hill (which had begun in the summer of 1925; see chapter below) at once recognized the pottery as Early Iron Age. He tried to prevent his father from digging any more until the site could be properly examined. Their conflict of wills was resolved by a compromise when Nowell pursuaded his father to allow him to have a patch at a time to excavate, while the vegetables had the rest. It took Nowell several years to get at the whole site, but it was eventually published in the *Journal of the British Archaeological Association*.

Professor Myres had a pointed grey beard, and looked, according to C.M. Bowra, like an Elizabethan seaman, with hard, very bright eyes, and a provocatively rapid speech. He was a man who saw the past in a full setting of archaeology, geography, anthropology and ethnology' (*Memories*, p. 103).

When Christopher first met him, although he was only fifty-five years old, he was already suffering from a spinal curvature: he was unable to stand up straight, although he moved as quickly as he spoke. Among his many responsibilities he was Editor of the Anthropological Institute's journal *Man*. He also served on their council, and regularly went to London for meetings, staying the night in a hotel close to Paddington station, so that he could return to Oxford on the milk train. Christopher used to see him coming in from the station as they went over to breakfast in the junior common room.

Lady Myres was by then a graceful, elderly woman with a fine aquiline nose and delicate features. She was very dignified and sweet-natured, and rather old-fashioned, with her long skirts sweeping the ground. She suffered from what was then known as 'hip disease': presumably an arthritic condition, which in those days was untreatable.

Through his parents Nowell knew a lot of people, and it was he who first introduced Christopher to Miss Taylor. Margerie Venables Taylor had been an undergraduate at Somerville in the days when women were unable to get formal degrees; they were merely given a certificate. While she was still a student she had been introduced to Haverfield, who was a senior student and tutor at Christ Church. Although Haverfield died five years before Christopher went up to Oxford, his influence on the archaeological world was such that it is worth recording something of the man who was really the father of all subsequent studies of Roman Britain.

Francis John Haverfield was born in 1860. His father, who had been ordained ten years earlier, after graduating at Oxford, was given three curacies; two in Somerset, and one at Shipton-on-Stour. It was in this third parish that his son Francis was born. Both his parents died when he was quite young, and at the age of twelve he was sent to a preparatory school at Clifton. He was painfully shy and awkward, and as he had very little aptitude for games he had a predictably rough time. That he was clearly different from his fellows became apparent the following year, when he gained a scholarship to Winchester. He won the Goddard Scholarship, and went up to New College in 1879.

Christopher used to go to tea with the elderly Professor of Exegesis of Holy Scripture at Magdalen, who had been at Winchester with Haverfield. Professor Turner, who had a house in Norham Road, 'enjoyed the company of decent young chaps who were also Christian', as Christopher said, and he would invite several of them to tea on Sunday afternoons. He told Christopher that Haverfield always seemed to have a different edition of the text they were studying – preferably a German one – which had different readings when there was any uncertainty in the text; and he would interrupt the teaching of the headmaster, Dr Fearon, to the delight of his companions. He was a prodigious worker, and at New College he got a first in Mods without any difficulty. However his lack of interest in philosophy, and the fact that he refused to give his full attention to anything that failed to interest him prevented him from getting the necessary class in Greats that would have secured him a fellowship. So in 1884 he took up a teaching post at Lancing College in Sussex. He spent all his holidays travelling abroad, almost always alone, and in term time he did as much writing as he could.

He was already contributing learned articles to periodicals, both in this country and on the continent, especially in Germany, and his meeting with Mommsen in Berlin led to his appointment as one of the Editors of the *Corpus Inscriptionem Latinarum* (known as *CIL*). This meant that he had to keep the supplement for Britain up to date; which he did until R.G. Collingwood took it over, and it was continued in the *Journal of Roman Studies*, which was edited by Miss Taylor.

Haverfield's initial appointment as one of the editors of *CIL*, only five years after he had sat for Greats, shows the depth and extraordinary range of his scholarship. He was becoming increasingly interested in epigraphy, and he published his ideas in innumerable papers and articles. Margerie Taylor became his research assistant while he was still at Christ Church, and there was much speculation at the time that she was hoping to become Mrs Haverfield. In the spring of 1907, however, when he was already forty-seven years old, he married Miss Winifred Breakwell. While they were travelling abroad on their honeymoon he received a telegram informing him that he had been elected Camden Professor of Ancient History: with it came a Fellowship of Brasenose.

On their return to Oxford Haverfield began building a house in Headington, which he named Winshields, because of his great love of the Northumbrian moors: Winshields is the highest point on Hadrian's Wall, 1,230 ft above the level of the sea. J. Collingwood Bruce, in his

Handbook of the Roman Wall says: 'The prospect from this elevation is very extensive in every direction. On a clear day the vessels navigating the Solway can easily be descried. Burnswark and Criffell, well-known heights in Dumfriesshire, come into view.'[27]

This house became a meeting place for Haverfield's wide circle of friends and colleagues, as well as for his students: and of all those, it was Leonard Cheesman, who had been one of his pupils and had become a Fellow of New College, who was closest to him. When, in the summer of 1915 Cheesman's name appeared on the lists of those missing in the Dardanelles, Haverfield said little; but it was clear to everyone that a light had gone out of his life. After the confirmation of Cheesman's death at Chanuk Bair, Haverfield continued to work, but he became increasingly exhausted both physically and emotionally, and that Christmas he suffered a cerebral haemorrhage. It was six months before he was able to work again, but he made a remarkable recovery, and with the armistice his spirits did begin to lift. But he had lost that inspiration and energy that he had always had in such abundance. In the summer of 1919, when he had recovered sufficiently to embark on a tour, he visited some of the sites on the Wall with Rostovtzeff, who, like many of his compatriots, had been driven out of Russia by the Revolution.[28] On their return to Oxford at the end of September he seemed brighter than he had done since the early days of the war. At midnight on 30 September, without warning, he had a sudden seizure and died instantly. Winifred, who had always been delicate, never recovered from her shock and grief, and within a year she also was dead.

One of Haverfield's *obita dicta* was that 'it is no use to know about Roman Britain unless you also know about the Roman Empire in general'. True to his beliefs he left his entire estate to the university, to be used 'for the furtherance of Romano-British studies'. A trust was set up, which is still carrying out his wishes, and his magnificent library was left to the Ashmolean Museum. He stipulated in his will that his library should be cared for by Miss Taylor, thus giving her a place, though at first a rather uncertain one, in the field of Romano-British archaeology.

She used to sit at a desk in the open library in what is now Room 1 of the Ashmolean Library, and it was there that Christopher first met her, in the autumn of 1924. She was to be a tremendous help to him throughout his time at Oxford; for when she learnt that he wanted to be an excavator, she wrote at once to a Dr Wheeler, who would be digging, in the summer of 1925, at the Roman fort of Brecon Gaer 'on the fishful river of Usk'.[29]

Christopher had had a brief experience of excavation that previous winter. He had helped cut a section across the Akeman Street, between Ramsden and Asthall, in Oxfordshire. He, Nowell Myres and Charles Stevens worked at weekends on the north-east corner of field 230 in the parish of Minster Lovell. Myres and Stevens cut five more sections in May, and they published their results in the *Antiquaries Journal* the following year.[30]

Robert Eric Mortimer Wheeler was a dashing young man of thirty-five when Christopher first saw him at the Brecon Gaer. After the strains of the war he was still in a rather nervous state; but he coped with his private stresses by escaping most evenings after the day's work on the site to sit on the banks of the river fishing till long after dark. He wrote of the excavation in his autobiography:

> On the whole, it was, I suppose, the happiest and least anxious of all my enterprises. Amongst my students there I have a vivid memory of two young Wykehamists from New College, Christopher Hawkes and Nowell Myres: one vital, ebullient and determined, the other more sedate and reflective, but with a lively twinkle in his eye. The one was a perfect antithesis, or rather, complement, of the other, and I like to think that this happy conjunction of the stars is a continuing phenomenon of a university where one is now the Professor of European Archaeology, and the other Bodley's Librarian.[31]

In February, however, before he had really begun serious digging, Christopher wrote to his mother with more plans for the already crowded long vacation:

> There is a Saxon Chapel on the top of Hills at Winchester – did I tell you this? – that some of us want to dig up: the idea is for some of us to go there in the summer holidays for a week or ten days, when no one is there, and get leave to sleep in College; it would be interesting, pleasant, and strenuous: I am to approach Williams cautiously on the subject when I go down this weekend. . . .[32]

The idea for the dig on St Catharine's Hill arose during the many conversations that took place in the rooms in Long Wall Street which Nowell shared with his friend Maurice Hugh-Jones. Charles Stevens had rooms above them, and Christopher often used to join them. Permission for staying in college was given by the warden and fellows, and plans were made for what was to be the first of four very successful seasons' work. The Hill (called 'Hills' by the school) was then still owned by the ecclesiastical commissioners, though not long afterwards it was bought by the college.

Christopher's spare time was almost breathlessly full. There were many other things besides archaeology. This year, for the first time, he accompanied his father on his annual visit to 'Canterbury Week'. Essentially a week for cricket, when Kent played two- or three-day matches in succession, the week was also enlivened by evening performances of two plays, which had been rehearsed in London, with the final dress rehearsals at the theatre in Canterbury on the Saturday before the week began. The performances were put on by the famous amateur club, the Old Stagers, to which C.P. belonged; and the cast was augmented by professional actresses. The producer, Jock Ledward, knew C.P. in another connection: he was the senior partner in the Hawkes's family solicitors. The father figure of the club was Ralph Alderson: though the nominal president was a Kentish nobleman, Lord Harris, who had been a Kent and England cricketer.

The club, by tradition, always stayed at the Fountain Hotel, close to the old Theatre Royal; but in 1925 the performances had been moved to the new St George's Theatre. Families and some female members of the cast stayed at the Royal Hotel, and it was here that Christopher and his mother spent the first week of August, enjoying the various activities in which C.P. was taking part.

Ralph Alderson used to attend the OUDS performances every year, talent spotting; and after seeing the production of *King Lear* in February 1927, in which Christopher played the part of the Earl of Kent, Alderson invited him to take a small part in the week that August. He was subsequently elected a member, and he still has the tie, and the sash that he used to wear with evening dress. He was too busy after the war to take part in any of the performances, and when he retired, he was again asked if he would go, but he declined, and finally they accepted his resignation.

The Opera Club was founded in March 1925 by Bobby Stuart and Jack Westrup, and Christopher was one of its founder members. The first opera they performed was Monteverdi's *Orfeo*, at the old Playhouse Theatre, during the first week of the Christmas vacation, 1925. Sir Hugh Allen, whose own interests were firmly planted in his flourishing Bach Choir, insisted that the newly formed Opera Club should not be allowed to perform during term. *Orfeo* was a tremendous success: 'The number of celebrities (Bantock, Barry Jackson, Ernest Newman etc.) that saw *Orfeo* was most flattering. The last night was a quite perfect performance – ending with a champagne supper *chez* Bobby Stuart. . . .'[33]

Dr Harris who was the organist at New College, gave them a lot of help and encouragement.[34] He had a good, light tenor voice himself, but he never sang in the choir: he used to coach them, playing the orchestral parts on the piano. 'Uncle Bill', as he was called, was a delightful character. Small and spare, he had fair hair and rather protruberant, pale-lashed eyes. While only in his forties already he had a slight stoop, and his manner was that of a rather older man, especially when faced with the exuberant high spirits of some of the members of the club, who once broke into Gilbert and Sullivan when a tuneful similarity overcame them. 'Uncle Bill' also tested the candidates for the Bach Choir and when Sir Hugh Allen retired in 1926, he took over its direction. However, by then Christopher had decided to resign for there was a clash on Monday nights between music and archaeology: archaeology won.

There was also the French Club, which he joined at once to keep the language up. The club had rooms at 51 Cornmarket Street, and although it had no dining facilities, unlike the OUDS, it was a pleasant meeting-place, and they had some interesting speakers. They also provided splendidly embossed writing paper, which he sometimes used.

In the spring of 1925, as the weather improved, the normal afternoon walks, which were Christopher's chief form of exercise, often gave way to trips on the river. He quickly mastered the more leisurely method of propulsion, and spent many happy hours punting on the Cherwell.

During the Easter vacation he went to Holland for a week with his father. C.P. was a passionate admirer of the Dutch school of painting, and he wanted Christopher to see why. They crossed from Harwich to the Hook, and visited most of the main galleries, beginning with Amsterdam, where they feasted their eyes on Rembrandt. Christopher was stunned by the sheer size and power of *The Night Watch*, but he was more attracted by the luminous interiors of Vermeer, with their serene and intimate exchanges: a young woman reading a letter, stately and pregnant; and the kitchen maid pouring milk from a rough, unglazed jug. It was a week of great happiness for them both.

On their return Christopher went down to Winchester for a week to do some more to the wall painting, and he also walked from Oxford to Monmouth with his friend Humphrey Beevor. They had intended to stay the night there with Freddy Hood, whose family had a house in the town, and Freddy was to have driven them as far as Cheltenham, to catch a train direct to Winchester; but in the end he had to go away, and they were put up for the night by the parish priest instead.

He was back again at Oxford by the end of April:

The term seems to have started well. Charles and Nowell have fixed up the excavation scheme, and signed an agreement with the Ecclesiastical Commissioners. The dates are to be 8th to 21st August – that's to say if it takes as long as a fortnight . . .

His birthday that year was full of surprises:

Alfred [Snell] has made me a really wonderful present for my birthday, but he said he couldn't wait till then; he carefully typed out all my Winchester plays, cut the papers, and had them bound in a handsome book. It must have been a vast work – they're a thousand lines each – and it's quite amusing to re-read them, though I do wish we had been able to perform the last one. . . . I don't know how to thank him. . . .

And on the actual day he received a letter. Reporting this to his mother, he wrote:

The great excitement is Uncle Owen, who writes explaining that he thought I was to be 21 this year, but finding his calculations were a year out, he sees nothing against a little healthy anticipation, and offers me a motor-bicycle on the spot! The only question is, what

THE BRECON GAER: EAST GATEWAY · · · · · · · *PLAN AND WEST ELEVATION*

= EARLY 2ND CENTURY
= POST-ROMAN RAMPART

NORTH GUARDROOM · · · SOUTH GUARDROOM

FORT-WALL

R E M W & C F C H
1925

SCALE OF · *FEET* · 1 0 1 · 5 · 10 · 15 · 20 · 25 · 30 · 35
· *METRES* · 0 · 1 · 2 · 3 · 4 · 5 · 10

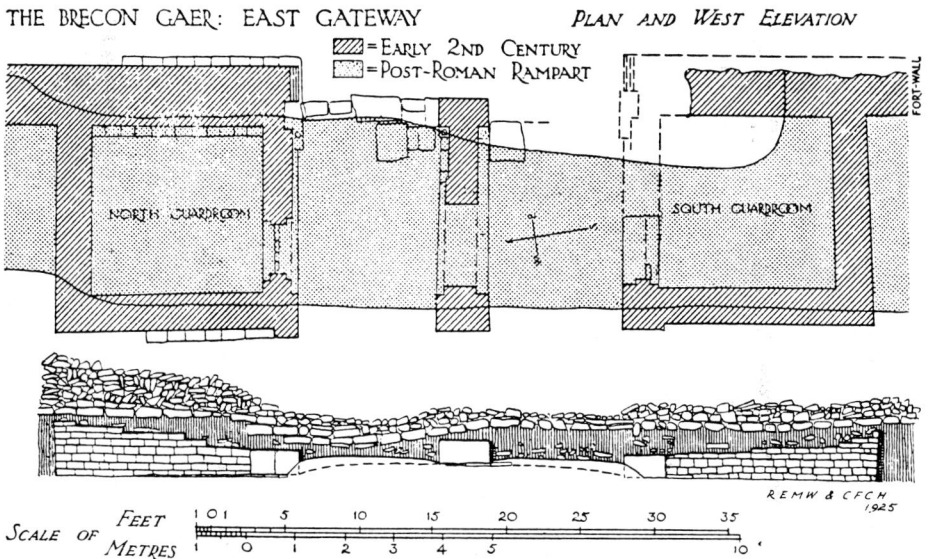

The Brecon Gaer: East Gateway. Site drawing by Christopher and Mortimer
Wheeler, 1925

make? – which will I please decide. Frenzied enquiries from my
motoring friends seem to point to a 2¼ h.p. BSA, but the most
authoritative person – Father Sargent – I haven't seen yet. He's
secretary of the O.U. Motor Club: a Pusey House priest – admirable
combination . . .

In his excitement, however, he failed to respond at once to his uncle's
letter. Not surprisingly, after some days, Owen consulted Uncle Frank.
The result can be imagined. Christopher realized how appallingly
ill-mannered his silence had been, and he wrote immediately to
apologize, explaining the reason for his delay – Miles Sargent had been
away, so his 'consultation' had been delayed almost a week – but there
was absolutely no excuse, and he was thoroughly ashamed of himself.
The offended uncle was pacified at once, and the machine he got was in
fact a 2¼ h.p. Raleigh, which he called 'Sir Walter'. It served him well
that summer for the first season's excavations at St Catharine's Hill.
  Even before the summer's activities, however, he had begun to
consider seriously a career in archaeology:

I am quite convinced that I ought to specialize in Ancient History and
Archaeology – it's so very far from being a dry-as-dust pursuit
nowadays. . . . O.G.S. Crawford is coming to Oxford this weekend,
and Charles and Nowell and I are dining him on Saturday. He urges
the archaeological life, but how can it support a man unless he is
attached to some place which gives a regular screw, like the B.M., or is

a don? The former would certainly be preferable, I think. I don't want to anchor in Oxford for good. We shall all have a long talk with Crawford about it: I'm very anxious to hear what he says. And I am thinking of approaching Fisher about the Museum. One thing I'm decided on – I'm not going to take up the bureaucratic side of the Civil Service, nor a legal career. . . .[35]

He had an opportunity of talking to Fisher not long after he wrote this letter. The warden often invited people to lunch – quite a frugal one – at his lodgings, as Mrs Fisher was often away in London on charity work, though their daughter Mary, who was still a schoolgirl at Oxford High, was usually there. After lunch they walked down to Mesopotamia, the tree-lined walk through the Cherwell's water-meads, embanked between the river's two arms. He asked Christopher what his ambitions were. This conversation bore fruit in the winter of 1927, when the Keeper of the Department of British and Medieval Antiquities at the British Museum took early retirement. Fisher was a Trustee of the museum, and he sent for Christopher to discuss his application for a post in the department.

Term ended on 13 June, and Christopher spent some time in London with his parents, before setting off for Winchester towards the end of the month, to work on the mural. He stayed this time with the Dean, Dr W.H. Hutton, who was a delightful man: a sort of eighteenth-century bachelor, who enjoyed entertaining, good wine and food, and amusing company. He had previously been Archdeacon of Peterborough, and before that he was Chaplain of St John's College at Oxford, where he had befriended such undergraduate luminaries such as Hilaire Belloc and Compton Mackenzie. He came to Winchester in about 1920, and his arrival transformed the Deanery. The previous incumbent had been rather stuffy and inhospitable. Hutton could not have been more different. He filled the house with young people every weekend: Nowell stayed with him once, and so did John Sparrow.

In July Christopher and Nowell set off together by train for Brecon, stopping in Hereford on their way, to have a look at the famous *Mappa Mundi*. They arrived at the boarding house in Brecon in the early evening.

The Roman fort of Brecon Gaer lies at the junction of the rivers Yscir and Usk, three miles to the north-west of the town. The site had been known as early as the twelfth century, when a charter of Roger, Earl of Hereford, records that, 'at the time of the Norman Conquest the deserted fort still bore obvious traces of previous occupation'.[36] From the seventeenth century onwards there were finds recorded by a number of antiquaries, and in 1908 Haverfield published his own findings together with a review of all the other evidence; but it was not until the summer of 1924 that a large-scale investigation of the site was undertaken.

It is assumed that the fort was founded by Governor Frontinus in about AD 75, but some opinions place it earlier, under Veranius or Suetonius, between AD 56 and 60. At first the fort was built entirely of timber, with a turf rampart. Early in the second century the central buildings were replaced by stone, and a wall inserted, with the stone gateways, in front of the turf rampart. A tombstone found near the fort is of a trooper of the *Ala Hispanorum Vettonum*, showing that this unit, from Spain, must have been stationed at Brecon at some time. The large fore-hall in front of the *principia* is a further indication of the presence of a cavalry unit. By AD 125 the garrison appears to have been much reduced, though the fort may have been kept on under a care and maintainence basis for longer: there is evidence of later structural changes.

The site of the fort is in 'a beautiful and sequestered spot in the Usk valley, lorded over by the Brecon Beacons'.[37] Wheeler admitted that 'in addition to its undoubted strategic advantages, he was attracted to the Brecon Gaer by his knowledge that the Usk swarmed with salmon and trout. He really treated the excavation as a background to a fishing holiday.'[38] He and his wife, Tessa, together with Paul Baillie Reynolds, had rooms at a lodging house in Brecon, which was kept by a widow, who had a young daughter.

Baillie Reynolds was an Old Wykehamist, whom Christopher had first met the previous year at Winchester, where he had briefly taught before moving to the University of Aberystwyth, to take up the post as Lecturer in Ancient History. He was soon to marry the beautiful elder sister of Christopher's Opera Club friend, Bobby Stuart. Later he joined the Inspectorate of Ancient Monuments, rising eventually to be Chief Inspector. At Brecon he was the only one who had motorized transport. The Wheelers had only push-bikes, as did Christopher and Nowell, so Paul used to take Tessa out to the site in his motor-cycle side-car with all the equipment. As well as working with her husband on the excavation, Tessa coped with all the administrative chores, which included the daily provision of packed cold lunches.

The lodgings were quite comfortable, and there was even an upright piano. Paul played it, and Tessa would encourage him and Christopher in jolly after-dinner sing-songs. Nowell, who was almost tone-deaf droned away cheerfully in the background. Rik (Wheeler) was seldom there in the evenings, preferring the quiet of the river, and his fishing rod.

The landlady's young daughter, who was photographed with both Nowell and Christopher (see opposite) had been carefully brought up by her English mother to speak without a Welsh accent. Although her late husband had been Welsh, she was determined that her daughter should follow her in speech. She used to complain when the child came home from school having picked up the accent from her friends. So it was characteristic of Wheeler that he was unable to resist the temptation to encourage the forbidden accent. Christopher was highly amused one evening to come upon his Director wickedly coaching the girl to speak

Christopher at Brecon Gaer, with the daughter of his landlady. Photograph taken by Nowell Myres

Nowell Myres at Brecon. Photograph taken by Christopher

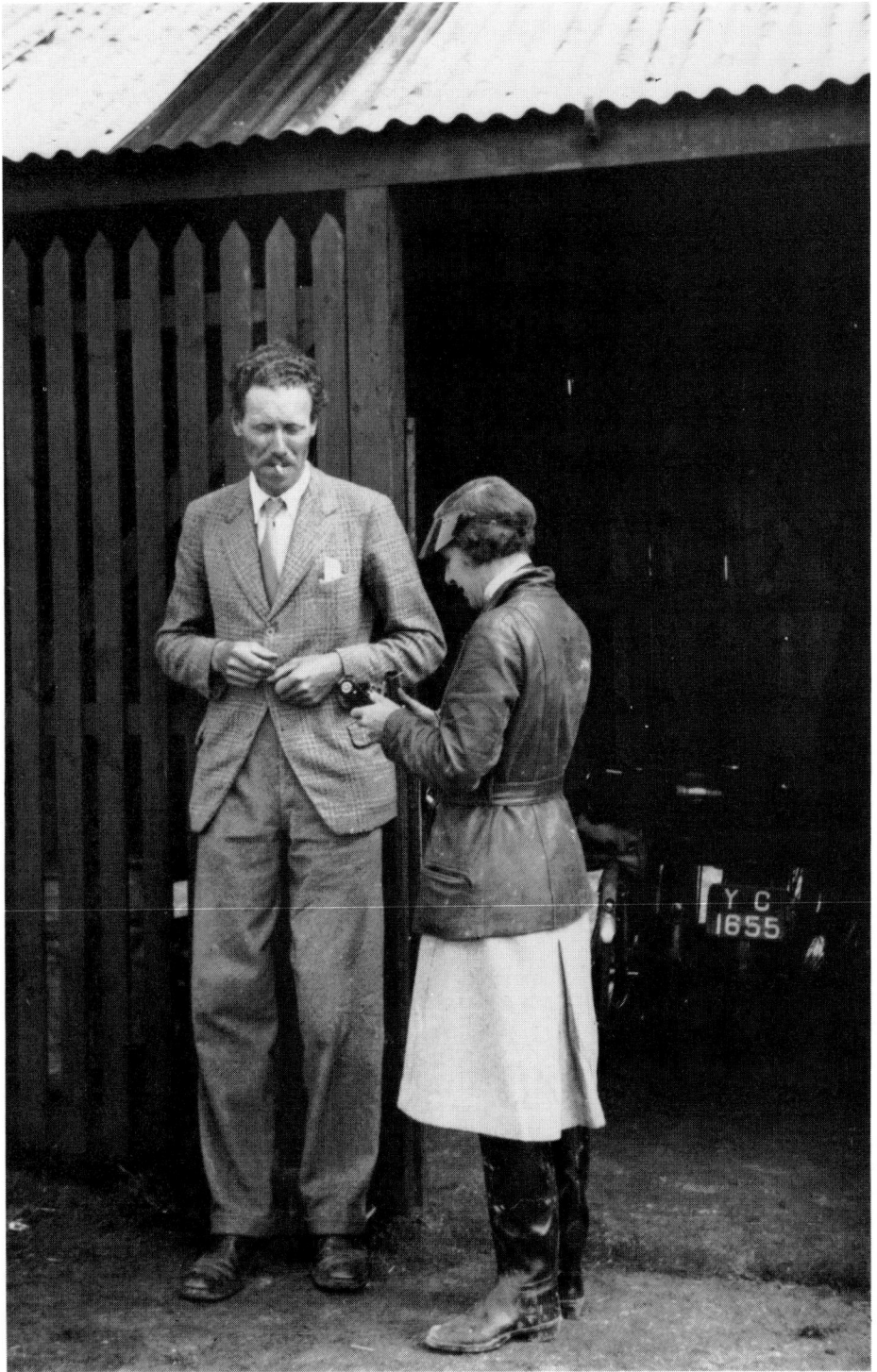

Dr Wheeler with his wife Tessa, in about 1925. Photograph by O.G.S. Crawford

with a pronounced lilt, which of course she adopted gleefully. Her mother never found out why her efforts were being thwarted.

Christopher was only able to spend eight days at Brecon, while Nowell stayed for a full two weeks; but he learnt a lot from Wheeler's methods. Their first day was spent in a frustrating search for a possible road surface outside one of the gates, perched on a ledge above the river. Christopher found one tiny piece of tile, which he kept to show Dr Wheeler when he came round.

'Give it to me!' he barked. With barely a glance he flung the fragment into the river.

This 'baptism' was very quickly followed by much better things for them both. Christopher was asked to measure and draw the frontage of the east gateway; and his original work, inked in by Wheeler (see p. 124), appears with both names initialled at the bottom, in the report which was published the following year.[39]

Apart from the Wheelers' ten-year-old son, Michael, the only visitors to the site that year were the newly-knighted Flinders Petrie and his formidable wife Hilda.[40] Although this was after Christopher had left to join his parents in Canterbury, he had already met Petrie in London through his Aunt Vickie: one of her many enthusiasms was Egyptology. She had visited the Petries in Egypt while they were digging, before the First World War, and, though she never did any digging herself, she spent hours copying heiroglyphs into a notebook. She also purchased a number of small antiquities from dealers, which she brought home with her. There were one or two objects at Campden Hill Square that Christopher can remember which must have been gifts to his parents after the trip. Vickie took him to hear Petrie give a lecture at University College, and he was introduced to the great man afterwards. He was quite tall, with a long white beard and fierce, intelligent eyes. As a child he had been rather sickly, so he had never been sent to school. His education was entrusted to a tutor. But gradually his health improved, and in his teens he began to take an interest in the earthworks and remains near his home at Charlton in Kent. His father taught him surveying; and in 1874 the two of them spent some days at Amesbury, making detailed plans of Stonehenge. Although the monument had been drawn many times, it had never before been accurately surveyed and measured. They did not complete the task until the summer of 1877, when the young Petrie also carried out other surveys of earthworks in southern England. These plans were all lodged in the map room at the British Museum. His interests soon turned towards Egypt, however, and in 1874 he published his researches on the Great Pyramid; but it was not until five years later that he first went to Egypt.[41] His career has been admirably recorded by his biographer Margaret Drower, who graduated in Egyptology and knew the Petries well.[42]

7 St Catharine's Hill Excavation, 1924–8

Nowell, Christopher and Charles Stevens arrived at Winchester on Sunday 9 August, having made the journey from Oxford together: Christopher on his newly-acquired 'Sir Walter', and Charles on a motor-cycle combination called 'Tancred', with Nowell and all the luggage in the side-car.

The first two seasons of digging were with volunteers, about ten of them – all from Winchester – though only four or five were there at any one time as they had limited space in VIII Chamber for sleeping. They had their meals in Thule Chamber, which had a small kitchen above it and which was part of the private rooms used during term by the college tutor, Mr Jack Parr. Here the cheerful Edie prepared their evening meals, and a breakfast of bacon and eggs. She worked for Mr and Mrs Dean, who ran the school shop, together with their daughter, Edna, and a young man. As Edie lived in Winchester, she was glad to be able to earn

St Catharine's Hill. Drawing by Diana Bonakis Webster from a photograph of the 1920s

some extra money in the holidays; but it must have been quite hard work catering for the hungry young men in such a tiny kitchen. She also provided the packed lunches for them to eat on site.

The warden and fellows had given them every facility: they had hot water for baths every night, and they were looked after by an elderly houseman, who kept the chambers clean and tidy, and lit the coke furnace for their hot water. He also made the beds. They were so tired after a day in the open air, doing heavy manual work, that they had little energy left for any other activities; and they were left completely to their own devices. Everyone else was away on holiday, including Monty, who never in fact visited the excavations at all. Only one of the dons, Mr Humby, who had volunteered to act as treasurer for the last two seasons when they worked with hired labour, did go to see what they were doing.

> St Catharine's Hill in the parish of Chilcombe near Winchester is a steep sided hill of oval form jutting out from the irregular edge of the chalk uplands that bound the middle Itchen valley on the east. Its summit, which lies just one mile south-west of Winchester Cathedral, rises 328 feet above sea-level; and the fall to the Itchen water-meadows on its western side is in places as steep as 1 in 3. . . .

Thus begins the report of the four seasons' work, which was published in a handsomely bound volume by the Hampshire Field Club in 1930, as volume XI of their *Proceedings*.

There is no record of the foundation of the chapel. It is first mentioned in 1284, when Edward I granted 'to John Pontissara, Bishop of Winchester, a quit claim to a quantity of disputed property which included the advowson of the church of Chilcombe with the Chapel of St Catharine'.[1] It was built some time during the first two decades of the twelfth century. It was a large aisleless cruciform building, which had originally been a small single-cell chapel, to which had been added the nave, crossing, and north and south transepts. There were also the remains of what was probably a hermit's lodging, consisting of at least two rooms. The walls were built of flint, with occasional blocks of chalk and Quarr stone from the Isle of Wight; and they found evidence to show that the walls had been plastered on the inside. There were no foundations as there was solid chalk within a foot of the old ground surface.

The chapel stood until the first quarter of the sixteenth century. John Leland, who visited the site some time between 1536 and 1542, wrote: 'Ther is a very fair Chappelle of St Catharine on an Hille scant half a mile without Winchester toun by south. This Chappelle was endowid with Landes. Thomas Wolsey, Cardinal, causid it to be suppressid.'[2]

As early as 1524 Wolsey had suppressed a number of small monasteries, transferring their endowments to his colleges at Oxford and Ipswich. It seems unlikely that the chapel fell at this time, as almost all the institutions then affected were monastic. The most likely date for the confiscation is some four years later, when Wolsey was appointed to the see of Winchester, by proxy, shortly before his fall, in 1529.

The first lay tenant of the site was Thomas Wriothesley (1505–50), who later became Earl of Southampton. 'He was one of the most unscrupulous of the new Tudor nobility.'[3] In 1538 he became coroner and attorney at the King's Bench, and he was granted a number of properties, which included the abbey at Beaulieu and Hyde Abbey in Winchester. 'He pulled down buildings with amazing expedition and sold the rich materials.'[4]

Wriothesley must have demolished the chapel before 1540, when his destructive activities came to an end: the surviving walls were buried beneath their own fallen masonry, and the centre became a grassy mound. The memory of the chapel quickly disappeared, and there is no mention of it in any of the seventeenth- and eighteenth-century maps of Winchester.[5]

In 1762 the mound was planted with fir trees by Lord Botetourt, who was Colonel of the Hampshire Volunteers, which had been called up during the Seven Years War with France, which was to end the following year. Up until the 1970s over a hundred trees were still standing: some of them firs, but most of them beeches.

Christopher was sufficiently interested in the dedication of the chapel to write to all the incumbents whose churches bore the same name, and he published his findings in a fascinating tailpiece to the medieval

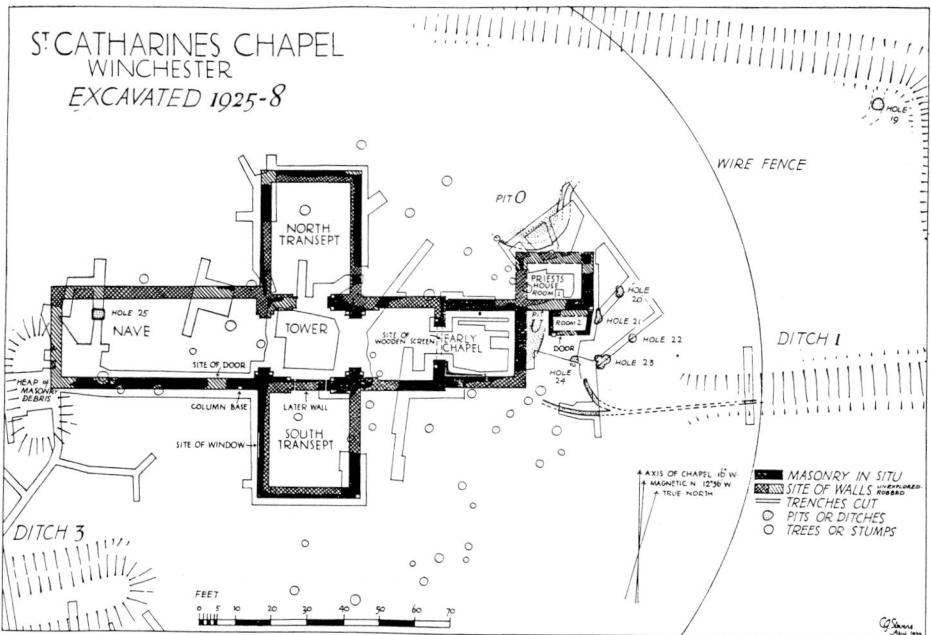

St Catharine's Chapel, Winchester. Site drawing by C.G. Stevens, April 1929

section of the report. In it he gives the story of the saint, which is worth quoting in full:

> The supposed date of the martyrdom of St Catharine is AD 307, although there are no historical records of her for some centuries afterwards. Her story may be said to begin with the discovery, in the early ninth century, of her supposed corpse on Mount Sinai. (Her name is from the Greek word for purity.)
>
> She was the only daughter and heiress of the 'King' of Egypt, who was himself descended from the father of the Emperor Constantine the Great. She was good, beautiful, and devoted to learning. When she was fourteen her father died (the date is supposed to be at some time at the beginning of the fourth century), and she reigned in Alexandria as sole queen, steadfastly refusing wedlock; for although as yet a pagan, she declared that she would be content only with a husband far above herself in all gifts of nature and grace, thus embracing, albeit in ignorance, an ideal which Christ alone could satisfy. In due course she was converted to the faith by a hermit, and resolved to become the bride of Christ alone. The persecuting Roman Emperor, Maxentius, then intervened, and set pagan philosophers to pervert her, but the result of the disputations which followed was the conversion of the philosophers themselves, who consequently suffered martyrdom at Maxentius' hands. The enraged Emperor condemned her to breaking on a wheel, but Divine intervention rewarded her prayers, and it was the wheel that was broken. Thereupon she was ordered to be scourged and beheaded, and this time the sentence was carried out. Her body was miraculously borne by angels to the grave on Mount Sinai, where it was found five centuries later, on the spot marked by the famous monastery which bears her name.[6]

The report goes on to say that there is unlikely to be a genuine source behind this popular myth, but Catharine received her pedigree and 25 November was celebrated as her festival. The cult is presumed to have reached this country with the ending of the First Crusade in 1099, and there are in England three churches dedicated to her where earlier building is known.[7] Among parish churches perhaps the earliest dedication is St Catharine Cree in London, which was in existence in 1108.

All the plans and drawings for the report were done by Charles Stevens, and apart from one by O.G.S. Crawford, all the photographs were taken by a professional photographer from H.W. Salmon of Winchester, except for one by Stevens, two by Mr Humby, and one with the combined expertise of Mr C.O. Waterhouse of the British Museum, and Mr G. Chaundy of the Ashmolean.

In 1927 an approach was made by the Hampshire Field Club, with the offer of financial help, if the amount they gave was matched by subscription, for excavation in the Iron Age hill-fort. A committee was set up under Dr J.P. Williams-Freeman, with a most illustrious Council, which included Sir Charles Close, who was then Director General of the Ordnance Survey (and Crawford's boss) as well as Crawford himself.

The Wardens and Fellows of both Winchester and New College made generous donations, and for the third season there was just under £200 to pay for a team of hired workmen, and the necessary equipment. £230 was raised for the final season in 1928.

Charles, Nowell and Christopher lived in college again, as they had for the first two seasons, going to and fro on their motor cycles, with Nowell still a passenger in the side-car. They were able to leave the machines unattended at the bottom of the hill, without any fear of theft or damage. The workmen started at 8 a.m., and they had to take it in turns to be out on site early to organize the work. Christopher would go up alone one morning, while the other two had breakfast, then he would be relieved by the other two, and he would go back to College to enjoy a late breakfast at about 10 a.m.

On the first morning the manager of the Labour Exchange came up himself with the men, who had been very carefully picked for the job – about twenty of them. One was a splendid, wiry old character called Mr Bolland, who wore a bowler hat which was green with age, dull yellowish corduroy trousers with both belt and braces, a moleskin waistcoat, and a red cotton handkerchief knotted round his neck. His trousers were tied below the knees with pieces of string, with the bottoms tucked firmly into his boots. Christopher solved the problem of his trousers flapping and getting in the way by wearing an old pair of his father's riding breeches with puttees, and he sometimes wore an old felt hat.

They had a wooden hut on the site for sheltering, storing equipment, and drawing in. On the first day Christopher and Nowell sat at a table in the hut, and the men were sent in, one by one, to sign on. Nowell read them a sort of contract, that they would undertake to carry out all instructions, and not pinch any of the finds; but they were told that if there was anything of value, there would be a bonus on top of the wages. They all signed. When it came to Mr Bolland, however, Nowell said: 'Will you sign here please Mr Bolland?' (they never found out if his name was actually Bolland or Bollard), and the old man grinned at them.

'I'm no scollard!' he said, solemnly making a cross on the paper. Nowell wrote under it, 'J. Bolland, his mark.' He was a superb workman, as tireless and efficient as any of the younger men, with whom he refused to mix, preferring to eat his lunch on his own, with his back turned away from the others.

The Hampshire Field Club paid them a visit one year (probably the final one), led by Dr Williams Freeman, who had succeeded Sir Charles Close as president. Freeman was immensely tall, with a little grey beard and a most commanding presence. He wore a panama hat, and made a speech to the assembled company, who were seated on the grassy slope at his feet:

Dr J.P. Williams Freeman on Gaer Hill, Hampshire, in May 1931. Photograph by Dr Stephen Coffin

I think I said in my book [*Field Archaeology of Hampshire* (1915)] that all these hill-forts were Bronze Age. Well, we've seen this afternoon that I was wrong. Our friends here have clearly shown that this is Iron Age, and I now recant and say that all hill-forts are Iron Age!

There was an enthusiastic ripple of applause.

Among the other local dignitaries was Heywood Sumner. This was the only time that Christopher met him, though they had an enjoyable correspondence some years later when Christopher was at the British Museum. Sumner was already seventy-two when he visited the excavations, but he had known the hill-fort for many years. In fact the first painting he exhibited at the Royal Academy, in 1881, was a view of the hill-fort. After Eton and Oxford, he qualified as a barrister at Lincoln's Inn; but after his marriage to Agnes, the daughter of W.A.S. Benson, he became more and more drawn into William Morris's circle. He worked as an illustrator and designer until the age of forty-four, when he grew weary of fashionable London. His wife had always been delicate, and they wanted to bring up their family (she had given him five children) in the country. They bought a plot of land on the edge of the New Forest, near South Gorley, and within a year the new house, which they called Cuckoo Hill, was ready for them. From that time onwards Sumner's interests became more and more rooted in the Hampshire countryside. He studied the earthworks and trackways, as well as churches and pottery; and his reports were not only full of information, they were also beautiful to look at, with his many highly idiosyncratic drawings, that are now so evocative of a more gentle and untroubled way of life. He remained at Cuckoo Hill until his death in 1940.

The Iron Age earthwork forms a complete ring broken on the north-east by the original entrance, which is flanked by the inturned ends of the rampart. It encloses a roughly oval area of some twenty-three acres, of which the highest point of the hill lies just north of the centre. The fortification consists of three parts: the rampart, a ditch immediately outside it, and a low bank on the outer edge of the ditch which was referred to as the counterscarp bank.

The finds from the excavation were presented to the Winchester City Museum, with the permission of the Ecclesiastical Commissioners (now known as the Church Commissioners), who owned the site. It was established from the pottery that the settlement on the hill, which was dated between the fifth and fourth centuries BC, was later followed by the earliest large settlement in Winchester itself, a site called Oram's Arbour, which more recent excavations show to have begun in the early part of the first century BC, when the settlement on the hill was abandoned.

Christopher was able to discuss his more recent conclusions on the excavation in a paper called 'St Catharine's Hill, Winchester: the report

Heywood Sumner at Cuckoo Hill. Photograph by O.G.S. Crawford, 1931

re-assessed', in a volume entitled *Hillforts*, edited by Dennis Harding , which was published in 1974.

For a description of the hill as it looked in the days immediately before the First World War, which would have been very much the same as it was when Christopher was at Winchester, one could do no better than this passage at the end of A.G. Macdonell's *England, Their England*.[8] It is an hilarious and biting satire on English country life, but Macdonell was himself a Wykehamist, and his affection for the place is clearly demonstrated in these lines:

> He had not begun to awaken when he climbed the first slopes of St Catharine's Hill, or when at last he reached the clump of trees on the top of the hill, and found a little grassy slope which fitted his back like a deck-chair at full stretch, and lay down and tilted his hat over his forehead and joined his hands behind his head.
>
> At his feet were the glittering streams of the Itchen, that small magic river of silver, dry-flies and trout. Beyond them were the playing-fields with their white dots of cricketers, and beyond them the tower of the College Chapel, and beyond that the slumbering leviathan, Wykeham's House of God. The air was filled with the little sounds, the tinkling of sheep-bells across the vales of the chalkland, the click of cricket ball on cricket bat, the whispers of the fitful puffs of wind in the trees behind him, megaphoned shouts of the coaches as the racing fours went up the stream with flashing blades; and from across the valley the bells of the Cathedral, deep and far, like the strong clang of Thor's anvil in Valhalla.
>
> Twenty or thirty feet below the grassy deck-chair on which Donald was by now half dozing ran the circular trench which the Britons dug as a defence against the Legions. The line of the Roman road was clear, a chalky arrow, as far as the blue horizon. . . . The English school whose motto put kindliness above flourishment of learning, lay among its water-meads, and all around was the creator, the inheritor, the ancestor, and the descendent of it all, the green and kindly land of England. . . .

8 Oxford, 1926–8

In early January 1926 Christopher was invited to a weekend house-party in Herefordshire:

> My stay at Wormelow was most delightful – though the girl Jane had hurt her ankle breaking a colt, and couldn't dance. Her mother had also hurt her wrist doing the same thing. The other guests were Elizabeth Lupton, a vast Irishman from Magdalen named Bull, and one Fletcher of Trinity, Cambridge. They're both old Etonians – both MacBryde *père* (killed in the war) and *mère* belong to old Etonian families: and Jane's guardian is no less a person than the Provost of Eton, who was staying at the house. It was tremendous to meet him – a most interesting and jolly old man, eternally smoking an old black pipe and playing Patience. . . .

In this letter to his mother (dated 8 January) he gave no further information about this encounter, but it made a deep impression on him. The 'jolly old man' was in fact M.R. James, whose exquisitely chilling ghost stories had already made him famous.[1] He read some of these stories to the party one evening at Holme Lacy. Monty James was not really as old as he seemed to Christopher at the time: he was sixty-four. Jane, the girl who was unable to dance, was the daughter of the artist James MacBryde and his wife Gwendolen. Christopher was wrong about Jane's father being killed in the war: he had died tragically as a result of an operation for appendicitis on the very day that Christopher was born. Gwendolen gave birth to their daughter towards the end of that year, and Monty James, who had been James MacBryde's closest friend, agreed to act as her guardian. Gwendolen remained a close friend and confidant of Monty James throughout his life. He wrote many beautiful letters to her, a number of which are quoted in Michael Cox's sensitive biography.[2] The first book of ghost stories, called *The Five Jars*, for which James MacBryde had completed four illustrations at the time of his death, contained a graceful preface as an act of homage to the author's friend.

Jane and her mother were living at a house called Woodlands, not far from Abbey Dore, and Monty James visited them there every year until 1929. He had been made a Trustee of the British Museum in 1925, an appointment which gave him much satisfaction; but at the time, Christopher's plans for his own future were still very vague. Even as late as November 1927 he was writing to his father:

I hadn't much opportunity of talking to you about it at the end of the vac, but I feel more and more drawn towards teaching as a profession, *vice* the BM. It should be a university rather than a school, I think, and a provincial university rather than Oxford. It means knocking up against a rather different type, which is all to the good, and much less routine work; with consequently far more time to do original work, that counts for bigger posts later on. And a long vac. every year isn't to be sniffed at. My subject of course would be Ancient History, on which, as you know, I'm going to concentrate principally in Greats . . .

Mods began on 4 March 1926, and the term ended on 14 March, after which Christopher went with his father for a holiday in Portugal. They stayed in Lisbon, making short sight-seeing trips and they were joined for part of the time by Aunt Vickie and Uncle Edgar, who were also on holiday. It was while they were staying at a hotel in the centre of Lisbon that a telegram arrived from Uncle Frank, congratulating Christopher on getting a first. Frank had seen the report in *The Times*: formal notification was awaiting Christopher on his return to Campden Hill Square. C.P. was overjoyed. He embraced his son warmly, and with tears in his eyes. Although Christopher was naturally delighted by the results, and gratified that his father should be so too, he was also rather embarrassed by this sudden display of emotion.

Shortly after the beginning of term came the General Strike. It began at midnight on 4 May, when the General Council of the Trades Union Congress had voted to back the miners, after the breakdown of negotiations. A formal state of emergency was declared four days later; and, as a precaution against violence, troops were sent to areas where trouble might have been expected. Undergraduates joined thousands of white-collar workers in driving trains, buses, and lorries carrying essential supplies.

'The University is rapidly disintegrating,' Christopher wrote to his mother, 'some to Hull, others to Bristol, others to Southampton and London, chiefly for dock-work. All men with cars here are under orders, and motor-cyclists like myself are standing by. By "all" I mean all who have volunteered on the Roll opened by each College. Those with special facilities for jobs at home, or who are specially needed there, have gone, or are going, down. Undergraduates are volunteering as secretaries and typists at the Town Hall. . . .' Christopher was sent to Wolverhampton several times to deliver pamphlets and despatches for the Master of Balliol College (the future Lord Lindsay). It was not until 12 May that the Chairman of the Trades Union Congress, Arthur Pugh, went to 10 Downing Street, and the strike was called off.

Having had his principal gift of 'Sir Walter' a year early, Christopher's actual twenty-first birthday might have been something of an anti-climax; but his friends produced such a splended array of gifts – he even got the three-volume quarto edition (1789) of Camden's *Britannia* from Nowell, Lewis, Hayter[3] and the two Llewellyn-Smiths, as well as a most imaginative selection of other gifts. He had a party, too. He went down to Winchester shortly afterwards and saw Maddie:

> She looks well, and likes her lesson folks, but the Colliers [the policeman and his wife with whom she had lodgings] have suddenly been ordered to live in married quarters in the police station in one week's time, as he is being given higher grade work; so after next Wednesday she will have no fixed abode, unless one is found meantime. . . .

Christopher had been invited to join the excavations on the site of the Roman city of Wroxeter near Shrewsbury by its director, Donald Atkinson. On 12 July Christopher set off in blistering heat for Shropshire. He left Campden Hill Square in the early morning, arriving 'safely, but very hot', in time for tea at his digs in the Abbey Foregate in Shrewsbury. He wrote a card at once to his parents:

> 4.15 p.m.
> These digs are most comfortable. The people are a nice young couple named Potter. The house – a good sized middle-class dwelling – is opposite the Abbey Church (mostly Norman). I like the town immensely. . . .

'The Old Work' at Wroxeter, Shropshire. Drawing by Diana Bonakis Webster, 1985

What he did not say was that the nice young Mrs Potter made him amorous advances, being bored with Mr P., who spent most evenings away from the house. She only caught him once –usually he managed to escape to his room in the evenings, where he read quietly. One of the books he had brought with him was Gordon Childe's *The Dawn of European Civilization*, which had come out the year before; it was this book that drew him first towards prehistory.

He described the work on the site in a letter to his mother: 'Wroxeter is most interesting and puzzling just now – an immense second-century Forum and Basilica built over the foundations of a destroyed late first-century baths.' (The early unfinished baths were thought to belong to the first century, but they have more recently been shown to be a cancelled first stage of the second-century Hadrianic plan.) In a letter to his mother Christopher described the director of the excavation, Donald Atkinson, who was at that time a reader in ancient history at Manchester:

> Atkinson is a quiet fellow, with much latent humour, and very learned and helpful, while being friendly and unassumingly chatty. Barnet, his assistant, is a comic old buffer, burly and outspoken, but a very humble admirer of Atkinson. My knowledge of pottery and excavating method is growing.
>
> There are twelve men and a tip-railway: corrugated iron sheds for museum and workshop, and we pore over the jigsaw-puzzle work of fitting pot-fragments together after tea. . . .

The Roman city of Viroconium is one of the very few which have never been built over. It lies on the west side of the road which runs south to Ironbridge from the main A5. Its central area was extensively excavated in the nineteenth century by Thomas Wright; his work showed that a great deal has survived of the second-phase Hadrianic bath-house east of the forum. It is dominated by the surviving wall known as 'The Old Work', which is the north wall of the *frigidarium* of the later baths. From 1912 to 1914 the Society of Antiquaries had financed an excavation on the opposite side of the modern lane, under the direction of J.P. Bushe-Fox, with Donald Atkinson as his assistant. Atkinson took over the direction for the four summer seasons, each four months long, from 1924 to 1927. It was during the cutting of one of the first trenches, in 1924, which passed diagonally through the main entrance of the east colonnade of the forum, that two fragments of stone slab were found, showing the lower parts of the letters 'A', 'S' and 'C'. The trench was widened in all directions, and eventually 169 pieces were recovered, so that the inscription could be reconstructed (see opposite). Translated it reads:

> To the Emperor Caesar Trajanus Hadrianus Augustus, son of the deified Trajanus Parthicus, grandson of the deified Nerva, Pontifex

Inscription from east entrance to Forum: scale $\frac{1}{18}$

INSCRIPTION AS FOUND

INSCRIPTION COMPLETED

C.E.A.A. Menzel del.

Drawing and Restoration of the inscribed tablet. Scale $\frac{1}{13}$

The forum inscription at Wroxeter

Maximus, holding tribunician power for the fourteenth year, consul for the third time, father of his country, the community of the Cornovii [dedicated this building].

The inscription can be dated to between 10 December AD 129 and 9 December AD 130. Christopher saw it in the main excavation hut, propped up on a makeshift easel. A replica can be seen in the site museum, and the original is on display in the Rewley House Museum in Shrewsbury, where the majority of the finds were taken after the excavations. There is also a copy of the inscription in the British Museum. The report on the excavations was eventually published during the last war[4] and Atkinson sent Christopher a copy of it. Christopher's letter of thanks, six beautifully written pages, must have meant a great deal to Atkinson, for he kept it inside his own copy of the report for the rest of his life. It passed, together with many other books and papers, to his friend, Graham Webster, whom he taught at Manchester, and whose own excavations at Wroxeter were to last for thirty years, from 1955 to 1985.

Atkinson's family came from Birmingham. He was born in 1886; and while he was at Oxford (at Brasenose College) he came under Haverfield's influence, digging with him at Corbridge. After graduating in classics in 1909, he got a job teaching classics at Stamford Grammar School, which he held until 1912, when a scholarship to the British School at Rome enabled him to study a hoard of south Gaulish samian from Pompeii, a report on which he published two years later in the *Journal of Roman Studies*. His first University appointment came about through the efforts of Haverfield. He was given a Fellowship in Roman Archaeology at Reading in 1913. He volunteered for war service in 1915, but he was always very reticent about it, and Christopher never found out what he did. At the end of the war he was made a Reader in Ancient History at the then Victoria University at Manchester. Ten years later he became its first Professor of Ancient History, remaining at Manchester until his retirement in 1951.

In 1932 Atkinson married his pupil, Kathleen Chrimes, who had been an honours graduate of Lady Margaret Hall, and whom he afterwards supervised for her doctorate at Manchester. She was a distinguished Greek scholar who later became a professor herself, but their courtship was beset with difficulties. First of all, for a professor to have a relationship with one of his students was considered to be improper; so when Atkinson tried to get his wife appointed as his assistant, to deal with the Greek while he concentrated on the Roman, this was too much for the authorities. Kathleen's position was made so uncomfortable that she took the first post that was offered – in Belfast: a lectureship in Greek in the Department of Classics at Queen's University, where she eventually became Professor of Ancient History. Although this solution was not ideal – it meant that she only saw her husband during the vacations – she had a very successful career.

On his retirement from Manchester Atkinson became honorary curator of the Corinium Museum at Cirencester, where he was able to catalogue the collection of some 8,000 coins, as well as organizing the reserve collections and arranging displays, with the help of a full-time custodian.

When he died, in 1963, no obituary of Atkinson appeared in any of the national periodicals. He had never received a *Festschrift*, nor any other public recognition. Whatever his shortcomings, it is difficult to understand such uncharitable dismissal of a lifetime of teaching and research; and with it the denial of a record of a man whose influence on those with whom he worked must alone surely have fitted him for acknowledgement.

In the middle of September, after the second season's work on the

'The Old Work', Wroxeter. Drawing by Diana Bonakis Webster, 1985

chapel on St Catharine's Hill, Christopher took charge of his first full-scale excavation, at Alchester, a small Roman town eleven miles north-east of Oxford. This project had been set up for him by Miss Taylor, and he was given sufficient money to employ a small team of labourers. He also had the help of several unpaid assistants, who were either friends or local enthusiasts.

The site, which covers an area of some twenty-six acres, lies just off the Bicester road in the parish of Wendlebury. It was mentioned in Stukeley's *Itinarium Curiosum*, and there is a reference to it in Camden's *Britannia* (p. 267). In 1892 Nowell's father, J.L. Myres, and his friend Percy Manning dug in the north west angle of the central crossroad. The excavation is also recorded in notes and plans which are in the Haverfield Library at the Ashmolean, together with a bibliography of the site.[5]

Christopher began digging on 8 September, and during the next four weeks he and his team uncovered an area of about 6,000 sq. ft. Christopher stayed at the pub in Wendlebury, the Waggon and Horses, which was handy, if a trifle primitive. The recent replacement of an outside water-closet with a brand-new, indoor chemical one added considerably to the comfort. He had little time for writing letters, but his two brief notes to his parents gave them a pleasing enough picture for them to pay him a visit:

> . . . We now have a row of shops facing the road, with a cobbled yard, and two houses behind. Quantities of pots – some of them rare and beautiful (none quite perfect, though), and a weight marked 'I:CAES:AVG', as well as coins etc.
>
> I had to sack a man who was idle last week, and have got a much better one. Such a healthy life: fresh air, beef and beer, and good company . . . [6]

The weather was good, too. C.P. and Ellie came down by train and took a taxi to the site from the station at Bicester. It was the only time they ever visited him on an excavation: although they were proud of what he was doing, neither of his parents ever showed any personal interest in archaeology.

Christopher had one very important visitor. R.G. Collingwood came to see them one afternoon, driven by his wife Ethel. This was a great honour, and Christopher showed him what they thought they had found – a middle-Roman-period occupation, with remains of stone walls, reposing on a bed of apparently clean gravel, which he took to be natural.

'Ye-es . . .' said Collingwood, in his funny, high, squeaky voice, taking his penknife from his waistcoat pocket. Very gently and carefully he scraped into the gravel, and at once produced some charcoal. The gravel surface had been purposely laid over an earlier Roman level, which Christopher had failed to reach. He was very chastened by this; and after

Collingwood's visit they removed the gravel and found sherds of very fine early samian, and a number of objects, one of which at least was undoubtedly military, in the early-period level of occupation, well back in the first century. He wrote up the excavation at once, and the report appeared in the *Antiquaries Journal* the following year.[7]

Robin George Collingwood was born at Coniston, in what was then North Lancashire, on 22 February 1889. His father, W.G. Collingwood, was himself an antiquary, as well as a fine draughtsman and artist, and was the friend and biographer of Ruskin. He published a number of important works, the best known being his study of Northumbrian crosses, all meticulously drawn, which is still the standard work on the subject.

His son Robin was educated at Rugby, and then at University College, Oxford, where he got a first in both Mods and Greats. His remarkable gifts were very swiftly recognized: in the summer of 1912, while he was still wearing his scholar's gown, he was interviewed by the Master and Fellows of Pembroke College, who made him a tutor in philosophy and ancient history. He attended Haverfield's lectures, and, like Donald Atkinson, he too served as an assistant at Corbridge, after which Haverfield put him in charge of an excavation on the Roman fort at Ambleside, in 1913. At the outbreak of war he was sent to London where he worked in intelligence at the admiralty; and in ihe autumn of 1918 he married Miss Ethel Graham, the daughter of the Laird of Skipness in Kintyre. His marriage, however, terminated his fellowship at Pembroke, as the college's austere statutes imposed celibacy on its fellows, but, after the death of the then Master of Pembroke, Collingwood was re-elected, becoming at the same time philosophy tutor at Lincoln College. He and his wife bought a house at North Moreton in Berkshire, which was about thirteen miles from Oxford. He used to spend four nights a week in college during term, always going home at weekends. This arrangement cut him off from much of the social life in Oxford, and it led to his reputation for being 'somewhat remote and mysterious'.[8] Later, however, they moved to Belbroughton Road in North Oxford, after his election as Waynflete Professor of Metaphysical Philosophy in 1934, which gave him a fellowship at Magdalen. Four years later he was made a Fellow of the British Academy.

In conversation Collingwood was always courteous and delightful; and he had an extraordinary ability to speak both freely and yet with absolute precision. As Christopher had chosen to specialize in Roman Britain, he was able to go to Collingwood for a term for tutorials, while he was working for Greats. This experience was not always entirely comfortable. On one occasion half-way through the term, Christopher had attended one of Collingwood's lectures, and the essay he produced that week was simply a rather ill-digested version of his tutor's own words. The explosion of displeasure was frightening. Collingwood shrilled at him for merely repeating what he had heard: 'That lecture was meant to make you think for yourself!' He was white with anger. It never happened again; indeed, it was the only time that Christopher ever saw him lose his temper, and it was over very quickly.

Collingwood suffered a stroke in about 1938, and went off on a cruise to recover, leaving his wife behind. He wrote a book about the voyage, called *The Log of the First Mate* (though Christopher never read it), and he also began writing his autobiography. This brilliant little book is in every way unconventional. He gives little information about the events and characters in his life, and a great deal of his beliefs and attitudes. Not surprisingly his forceful opinions on some of his colleagues led to the book being 'regretted' by many of them, who found themselves impaled on the sharp end of his wit. To make matters worse, when he returned from the cruise, he persuaded Ethel to divorce him, so that he could marry a much younger woman. This excited a great deal of moral indignation at the time; and as a result his obituary, written for the British Academy by R.B. McCallum, simply stated that he had 'declined' in his later years. No mention was made of the divorce, or of his subsequent remarriage.

Collingwood resigned his professorship in 1941, and he retired to the house at Coniston which he had inherited on the death of his father nine

R.G. Collingwood. Photograph by Lafayette. Published in the *Proceedings of the British Academy* XXIX (1943)

years before. He died there in 1943, and is buried beside his father in Coniston churchyard. Christopher's last letter from him was written on 27 March 1941. The handwriting, though still precise, is so minute that it is difficult to read, but the style is unmistakable:

15, Belbroughton Road, Oxford.
My dear Christopher,

The University is in vacation: when it meets again the news will comfort it: at present I am not (being a poor writer) circulating it, but not because I wish it to remain unknown: for it is known to many.

I am living, however, close at hand. The address from which I shall carry on my activities being South Hayes, Streatley, Berkshire.

It is three years since the superincumbent sword of Damocles became clearly visible, and here I am driving a pen, though not well: driving it better as the weeks progress, and going for longer walks. So I hope that in the course of time I shall be fit, if not to lecture again, at least to write again, and to deliver with it all that I have to say. I don't look forward to complete inactivity, or to an activity that leaves Oxford out of account. The half-written book over which I acquired the paralytic stroke is the best thing I have written yet, and I look forward with pleasure to going on with it one day.

Your good wishes are very welcome, and help me not to feel (if I had been inclined to feel it) that I am leaving Oxford a broken down old man, good only for leisure; but to be conscious of the support which a senior but not yet decrepit man may receive from his juniors – which is of course his strength.

Yours sincerely,
Robin Collingwood

Looking back in his fiftieth year Collingwood described his life's work as being 'an attempt to bring about a rapprochement between history and philosophy'.[9]

In his earliest book, *Religion and Philosophy*, which was published in 1916, he declared that the two disciplines were actually 'the same thing', but his subsequent work in both subjects led him to modify that statement. He was fundamentally a philosopher who applied his superbly precise and rational mind to the study of history; and it is probably for his work on Roman Britain that he is best remembered. In 1936 he and Nowell Myres contributed a volume to the *Oxford History of England*. In the preface he explained that the work was not a collaboration, but two quite independent studies. Myres followed Collingwood's Roman period with a study of the English settlements – the Angles, Saxons, and the Jutes from the Continent. This book, known to all archaeologists simply as 'Collingwood and Myres', was the unassailable statement of all knowledge on the subject for decades. It was to remain so until Sheppard Frere published his *Britannia* in 1967;

and still later came Peter Salway's revised version of the *History of Roman Britain* in the same *Oxford History of England* series, which appeared in 1981.

Collingwood took over the mantle of Haverfield in the publication of all the inscriptions found in Roman Britain, in collaboration with Richard Wright, who continued to work on alone after Collingwood's death. The inscriptions were published in the *Journal of Roman Studies* every year, up to the foundation of the journal *Britannia* in 1970, by the Society for the Promotion of Roman Studies. Since then the yearly intake of inscriptions, under the joint editorship of Mark Hassall and Roger Tomlin, has been published in this periodical.

Although Christopher was becoming more and more interested in archaeology, he only began to drop some of his other interests towards the end of the Michaelmas term in 1926, when he found that his voice was beginning to show signs of strain:

> . . . A rather sickening thing has happened since I wrote: 'assiduous attendance' at rehearsals is beginning to tell on my voice, and I've had to offer to resign my part: the committee have arranged that I'm to sing at the matinée on Friday (Sunday is press night), and that my understudy, who, having only been in the club a fortnight, hasn't had time to wear himself out, is to take it every other night. Moral – don't grind your principals into singing in the chorus as well . . . I'm resigning the Opera Club secretaryship after this term. It's all too much. . . .

Christopher's enthusiasm for the theatre remained undimmed, however. C.P. had spoken to Gyles Isham, whom he had met through his acting circle in London, about the possibility of putting Christopher up for membership of the Oxford University Dramatic Society (OUDS), and Isham had said he would be delighted to propose him. Gyles Isham was 'a romantically handsome baronet's son from Magdalen' who had had a remarkably successful four years with the society.[10] His performance as Hamlet in 1924 had been greeted with rave reviews. *The Times* proclaimed that 'no performance of the Oxford University Dramatic Society during the last quarter of a century has attracted greater attention'. The *Daily Express* was yet more lavish with its praise: 'Wonderful new Hamlet!' it shrieked, 'Genius of Oxford University'. Isham was compared favourably with Irving. There were, though, some hostile reports from critics who were irritated by the lyrical outpourings of their colleagues. Christopher only met Isham once, in 'Sligger' Urquhart's rooms.[11] He had asked Christopher if he would like to become a member of the OUDS, saying that he had seen his father in London, and he had promised to recommend him if he wanted to join the society. Christopher was naturally delighted, and shortly afterwards rehearsals began on one of the most taxing of all Shakespeare's plays – *King Lear*.

'Ingenious lighting is to be the keystone of Komisarjevsky's production,' he wrote to his mother, soon after the first rehearsal, at which the great Russian producer had remarked to the assembled company: 'A professional cast would need three months to rehearse this play: you, three years: and you have three weeks. So we cannot act the play, we must just try to speak it.'[12]

Theodore Komisarjevsky, who was born in 1882 into an aristocratic Russian family, had been the Director of the Imperial State Theatres in pre-Revolutionary Moscow. He had been responsible for staging the first performances of some of Chekhov's plays, as well as producing operas. He fled the Revolution, like so many of his compatriots, in 1919, and settled in London, where his fiery and unpredictable talents were greatly valued. Rather surprisingly, he had never before been asked to produce any of Shakespeare's plays before he was approached by the OUDS in the autumn of 1926; but he was not at all dismissive of the work of amateurs. In fact he always said that he considered them to be much less selfish than professionals. For the title role he chose Harman Grisewood, with Denys Buckley, who was president of the society, as Gloucester,[13] Peter Fleming as the Duke of Cornwall,[14] and Christopher was given the part of the Earl of Kent. According to Duff Hart-Davis, who was Peter Fleming's godson, and wrote his biography,[15] his performance wasn't much of a hit: 'He looked like a hurriedly constructed fifth of November Guy Fawkes.'[16] He did, however, get himself quite spectacularly cut one night during a fight with his servant, who was played by the young Osbert Lancaster, who had just come up to Lincoln College. Lancaster's strict adherence to the precautions laid down by the university's sabre champion, who had coached them for the fight, got him through all the performances very well. Peter Fleming was less cautious. Helmetless on one occasion he received a crack on the head from his opponent's 4 ft steel blade; and on another evening he forgot his mail gauntlet and received a nasty cut, which must have added considerable drama to his exit line 'I bleed apace!'[17]

Christopher, as the Earl of Kent, added a further touch of reality to the proceedings. In the scene where Kent abuses Goneril's pretty boy steward (who was played by R. McNair Scott), he twice got carried away by the dramatic power of the words, and kicked the unfortunate young man right off the stage. What made matters worse was that the arrangement of the stage, which normally slopes gently up towards the back, was cunningly set out in a series of terraces, so that when you got to the wings on each side of the stage, the carpenters' work stopped abruptly, and there was a drop of a couple of feet to the lower level. On the second night, when Christopher repeated this painful exercise, McNair Scott, not surprisingly, was very angry indeed. Christopher's three subsequent performances were executed with rather more restraint.

The part of the Fool was originally to have been played by John Betjeman.[18] There are several versions of the events which led to his expulsion from the cast. One account has it that, until he lampooned the OUDS in the university newspaper *Cherwell*, he had been going to play the part of the Fool. Humphrey Carpenter says that, according to John Fernald,[19] who actually played the part of the Fool in the five performances, he had simply been forbidden to do any more acting because of interdiction by his college.[20] However, Christopher's recollection is rather different. On the evening of the first rehearsal the wretched lad was so nervous that he had sought refuge in a nearby hostelry, and was so drunk when he arrived that he had to be firmly led away. His part was taken over by Fernald, who had been cast as Cornwall, thus bringing in Peter Fleming to take over his part as the Duke. It is probable that all three reasons contributed to Betjeman's ignominious departure.

The stage set was highly dramatic, built up with the platforms, nicknamed by the cast the 'Mappin Terraces', after the terraces of that name in Regent's Park Zoo. There were also two very clever lighting systems, and a gold panorama cloth so that the heath could immediately be transformed into the interior of the palace without any elaborate changes of scenery. Komisarjevsky went on to develop his ideas even further, when he was responsible for a number of highly controversial productions at Stratford, including *The Merchant of Venice* in 1932 and an extraordinary version of *Macbeth* with aluminium scenery and vaguely modern uniforms. In 1936 he produced J.M. Barrie's play, *The Boy David*, which was a failure; and after this disappointment he left for America, where he remained until his death in 1954. He was married for a short time to the actress Dame Peggy Ashcroft.

Osbert Lancaster recalled that 'at Oxford in those days women played a very small part in our lives'. There had been female students in the university since the 1870s, of course; and they were naturally invited to balls, concerts, picnics, and punting on the river. But it is difficult now to understand the absolute innocence which was so much a feature of the lives of young men and women at that time. Christopher remarked: 'In retrospect one might have done better from the worldly point of view if one had been less innocent. But at the same time, from the point of view of morality, there's a lot to be said for innocence. A lot of temptations are necessarily beyond you.'

Shortly after the OUDS production of *King Lear* Christopher got a letter from an old Wykehamist friend, Emrys Lloyd, who had gone to King's College, Cambridge. Lloyd wanted to visit Greece during the Easter vacation in 1927, and he asked Christopher to go with him. Term ended on 19 March, and Christopher planned to go on a weekend retreat at Pusey House immediately afterwards, leaving Oxford on 22 March. Lloyd wanted to leave on 1 April, but as C.P.'s birthday was on the third, Christopher delayed their departure until the following day.

In a letter to his mother written in the middle of March he gave her a detailed plan of the proposed trip, with a sketch-map. He had discovered that it would cost £54 to travel on the famous Orient

Express, via Vienna, Belgrade and Salonika, so they took a train to Venice, and from Brindisi they went by boat to Athens. The return fare came to about £25. He had also taken advice from his tutor, Christopher Cox, who was well known at the British School in Athens and suggested that they should both register there as students on their arrival, as the school provided excellent maps and guides, as well as information about finding suitable accommodation.

On the train from Paris Christopher almost repeated one of the incidents that had occurred on an early holiday with his parents in Switzerland: he got out of the train at Sens to get a drink. Lloyd was far too sensible to follow, and almost at once the train began to pull out. Christopher only just managed to climb on board before the train left the station. They spent two nights in Venice, and then boarded a steamer to take them to Piraeus, the port of Athens. They had already booked rooms at a hotel there, so the next thing was to find a travel agent who could provide them with transport. They found one: an immensely cheerful Alexandrian Greek, who fixed them up with a mule and a mule-boy. They would have to walk most of the time: the beast was to carry their belongings, and the boy would act as a guide.

Having dealt with the practicalities, they were eager to climb the Acropolis to have a look at the Parthenon. They both had cameras, and Christopher kept most of his negatives. Unfortunately some of them

Athens: panorama of the Acropolis from the south-west. Photograph by Christopher, April 1927

have rolled up, and it was impossible to print from them; but the ones that did survive give a very good idea what the place was like in 1927 – views that are almost unrecognizable to the present-day tourist, who is no longer allowed to get anywhere near the Parthenon. The marble has suffered so much from air pollution, and from the constant battering of feet that drastic measures have been required to prevent any further deterioration.

After they had seen something of Athens itself they made trips out, first to Eleusis, where they were lucky enough to meet up with an American lady and her daughter who had hired a car. They went with them to visit Sounion and Marathon and also on a day trip by boat to Aegina. On the fifth day they took a Greek ship back through the Corinth Canal to the little port of Itea, from where there was a bus that took them to Delphi. They booked in at the rest-house, and that night Lloyd became ill. He developed a high temperature, and Christopher was sufficiently alarmed to go out first thing in the morning to find a doctor. By an extraordinary stroke of luck the Hellenic Travellers' Club, which had spent the night on board its cruise ship in the harbour at Itea, arrived in two coaches, for a visit to the sanctuary. Christopher rushed towards this unmistakably English party, and to his amazement and relief he spotted the familiar snow-white hair of Mr Bather, who was in fact one of the party's leaders. Mr Bather had taught Christopher during his first years at Winchester, which had not always been very happy; and his surprise at this encounter was manifestly increased by Christopher's appearance. He had dressed very hastily, in his anxiety to get help for the ailing Lloyd; his shirt, and a pair of crumpled cotton trousers were accompanied by a pair of exceedingly battered patent leather pumps, which he was using as slippers, as they had long passed their use for more gracious occasions but were very comfortable, and light to carry about. Mr Bather's beady eye fell upon them at once: 'Pumps!' he exclaimed, 'Typical of you, Hawkes, in a place like this!' But he very quickly responded to Christopher's explanation, and it was arranged that Lloyd should be taken back to the ship with the party, to be cared for by the ship's doctor. They were on their way to Athens, and Lloyd was treated for what turned out to be a bad dose of influenza. He was taken back to the hotel in Athens to recuperate, while Christopher went on alone, by steamer, across the Gulf to Patras, from where he went by rail to Olympia. He was met there by the mule-boy; and though he spoke no English, Christopher's classical Greek, with the help of a phrase book of modern Greek, enabled them to get along very well together.

At Olympia he visited the remains of the classical sanctuary and the stadium, and in the main hotel there he met a very quiet and modest Danish professor and his wife. They began talking in the bar before dinner, and went into the dining-room together. There they found an enormous table in the middle of the room, elaborately decorated with rose-buds which formed the words 'sto kalo Karo' (roughly, 'all the best,

The Parthenon: western front seen between the column of the Propylaea. Photograph by Christopher

Karo'). It was a birthday party, and a big one. The guests soon began to arrive, very high-spirited and noisy, led by the celebrated German archaeologist Georg Karo, whose birthday it was. Christopher and the Danes were squashed at a small table in one corner of the room, scarcely able to hear themselves speak. There were speeches, gales of laughter, and applause accompanied by a hearty Germanic stamping of feet.

From Olympia they made their way southward down the valley to the port of Kalamata, where they stayed the next night. In the morning they started early for the high Langada Pass, stopping on the top at a village. It was Easter Eve, and the whole village seemed to be crammed into the tiny church. The service went on all through the evening, until the bells rang out for midnight, and the priest emerged from the sanctuary loudly proclaiming: 'Christos Anesti! Christos Anesti!' ('Christ is Risen!'). Then the feasting began. In each household one or two of the women had stayed behind to prepare the Paschal lambs, which were roasted on spits over open fires, in Biblical fashion, with 'his head and his legs, and the appurtenance thereof . . .' The beasts were then jointed and put into pots with wine and sprigs of fresh rosemary.

Christopher was lodging with the headman of the village and his family, and he went back to the house with them to join in the meal.

The Parthenon: eastern front. Photograph by Christopher

While he was munching his way through a generous portion of meat, the wife appeared from the kitchen, and approached him with an alarming looking morsel impaled on the end of a large fork. '*Encephala!*' she shouted, waving the steaming offering at him. It was a great honour, and Christopher dutifully ate it, declaring it to be most delicious. The word for brains is the same in both classical and modern Greek, so he knew exactly what he was getting: the idea was a lot nastier than the actuality.

After visiting Mistra, where Christopher saw the glorious Byzantine frescoes, they went down into Sparta, where he said a grateful goodbye to the mule-boy. He stayed the night in the town, but there was little of interest to see there. The next morning he was able to get a lift as far as Tripolitza in the car which was used to deliver mail, and from there the train took him down off the plateau towards Corinth. It was a very steep incline, of several hundred feet, and the single track ran in a huge curve towards the coast. Alarmingly the driver took the brakes off, shut down the steam, and simply free-wheeled as they went down. From his carriage window he could see, at the lower end of the great curve, another train labouring its way up the slope towards them, on the same single track. Of course both drivers knew exactly what they were doing: they met precisely at the point where the track doubled, at a little wayside station. Lloyd was waiting for Christopher at Corinth.

The next day they went down into the Argolid and thence to Nauplia, which was then no bigger than a village, on the coast not far from the Mycenaean rock-citadel of Tiryns. Staying in the little hotel at Nauplia was another English visitor. Miss H.L. Lorimer, who, like Miss M.V. Taylor, was never called by her Christian name, was a research fellow at Somerville whom Christopher knew only by her reputation as a scholar. He and Lloyd enjoyed her talking to them, and telling them what they would see at Tiryns. She was still around at Oxford when Christopher returned as a professor after the Second World War. She called on him at his rooms at Keble to present him with a copy of her newly published book *Homer and the Monuments*, which she had dedicated to Gilbert Murray.

After Tiryns they made another excursion from their base at Nauplia to see the theatre at Epidauros, which is famous for its accoustics. Christopher climbed to the top tier, and Lloyd stood below him in the middle of the orchestra, where Christopher's delivery of some heroic lines of Sophocles far above was indeed clearly heard by his companion.

By the next afternoon they had moved on to Mycenae, where they signed their names in the visitors' book at the much-described guest-house, 'La Belle Helène de Menelaus'. The inn had been run by a remarkable character known as Agamemnon, with his brother Orestes, and their sister Elektra. This visitors' book, kept by Agamemnon, whose real name was Spiro, contained some curious names, not all of them archaeological. In the 1960s visitors could see, among others, the names of several Nazi leaders, including that of Heinrich Himmler. Christopher wrote an inscription in Latin – just three words, '*Dum spero, Spiro*', which produced a rather unkind response from a fellow Wykehamist, J.D.S. Pendlebury, who visited the site not long after. He declared that Christopher's writing in Latin was 'showing off'.

Leaving the Argolid, Christopher and Lloyd returned to Corinth, to see the American excavations in the Agora. The place was deserted, though the excavated area had been left open, and they were able to walk round it. Next day they climbed right up to the Acro-Corinth, which is much higher than the Acropolis of Athens. The contents of the Byzantine fortification at the top had been robbed by the Turks, but the most breath-takingly memorable thing about the place was the tremendous view from the top. 'It was like having a map spread out in front of you,' Christopher remembered, and the place was bathed in the unforgettable colours of a late afternoon in spring in that perpetually lovely country.

They spent so long on the top that they had to run towards the end of their descent to the wayside station from where they were to catch the train to Athens. They actually arrived in good time, and were congratulating themselves on being early, when, as so often happens in Greece, the train came in – early. They were lucky to catch it at all.

The journey home was uneventful. Christopher stayed in Paris for a couple of days to see his sister, who was at a finishing school there, while Lloyd went straight back to England. Penelope objected strongly to the clipped military moustache that Christopher had when he

Athens: the Dionysiac theatre below the Acropolis rock. Photograph by Christopher

arrived, and she made him shave it off at once. He had not shaved at all while he was in Greece, but the beard had become rather scratchy and uncomfortable, and he had got rid of that on the last morning in the hotel in Athens, and tidied up the moustache in imitation of his father's. He has never sported any facial hair since.

During the seven terms Christopher had to prepare for Greats, his tutor for ancient history was Christopher Cox, and for philosophy he went to H.W.B. Joseph and A.H. Smith (who later became Warden of New College). Joseph was an austere logician. C.M. Bowra described him as short and stocky, with 'a large head and a pronounced jaw'; he was 'totally devoted to the College, and gave to his teaching an energy and care which would have destroyed most other men' (*Memories*, p. 99). Maurice Hugh-Jones, who shared rooms with Nowell Myres on Long Wall when Christopher first went up in 1924, recalled that if you got past the third sentence without interruption in your essay, you were doing exceptionally well. After Christopher had left Oxford he returned quite often to see his friends who were still there. One afternoon he bumped into his old tutor in New College Lane: 'Ah, Hawkes . . .', he said, 'Let me see . . . you went to the British Museum, didn't you? Which department?' Christopher told him that it was the Department of British and Medieval Antiquities.

'British and Medieval WHAT??' he exploded. 'It's a false logical division!' And so it was. Many people found Joseph too much to cope with; but to Christopher his razor-like mind was distinctly stimulating; and a healthy respect for precision in language, in both speech and writing, has remained with him ever since.

Towards the end of the previous June (1927) Christopher was asked to give the presidential address to the Archaeological Society. His subject was the Siege of Oxford – or rather Oxford all through the Civil War (1642–6) with special reference to its fortifications and remains. He wrote to his mother, telling her that it was 'a bigger subject than I had suspected. The paper took nearly one and a half hours to read!' He had had some slides made, and he reported to his mother that he felt it had gone reasonably well, though he was finding Oxford a trifle oppressive: 'I am thinking of running down to Winchester later today,' he added. He must have gone to see Maddie while he was in Winchester, though he makes no mention of her in this letter. The first reference to her decline came in the following February, although there may have been letters which have not survived. Poor Maddie suffered a total collapse, and she had to be taken to the County Mental Hospital at Basingstoke, where she died on 22 February 1928. Christopher wrote to his mother the following day:

> I think it is a cause for great relief; and I find the fact that her complete breakdown had already occurred and become permanent breaks the force of what otherwise would be one's shock of grief, by the mere fact of having caused so much of it already. The church is Holy Trinity, North Walls: the Rector changed about the time I left Winchester, and I don't know the new one's name, but the Rectory is in St Peter's Street. I am sure all the arrangements will be all right.
>
> It is obviously right to be calm and principally thankful for all she has done for us in the past – an immense amount. I will be at Mass with intentions for Requiem on Saturday. . . .

If this letter seems rather hard and unfeeling, one has to remember that Christopher's upbringing had instilled in him the most exacting standards of self-restraint, which had been further reinforced at Winchester. His life-long ability to make the best of things, even in the cruellest of circumstances, can sometimes make him appear to be insensitive; and his refusal to admit weakness must have puzzled many whose powers of endurance were less than his. Undoubtedly he grieved for Maddie. She was so much a part of his childhood that her death cut him very deeply, although he had naturally grown up and, in some respects, away from her, when he left Winchester. The very fact that he remembers so little of that harrowing time is probably a direct result of his protective ability for burying things which cause him distress.

On 27 April 1928 he went down to Winchester to give a lecture, and while he was there he went to see the Colliers, the policeman and his wife with whom Maddie had lodged before her final illness. He wrote to his mother after the visit:

> I think it would be a good idea if you went there on your way home from Beaulieu: they let it be seen, without saying so in so many words, that they could not understand why your early-made promise to go there has still to be carried out. The fact is there is a much larger amount of Maddie's stuff still with them than, I think, we guessed. If I remember rightly, two large hat boxes, a fair-sized wooden box, and some bulky paper parcels. These I left, as it seemed to me that you could profitably go through the contents (very miscellaneous, I should think) on the spot, and only take away a selection. The books, however, we packed in a sort of attaché case there was, and I brought them away and have put them in your bedroom.
>
> They were very nice, and not at all peevish – but I should not put off your visit longer than you can help. . . .

At Oxford, shortly before the end of the previous term, Christopher had been exposed to infection with mumps, and the college authorities had let him go home for the rest of the term, rather than risk an epidemic. In the event he escaped the highly unpleasant disease, and spent the time working quietly at Campden Hill Square.

As the time for his finals approached he had fewer opportunities for writing letters. He sent a note home on 2 April saying that he would be home on the fourth, as he had an informal interview with Reginald Smith at the British Museum at noon that day, with the exam and interview on the following day. He had been encouraged to put in for the post by H.A.L. Fisher, in his dual capacity as warden of his college, and trustee of the museum. The keeper whose early retirement caused the vacancy was O.M. Dalton. There were three candidates: Christopher and another from New College, Basil Gray, and A.G.O. Matthias, who came from Pembrokeshire, and had done some work at the National Museum of Wales.

The interview itself was carried out at the headquarters of the Civil Service Commission in Burlington Gardens on Tuesday and Wednesday 15 and 16 May. The documents Christopher received beforehand are engagingly particular in their instructions to candidates, who were required 'before proceeding to their seats to lay aside their hats, umbrellas, and any books, papers, or other appliances, the use of which is not expressly granted to them'; 'perfect silence must be preserved in the examination room: any candidate guilty of disorderly or improper conduct in or about the room will be liable to exclusion from the examination.'

The interview before the selection board was held on the afternoon of 16 May. Christopher remembers the occasion vividly:

> I was ushered into the examination room, where there was a large

table at which the Chief Commissioner was sitting, with Sir Frederic Kenyon on one side, and Reginald Smith on the other. There were a couple of other people there too, but I didn't discover who they were. Kenyon began it by asking some questions, and then handed over to Smith, who said, 'Mr Hawkes, you've said you've had to do with excavations, I understand – are you aware that this is a very different sort of thing from museum work?' So I said, 'Well, there is this in common, you have to write up your finds in your report of an excavation, and that is museum work, surely.' I must have got good marks for that. 'Can you draw?' Smith went on. Sir Frederic interrupted impatiently at that point: 'We *know* he can draw – he did a wall-painting at Winchester. . . .'

He was then shown a flint implement: 'Did I know what that was? I told them it was a Paleolithic hand-axe. It was. . . .' There were no more questions. As third of the four candidates he had to wait while Matthias was examined – Basil Gray was before him. Christopher got the job; but there was a rule at that time that if there was a close runner-up for a post, and if another vacancy came up within a year, then the second applicant was automatically given the job. This happened in Basil Gray's case. From the Department of Printed Books he moved to the Department of Oriental Prints and Drawings (embracing Persian miniature painting), and next to a broader charge of Oriental antiquities, extending it as keeper, from 1946, throughout their range.

Christopher took his Greats in June, and he wrote just one hasty letter to his mother before he finally came down:

Pickford is starting removal from here on Monday [the letter is simply marked Saturday] so expect my things about Wednesday. My viva was MOST hopeful – brief (four minutes), jocose, amiable, and on Roman Britain: I feel more optimistic than I have at all previously – it was really a great relief. . . .

Throughout his time at Oxford Christopher's interest in the opposite sex had been for the most part a brotherly one. He had, of course, made a number of women friends, and he enjoyed their company greatly, but there was never a close emotional involvement except with one girl, whom he met through Nowell Myres's sister, Rosalie. Pamela Walter, who was then an undergraduate at Somerville, was a quiet, solitary girl, and she had a dog, a beautiful black standard poodle called Babette, which was in itself unusual for an undergraduate in those days. She was not allowed to keep it in college, but she used to take it for walks in the early morning, enjoying the silence and her own company. The attraction that Christopher felt towards her passed before very long into a sort of brotherly affection. He sought, perhaps, something of the companionship of a sister, as he did in most of his relationships with women, rather than that of a partner, even of the most innocent kind. It was not until June 1928, during his last Commemoration week at Oxford that he first fell seriously in love.

Daphne Lambart, whose mother was a first cousin of May Lupton, the wife of C.P.'s old Cambridge friend, Cecil Lupton, was staying in Oxford at the Eastgate Hotel with her sister Veronica for their brother's gaudy at Radley. The two Lupton girls, Elizabeth and Marjorie, were also in Oxford, at Christopher's invitation, with his mother and sister, and they were joined by Daphne and Veronica for the OUDS Ball, which was held in the Town Hall. There was a wonderful cabaret with Sophie Tucker, 'the last of the red-hot mommas', singing 'Fish Gotta Swim' and 'The Man I Love'. Among the other members of the party were Vyvyan Stopford, who later married Marjorie, and Patrick Hamilton-Baines, who later became a friend of Veronica's. It was gloriously hot and sunny the next day, and they all went on the river. Christopher was enchanted by Daphne, who was blonde and very pretty, and his last week at Oxford passed in a flood of excitement and happiness.

In the week immediately after, he left for a short holiday on his own in northern France. He had wanted for some time to see the great cathedrals, especially those of Rouen, Caen and Chartres; and above all he wanted to see the Bayeux Tapestry, on which he had based his wall-painting in Thule Chamber at Winchester. He wrote at once to his father:

> I have only just arrived, and it is one of those very few really marvellous places which have so much beauty in them that one is almost afraid to start 'going round' them: I can only contemplate this cathedral – and the outside of it at that. It is the XIIIth century at its best – the time of St Louis, I suppose: the thing is simply indescribable. And the inside, where the glass is the most perfect in the world, I can, till tomorrow, only imagine.
>
> It is an exquisite evening, too; perfect for sitting under the thing with its two great west towers simply dominating.
>
> There is the usual cheerful French rowdiness in the middle distance, and the town is most delightful, with numerous small churches of great beauty, and many odd old houses.
>
> The jangling row of Rouen, which is a pretty big city, is well left behind. I came from there this afternoon, through Paris, really a long way round, but two hours quicker than the cross-country 'train omnibus'.
>
> I have been very lucky in hotels, having found in every place a most satisfactory one, something between the 2nd and 3rd order, with a large Madame in the caisse, and good buttery food. The prices are easy enough – about 20 fr. a night – and an average of 15 fr. for a meal.
>
> My plans are taking shape more now: I shall go from here west to Le Mans, then north-west to Avranches, and home by Bayeux and Caen.
>
> There was a cruiser squadron visiting Rouen, and many sailors, drunk and sober, and Feux d'artifice on the Seine one night. I am dropping into as many conversations as I can, and am already more fluent than I was. . . .

On his return to England in early July Christopher stayed briefly at Campden Hill Square, picked up 'Sir Walter' from the garage, and set off on it, as had been previously arranged, for Caerhūn, where Paul Baillie Reynolds had invited him to join the dig. But on his way there, just a little north of Shrewsbury, was Daphne's home. She had got him her parents' invitation to stay there for the weekend. The house was at Baschurch, and she was waiting there for him at the gate. He sent a letter to his mother from the Caerhūn estate office, near Conway:

> I got here today through the Welsh mountains after the most pleasant and delightful weekend with a really charming family. The Archdeacon is a big, happy, good-humoured, grey-haired man, with a direct, cheerful smile and a ready wit and a sound head: sort of Catholic without half-heartedness or wooliness. I liked him very much, and we seem to get on very well.

The archdeacon, though Anglo-Catholic indeed, much disliked the use of outward trappings of 'High Churchmanship' just for their own sake.

Christopher and Daphne spent one afternoon exploring the Berth at Baschurch. She wanted to show him the site, which is a ring-shaped earthwork, reached by a causeway, in the middle of a marsh, now dry. There was a punt moored on the part of the big ditch that is still full of water, called 'The Mere', and he and Daphne spent a happy afternoon lazing in it, in the sunshine.

While he was at Caerhūn a telegram arrived for him at the estate office (used as a poste restante by the Reynoldses) from his tutor Christopher Cox, with the news that he had got a first in Greats.

He stayed again at Baschurch in October, taking a few days leave from the museum. He went with the family to Sunday evensong at Ellesmere College, one of the Midland division of the Woodard Schools, of which the archdeacon was provost; and he and Daphne climbed the Wrekin to see its prehistoric hillfort. She enjoyed being shown new things about the countryside she knew, though Christopher had yet to recognize that her interest was mainly for his sake, whereas to him the study of landscape and its history had already become a passion. She also came to see him in London once or twice; and at Oxford, when he was one of the many to receive the BA, she came from London to watch the degree ceremony in the Sheldonian.

Towards the end of the year she accepted his proposal of marriage, and an announcement of their engagement appeared in *The Times* on New Year's Day 1929. He went to stay with the family almost immediately afterwards; and, as her fiancé, escorted her to the Shrewsbury Hunt Club Ball. Only a day or two later Daphne tearfully told him that she couldn't marry him. He prevailed on her to wait a little while, desperately hoping that she would change her mind; but when he lunched with her father in London some little while later, and he asked the archdeacon if he thought there was a chance, the answer, though kindly, was oblique, and gave him no encouragement. Yet still he hung on until some time in February, when Daphne insisted that he should place another announcement in *The Times* stating that the marriage would not now take place. It was all very painful for him, for the uncertainty had told on his nerves, so that when the final refusal came there was also with it a sense of relief, for by then he had come to realize how little they had in common. For him it was of vital importance to be able to share his interests with his partner, and he had already seen what appeared to be the ideal archaeological marriage in Rik and Tessa Wheeler. Tessa was the perfect organizer and companion. He realized that Daphne would never share his life in the way that Tessa shared in her husband's.

Christopher threw himself into his new life in London, with a rapidly increasing circle of friends, and it was not long before the shadow of disappointment was replaced by one of the happiest periods of his life.

Before he had left for the French holiday Christopher had written a letter in which he tried to explain to his mother how he felt about living at home :

> About my abode in London, I think I am quite sure that, as enlarging the house is quite out of the question, it will be infinitely better for me only to stay at home while on the look-out for somewhere else to live. Home will be very much as his College is to a man living at Oxford in digs. To get into the habit of being self-supporting and self-reliant, and to bear the responsibility of independence, is, I am convinced, vitally important. If there are expenses I must learn how to meet them half way. If there are difficulties, I must learn how to overcome them. If I were to remain at home I should get into the habit of relying on other people for a thousand little things for which a grown man ought to rely on himself. . . .
>
> My sleeping and having breakfast in the house makes very little difference to the companionship of the family, which we all want to enjoy. That companionship comes and will come naturally and freely because of the love behind it, and surely has no need of artificial guarantees of bed and breakfast. . . .

Not unnaturally he was eager to get away from home and make an independent life for himself, with a circle of friends who were not drawn so much from the family circle. His father understood exactly how he felt, but he also knew that Christopher would be earning a very small salary, and it would be better for him to live at home to begin with, saving as much as he could, until he was able to afford a place of his own. When, after about eighteen months, he finally declared that he could no longer go on living at home, his mother was upset. But she could see that it was right for him to leave; and, mastering her feelings, she set about finding him a flat, and very quickly found one close to Lancaster Gate tube station. It was on the third floor of 7 Gloucester Terrace, Paddington. He moved in on March quarter-day 1930.

9   London, 1928–33

In 1943 in his introduction to *A History of the British Museum Library*
by Arundell Esdaile, Sir Frederic Kenyon wrote:

> The British Museum is, next to the British Navy, the national
> institution which is held in most universal respect abroad. A visit to it
> is almost obligatory on travellers to this country; and foreign scholars
> regard it with a reverence which they sometimes extend to the
> temporary custodians of its treasures.

Whether one agrees with these sentiments or not, they do give a very
clear impression of the world in which Christopher took his place on 1
September 1928. His appointment for the first two years was
provisional: the post as assistant keeper (second class) was confirmed by
the trustees on 28 June 1930. There were twenty-three assistant keepers
(second class) and seventeen first class ones, with five keepers and two
deputy keepers under the director, Sir Frederic Kenyon. It is interesting
to note that the director's salary then was just over a third of that
received by the Headmaster of Winchester College in 1912, when Monty
Rendall took up the post.

The museum was founded in 1753 by an Act of Parliament which set
up a trust to house the private collection of Sir Hans Sloane. Sloane was
a baronet who had lived in Chelsea. A life-time bibliophile, he had
offered his collection (catalogued in forty-six volumes) to the Crown for
the sum of £20,000. The Act then established a body of trustees, headed
by the Archbishop of Canterbury, with the Lord Chancellor and the
Speaker of the House of Commons as principals. Among the other
trustees were the First Lord of the Admiralty, the Bishop of London, the
Master of the Rolls, the Attorney General and the Solicitor General, with
the Presidents of both the Royal Society and the Royal College of
Physicians. To these were added, in 1824, the Presidents of the Royal
Academy and the Society of Antiquaries. Five years after the founding
the first statutes were drawn up, and on 15 January 1759 the British
Museum was opened.

The present building, with its fine neo-classical front, stands on the
site of Montagu House in Great Russell Street. This first house, built in
1674, was destroyed by fire on the night of 18 January 1686. Rebuilt
immediately, to the same design, it housed the museum until 1874,
when it was replaced by Sir Robert Smirke's noble façade.

Christopher in 1928

Sir Frederic Kenyon was appointed director of the museum in 1909, when the new King Edward VII Building was under construction. This occupied the first five years of his directorship, and it is interesting that its opening, and that of the new Royal Library in Berlin, were the last state ceremonies to be carried out by George V and the Kaiser respectively. This new wing housed on its upper floor the exhibition gallery, as well as the students' room and the Department of Prints and Drawings; and on the main floor, divided between the sub-department of ceramics, and the other medieval and later exhibits (including two separate bequests, the Franks and Waddesdon), was the Department of British and Medieval Antiquities. The rest of its collections consisted of British and other prehistoric, Romano-British, Anglo-Saxon and post-Roman objects, with Early Christian and further European items dated to before 1100. All these, except for sculpture (which was shown with the Roman material from outside Britain), were in the older, south-east quarter, including its late-Victorian 'White Wing', and here were the department's offices. But the internal door to the director's and general offices, in the south-west quarter was where Christopher had to present himself: to meet the assistant secretary, swear allegiance to the trustees and receive his house-key, before being led to the British and Medieval Department, to start his first day's work.

He had been instructed to arrive at 10 a.m. sharp. Never an easy nor an early riser, he nevertheless arrived on time. The outer office was empty and silent. Eventually, at about 11 a.m. the assistant secretary arrived. He was extremely cordial. Christopher swore his oath on the Bible, and was taken to his department. There was nobody there either. Alec Tonnochy was the first to appear. He was responsible for the Early Christian and Medieval material, and he greeted Christopher warmly, but he could not show him anything to do. Rather than hang about uncomfortably, he decided to get on with his own work, writing the St Catharine's Hill report. Some days later the Keeper of the Department, Reginald Smith, returned. Smith had of course been on the interviewing committee when Christopher was appointed; and he cordially offered his congratulations to Christopher on his success in gaining a first in Greats. About a fortnight later Tom Kendrick appeared. He had been digging in Cornwall, in the stone-built Iron Age village of Chysauster, with an American friend of his, Hugh Hencken, who was a lecturer in European archaeology at Harvard.

Kendrick radiated warmth, and Christopher responded at once. They struck up a friendship which was to last undimmed until Kendrick's death in 1979. The family came from Birmingham, though Christopher never learnt much of his background in spite of the closeness and sympathy that grew between them. He had been at Charterhouse, and then Oriel College, Oxford; but within a year at the outbreak of the First World War, he had enlisted in the Warwickshire Regiment, rising to the rank of captain. He was severely wounded in 1916, in the Battle of Delville Wood, when his leg was blown off above the knee, and he also lost two fingers on his left hand. He suffered a great deal of pain for the rest of his life, but he very rarely complained, and he would never talk about the war. Later, when he was keeper, the door of his room was usually left open, and on more than one occasion Christopher heard him groaning with pain. He had to prop his leg up on a tall hassock to take the weight of the artificial leg which was strapped to the stump of his thigh. You could always tell who was coming into the room: because of his game leg Kendrick's step was instantly recognizable, just as Smith's approach was announced by his loudly squeaking boots.

In 1918 Kendrick had returned to Oxford to take the diploma in anthropology, after which he joined the Department of British and Medieval Antiquities, becoming its keeper in 1938, on the retirement of Reginald Smith. Although there was a harder side to his nature, and he could at times be unexpectedly rude, Tom Kendrick had immense charm, and he knew how to cope with the prickly nature of his keeper in a way which took Christopher some years to learn: Reggie Smith was not an easy man to work for. Kendrick humoured him, and on the whole managed to keep the peace, though there was at least one unpleasant and explosive clash between the new assistant keeper and his chief. Before the war Smith had been a distinctly different character, but by the mid-twenties he was often irritable and intolerant. He suffered from chronic indigestion, and was forced to live on a bleak and restricted diet, which included quantities of arrowroot and a constant supply of charcoal biscuits. Allowing precisely forty-five minutes, he got on the No. 38 bus down Shaftesbury Avenue, and took his frugal lunch at his club, the St James's. This timing was strictly imposed on the other members of the department, which reduced the scope of their lunch-time relaxation considerably. Christopher often went to the Lyons Corner House on the corner of Tottenham Court Road, where he was able to get 'roast beef and two veg, with baked rice' for a shilling.

Less well known than Tom Kendrick's several books is the photographic collection that he made of the pre-Norman Conquest crosses throughout England, which he formed gradually by making expeditions to photograph them from 1936 onwards. He used to take friends with him on these trips, among whom was a young scholar from Munich named Ernst Kitzinger, who was to become a good friend of Christopher's. He subsequently went to live in America, returning on his retirement to live a few minutes' walk from Christopher, in Oxford.

One of the friends he saw during those restricted 'lunch-hours' was a girl whom he had first met at Beaulieu, while he was staying with his aunt and uncle, Dorothy and Owen Bayldon, at their first home there, Dock House, in the summer of 1921. Verity Mills, whose father, Colonel Dudley Mills, had a house on the further side of the Beaulieu River, was invited to tea one afternoon while Christopher and his father were staying, and she danced for them on the lawn. She was a lovely girl of about fifteen, with china-blue eyes and curly, golden hair. She was very graceful, and though not as stunningly beautiful as her elder sister

Ottilie – who was very slender, while Verity was still girlishly plump – her unaffectedly sunny nature endeared her to Christopher, as indeed it did to all who met her.

During Christopher's first year at the museum, Verity's parents moved to a house in London, and Christopher was invited to a house-warming party given by her parents. He there discovered that Verity was at the LCC School of Arts and Crafts in Southampton Row, not far from the museum. She suggested that he should bring sandwiches to eat with her and a group of her friends, in the large entrance-hall, where there were also facilities for making coffee. This arrangement was much nicer than a solitary lunch in the Lyons Corner House, and Christopher used to join the group quite often.

Among Verity's friends was a delightful young man who also became a close friend of Christopher's. Lynton Lamb had been a student at the School of Arts and Crafts, but was by then working as an illustrator at the London office of the Oxford University Press. He and Christopher sometimes dined out together in Soho, and their friendship was only

After the Foster-Wilberforce wedding. From left to right: G.F. ('Bogie') Higginson, Ean Stewart-Smith, George ('Gerry') Young, Lesbia Cochrane, Christopher, and Bickham Sweet-Escott

sadly broken some years later by Lamb's premature death. Another part-time member of the group was Victor Pasmore. After leaving Harrow, he had got a job in local government at County Hall, painting only at weekends, and attending evening classes at the school. He was later taken up by the then Director of the National Gallery, Sir Kenneth Clark, who recognized his gifts, and he was able to leave local government in 1937, to concentrate on his painting. Pasmore was about three years younger than Christopher, and rather eccentric. They were all very much aware that he was both talented and unusual. He would bring his pictures along to the school, but would never allow anyone to visit him at his studio.

Another member of the Art School group was George Churchill. It was through him that Christopher came to enjoy two idyllic holidays in Italy. George's mother, Stella Churchill, was a doctor. She had qualified before her marriage, but her husband's career in the Consular Service (he was the British consul in Naples for some years) took her to Italy. Her two children were born there, and she never lost her love of that country. When her husband died she returned to medicine, and when Christopher first met her she was working part-time at the Great Ormond Street Hospital for Sick Children, living in a house at Strand-on-the-Green. Every year she used to take the *Castello Brown* (so called from its former owner, Francis Yeats-Brown, the writer on India), on the Riviera at Portofino for the Easter holiday, and she invited a group of friends to join her. She asked Christopher to go in April 1930. He wrote to his father on 2 April:

> The journey by the St Gotthard to Genoa was a reasonably good one, and now here everything is ideal. Donna Stella, as we call her, is the most charming and sympathetic character. I have learnt the mandolin already, and we mess about in boats, scramble about the mountains, laze about with books, and join in dinner-table conversations full of the flow of soul and reason. The place itself is marvellous: its shell is the old Genoese fort that dominated the little harbour, and you go down a zigzag path, through olive-yards, in terraces. From the garden or the windows you look straight down on Portofino, like a painted toy village. The place has its own little quay, and the best way over to the port is by water.
>
> It is all a little too lovely to be true. . . .

One of the first tasks that Christopher was given in the Department of British and Medieval Antiquities was not archaeological at all. During the Edwardian period its keeper, Sir Hercules Read, had a friend whose name was Montague Guest. Monty Guest was not only a friend of Read's, he was also a friend of Edward VII; and as the king was one of the trustees of the museum, and in fact attended quite a number of meetings, there was considerable pressure on the department to deal with his friend's bequest – an enormous collection of tokens. There were many kinds: trade tokens and club badges and passes, and there was a vast collection of coin-like passes which were the forerunners of theatre and concert tickets, either hired for the evening, or bought as a season ticket for a series of performances. O.M. Dalton, the previous keeper before Smith, had begun the catalogue after the war, under the direction of Sir Hercules; but when Read's health broke down, in 1921, and he was forced to retire to the south of France, where he died seven years later, Dalton became weary of the wretched things, and the project lapsed. He wanted to do the Early Christian catalogue, and he published, among other things, the catalogue of the Oxus Treasure, of mainly Persian silver. When Smith became keeper, the director reminded him that there had been an undertaking, signed by the trustees, that these tokens would be published, and it fell to Kendrick, Tonnochy and Christopher to complete the catalogue. Tom Kendrick did the sporting tokens, Tonnochy had the societies' and institutions'; Christopher fared rather better, with the theatre tokens, which he found exceedingly interesting. Many of them went right back to the eighteenth century, and some were of silver, quite large and impressive, and beautifully made. This labour took them a year; and it was followed by another immense collection, this time of flints.

Dr Allen Sturge was in general practice at Icklingham, near Mildenhall. He and his wife were both devoted amateur prehistorians, and they used to spend all their spare time walking over the fields with stout canvas bags, collecting flints. They bought from dealers, too, not only in this country but also from many sites in Europe and beyond. When Sturge died, in 1918, his entire collection was bequeathed to the museum. From Britain alone there were 86,425 flint implements, together with Sturge's own glass-topped display cases which had been brought from his home, and the whole collection was set out in a huge room in the basement.

The arrangement was that once or twice a week Christopher had to go down to the basement with Bowles, the clerk, to make a selection for Smith of between a dozen and eighteen examples, out of which Smith would make his own selection of perhaps eight or ten. These were then handed over to C.O. Waterhouse, the illustrator, who would draw them. Waterhouse did have a small office in the museum, but he took most of his work back to his home in Walthamstow. Smith wrote the descriptions, and it fell to poor Christopher to count the entire British collection for the catalogue when the drawings and descriptions had been completed. He was assisted in this by Bowles and a very tall clerk whose name was Chivers. It was a colossal job.

He was saved from having to work on the foreign material for the second volume by the arrival of a retired solicitor from Edinburgh named Edward Alexander. Having been widowed, Alexander had decided to come to London, and, following up his enthusiasm for stone implements, he had offered his services to the museum. They were gratefully accepted. Not only did he find satisfaction in working at the museum; he also found a wife. Kendrick had brought in a very sweet-natured, red-haired widow, Mrs Eileen Michell-Clarke, to help in the department. When war broke out in 1939 she and Alexander were married, and not long afterwards they retired to Torquay.

When the Sturge Collection had been dealt with, in January 1934, Christopher began a job which he was to carry out for nearly five years. This was the reason for the question at his interview about his ability to draw. He was to keep the accessions register, making a careful sketch, with measurements, of every newly-acquired object for identification should the number painted on the object itself become lost in cleaning or conservation. He was good at drawing, and did the job most conscientiously, though he soon began to find it tedious. Drudgery, however, was brightened from time to time by visitors. As well as the schoolboys who brought in their finds for identification, scholars and archaeologists from this country and from the Continent, some of them celebrated, would call in to see their colleagues when they were in London. It was an ideal meeting place, and he was to make some life-long friends this way.

His duties during these years also included gallery work, which they all had to do; arranging displays, and looking after the objects. The cabinet-maker, Mr Thomas, had a workshop 'somewhere in the bowels of the museum', and he was responsible for making the plinths and inner furnishing of the display-cases. The labels, like the numbers on the objects, were done by Mr Steele: he was given the wording, which he delicately copied with a brush either on painted blocks or strips of wood or metal, or on a kind of plastic called ivorine, which was normally used for piano keys, imitating ivory.

Christopher arranged the Bronze Age hoards, as well as the Iron Age collections and all the Roman, while Kendrick organized the Anglo-Saxon and the foreign collections of that period, and Tonnochy the Early Christian and medieval. By the time Christopher arrived Smith had given up gallery work, though he had done nearly all of it earlier on. His great contribution was the exhaustive series of five guides, which were for many years a sort of 'Gospel set' for all those interested in the subjects. Then, at any time of the day, up till 4 p.m., there was an intermittant trickle of people with enquiries. Objects were brought in for identification; and one particular enquiry after the war Christopher remembers vividly:

> A doctor from the neighbourhood of Mildenhall came in with a silver spoon. Well, there's a typology of late-Roman silver spoons, and you can date them by their shape. This doctor came back again after a week or two, bringing some more silver objects. Gradually I coaxed him into admitting that there was in fact a very large number of items. . . .

The finding of the Mildenhall treasure was first reported in *The Times* on 24 June 1946, though it was revealed at the inquest, which was held on 1 July, that it had actually been discovered some four years earlier. Two farm workers, Mr S. Ford and Mr G. Butcher came upon it accidentally while they were ploughing a field. Their employer believed the plates they had found to be of pewter or lead, so he kept them in his house. The elaborate decoration, unnoticed at first because of the dirt, was only revealed later when the objects were cleaned. The collection was declared Treasure Trove, which meant that it was Crown property and it was thus acquired immediately by the museum. By 20 July the magnificent silver tableware – thirty-four pieces in all – was put on public display; and a handbook which was prepared by the assistant keeper, John Brailsford, one of Christopher's two successors, with a preface by Kendrick, was published by the trustees the following year.

Shortly after he began work in the museum, Christopher was asked by Wheeler to become Honorary Secretary of the Royal Archaeological Institute. This he willingly undertook, though it was a further addition to his workload. Museum staff were allowed one half-day's holiday a week: they worked Saturday mornings, as this was the only day on which many people could bring in objects for identification. If you took an afternoon off during the week, you had to work on Saturday afternoon instead. The Royal Archaeological Institute (which met at the Society of Antiquaries' rooms in Burlington House) had afternoon council meetings once a month, so that in those weeks Christopher had only Sunday free. There were meetings of the Society of Antiquaries, too: he became a fellow of the society in January 1932, but he had been attending their meetings for some time before his election. In those days meetings were held in the evening, from 8 p.m. till 10 p.m. – with half an hour for tea or coffee afterwards – which gave just enough time for suburban members to catch the last train home.

When Wheeler took over the editorship of the Institute's *Archaeological Journal*, he was faced with the task of bringing out three volumes in rapid succession, as the previous editor had fallen behind with the publications. Wheeler badly needed material. At his behest, in April 1930, before his holiday at Portofino, Christopher made a trip to museums in France, with his new friend Gerald Dunning. The purpose was to update the work of Arthur Evans (1890) and J.P. Bushe-Fox (1925), on Belgic Gaulish origins for southern Britain's Late Iron Age culture, and so give Wheeler comparative material for the pre-Roman portion of his own excavations at the otherwise Roman city of Verulamium , outside St Albans. The result was virtually a monograph of almost two hundred pages, called 'The Belgae of Gaul and Britain', which Christopher and Gerald Dunning published jointly in the *Journal* for that same year.

Gerald Clough Dunning was born at Knighton, in the Isle of Wight in 1906. While he was at University College, London, he joined its archaeological society, and not long afterwards he fell in with Wheeler. His first post was jointly funded by the Ministry of Works and the

Gerald Dunning in later life.
Photograph given by his daughter
Tessa

Society of Antiquaries as their first salaried watcher of commercial
excavations in the City (what would now be called rescue archaeology).
He was paid a pittance, but it gave him a room at the old London
Museum, where he could work on his own material, as well as the finds
that Wheeler wanted him to draw. Both he and Christopher spoke
French, which, of course, helped Wheeler to decide to send them to
France to collect material. Dunning covered the provincial museums in
the north, while Christopher went straight to St Germain. He was looked
after by Raymond Lantier, who had recently returned from Algiers,
where he had been Director of the Musée du Bardo. Lantier was very
kind and hospitable. He invited Christopher to his home to meet his
wife, and he also introduced him to the aged *conservateur-en-chef*, M.
Salomon Reinach. Having no time to talk to him at once, the old man
asked him to call in the afternoon at his home in Boulogne-sur-Seine.

   This was a great honour. It was also something of an embarrassment,
as he had very little money, and the visit involved him in a taxi ride
right across the Bois de Boulogne. He arrived at the gates – barred and
spiked forbiddingly, with a long bell-pull. An eye peered at him from
the half-shuttered window of the lodge, and he was asked to say who he
was and what he wanted. The porter admitted him, and he was led

along a tree-lined path to another door, which was firmly closed. There were bells jangling as he approached to give due warning to those within: clearly M. Reinach was much concerned with security. He was ushered into a darkened library with tables down each side in front of the bookshelves, on which there were atlases and folios spread out. At the far end of the room, with the blinds shuttered and draped against the bright sunshine outside, sat the little old man in a skull-cap, under a green-shaded electric lamp. By this time Christopher was very nervous indeed. A chair was indicated, and he sat down on the edge of it, unsure what to do next. Before he could speak, Reinach said, '*Eh bien, jeune homme, êtes-vous Glozelien? ou non?*' Not waiting for a reply, he went on, '*Connaissez-vous Arthur Evans? Il m'a trahi!*' He referred, of course to the celebrated site of Glozel south-east of Vichy in the Massif Central, where extraordinary clay objects had been discovered, with incisions on them, which appeared to be alphabetic. An international commission had investigated the site two years earlier and cast grave doubts on its authenticity. Reinach was convinced that they were genuine. He had published a book called *Le Mirage Oriental*, in which he stated his belief that the civilization of Western Europe was older than that of the Near East. These finds had been greeted by him as proof that he was right, so he was still smarting under the dismissal of the archaeological world, including Sir Arthur Evans and O.G.S. Crawford. There was an awful, embarrassed silence as Christopher tried to think of something appropriate to say. The interview limped on for a little, but, as soon as he decently could, Christopher took his leave and escaped into the warm afternoon sunshine to return to Paris and tell this experience to Dunning, whom he was due to meet that evening.

The Wall Street Crash on 24 October 1929, with the financial panic which followed it, had a disastrous effect on the British economy as well as the American. Uncle Frank had invested his considerable fortune in rubber. Almost all of it was lost. They had to leave Empshott after struggling on there for about a year. Christopher wrote to his father in January 1931:

> . . . How very sad about Empshott . . . but as you say a clean sweep is the only thing that will give him a chance to get started over again without a prospect of being unable to get over harping inwardly on his troubles. Aunt H.'s placidity has certainly solid virtues in a case like this!
>
> After all, so long a life living on investments without a *fixed job* is bound to carry with it the chance of a thing like this happening; even though you do devote your leisure with all the energy he has shown to helping and being good to others. It is rottenly bad luck, though, and I am awfully sorry. . . .

Empshott Lodge was leased from Sir Heath Harrison, who was extremely kind, allowing them to stay on until they were able to find another house in a small settlement called Hill Brow, near Rake in Sussex, which lies above Liss, on the Hampshire–Sussex border, not far from Petersfield. They had to sell most of their furniture, as it was quite a small place, and there was wilderness instead of garden. But Frank and Helen set to very cheerfully and transformed it. Christopher stayed with them on several occasions, though his busy life no longer allowed much time for relaxation or family visits.

In June 1930 he began the first season's digging at Colchester. Earlier in the year he had been delighted to be asked by Sir Charles Peers, who was both President of the Society of Antiquaries and Chief Inspector of Ancient Monuments, if he would carry out an excavation on the site of the intended bypass at Sheepen, north-west of the town.

In 1843 a local watchmaker, William Wire, who was a keen antiquary, recorded in his diary that the farmer, Mr Ball, had discovered some pits, one of which had a hard floor and some Roman pottery in it. Two years later specimens were sent to the Archaeological Association. They included a number of coins, a so-called 'Celtic key' of iron, and some fragments of glass.[1] The next discovery was made in March 1877. Five second-century Roman pottery-kilns were found in the south-west corner of the hill-top field which was afterwards known as 'the Potter's Field'. There were finds also in 1905, when a water-main was laid along the Sheepen Lane, and again when another was laid in 1926, which went across field 613 at the foot of the hill. In the following years Rex Hull, the curator of the Colchester and Essex Museum, got his assistant E.J. Rudsdale and a friend of his, George Farmer, to keep watch on the large old hillside gravel-pit. They recovered a quantity of pottery, bronze objects and coins, all of which were presented to the museum.

When the plans for the Colchester bypass were produced in 1929 it became obvious that there would have to be an excavation along its line, and a committee was formed with Annie, Viscountess Cowdray, as president, and Sir Charles Peers as chairman, to initiate the dig. It was decided that J.P. Bushe-Fox, who was then Inspector of Ancient Monuments for England, should be the nominal senior director, visiting the site occasionally from his excavations at Richborough. Christopher was to be in charge of the work on the bypass line, with Roger Simms, a relative of Sir Charles, as his assistant; Hull took a site south-east of it, in a field due to be levelled as a sportsground.

Sheepen Hill and its foot, between a half and a quarter of a mile outside the Roman *colonia* beneath the core of Colchester town, lie south of the river Colne, protected on the west, as the excavations showed, by the innermost of the extensive array of dykes. These dykes protected the whole area, which was occupied as the native capital centre for about thirty years before the Roman conquest in AD 43. The seemingly older site at Gosbecks is two or three miles south-west of it. For nearly twenty years after the conquest Sheepen was mostly an industrial area, associated first with the army, then with the building and early years of the *colonia*. Later on came kilns for the production of

Roman pottery. The legionary fortress was not discovered until after the last war beneath the *colonia*.

The workmen employed on the site for Christopher's excavation were carefully chosen from the Labour Exchange. The first season he had an excellent foreman, Mr Hammond; and there were also a number of skilled helpers who were unpaid. When Christopher arrived at Colchester he was met by Philip Laver ('a funny sort of man with a grey goatee beard . . .'), who took him to the museum to meet Rex Hull. He also met Hull's chief assistant, H.W. Poulter, a retired mining-engineer who had worked in Spanish America. He was a genial and roguish Yorkshireman with a twinkle in his eye and a glossy black moustache and pointed beard. Poulter had a friend who owned a small private hotel on the north hill of the town, called The Peveril, and it was there that Christopher lived during the first year of the excavations.

He took all his leave allowance from the museum, which was about five weeks, after which it was arranged that Nowell Myres, who was then a tutor at Christ Church, should take over the site for the next month, while Christopher returned to London. Nowell brought with him a party of volunteers from the Oxford University Archaeological Society, one of whom, Betty Murray, was the best friend of the daughter of Dr Ruth Bensusan-Butt, an old friend of Dr Stella Churchill's. She stayed with them at their beautiful house in Colchester, The Minories.

When Nowell had finished, and Christopher had returned to take his place, there was so much material that there was no room for it in the museum at Colchester. They appealed to Wheeler for help, which he readily gave, allowing them to use the big stone-flagged basement kitchen at the London Museum, then in Lancaster House. Nowell hired a lorry and driver, and he and his wife Joan set off with the full load of pottery and artefacts for London. They had got as far as Brentwood High Street, when the lorry broke down. It took them some time to get it going again, so they didn't arrive at the Museum until after 8 p.m. that night.

This basement was very useful during the autumn and winter for Christopher: he was able to work on the material for two or three hours after he had finished at the British Museum, and had a hasty meal at Lyons in Piccadilly Circus.

The financial state of the excavation was quite healthy that first year, as he wrote to his mother:

> . . . we have enough money to go full steam ahead till I go, and then finish filling in afterwards, with about £75 in hand over the winter. The Corporation have promised another £100 in March. The By-Pass won't be on us till next autumn at the earliest. It is turning into the makings of a first-rate squandering scandal. Its line has clearly never been properly surveyed – the $\frac{3}{4}$ mile of intermittent bog is still staring them in the face. They have to shift sewers, water-mains, and whatnot, which they failed to find out were in the way. The Ministry of Transport have passed none of the detailed engineering plans, and

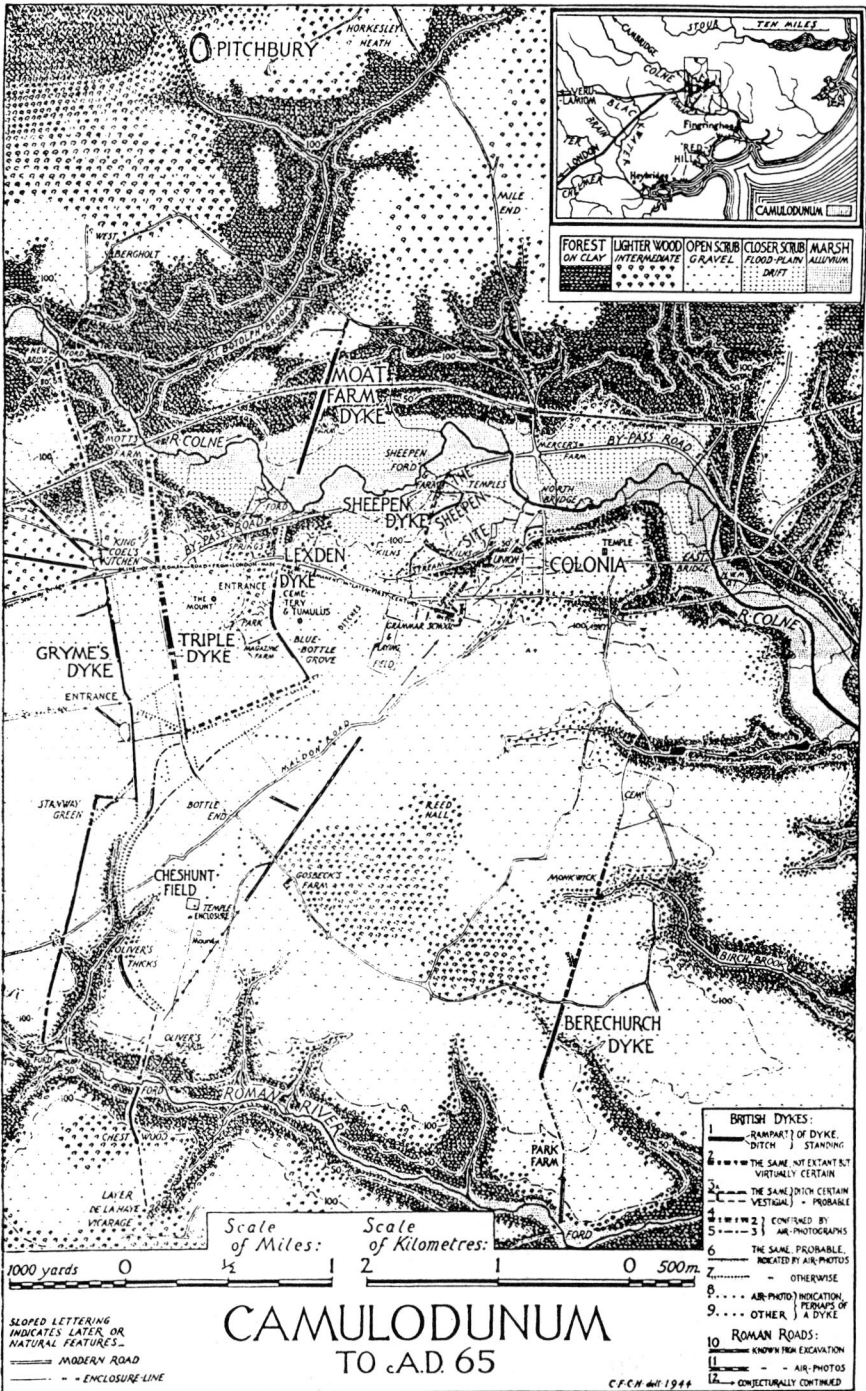

Plan of Camulodunum (Colchester) by Christopher

accordingly, none of the detailed estimates. If they ever carry it through, it will take five years, and cost well over a million I should say. Meanwhile we can dig in peace, and should finish the road line in one season more – next year – after this.

They worked on the site from 8 a.m. till after 5 p.m., when the workmen left, with Sundays free:

We have taken a whole day off from the dig today and motored 60 miles in lovely weather to visit the Wheelers at St Albans. Calkin, the Prep-school master from Bournemouth, who is a volunteer, has an Austin, in which he took Simms and me.

You know the site of Verulamium – it lies between St Albans Cathedral and Gorhambury Park (which is for sale this week, incidentally), and is most beautiful, all set about with enormous trees. Well, there they were, Wheeler, Tess and young Michael, with the Reynoldses (Paul Baillie R. with whom I went two years ago to North Wales, you remember) and various others, young men and maidens, some of whom I knew – one was Kathleen Kenyon. Of course the dig is enormously interesting, and is being brilliantly done. Still, though

Camulodunum in 1931. Photograph by L.G. Cosser

the Roman and post-Roman stuff is quite first-rate, the pre-Roman remains they were after, of the sort that takes up nearly one's whole time here, have so far eluded them. Altogether it has been a delightful Sunday.

We have had a lot of visitors – on Friday Bushe-Fox made an official visit, duly accompanied by Aileen Henderson,[2] with a pleasant middle-aged couple, the Walkers, who work for him at Richborough, as chaperonage.

The ill winds seem to have blown themselves entirely away – he was in his most genial mood; agreed to everything; stood both Simms and me a lunch with all his party at the Red Lion; and altogether the whole day was a great success, ending by their being our guests at tea. He even spoke affably of Wheeler! So everything is now all right in that quarter – largely, I cannot help believing, owing to the good offices of Aileen H., for whom he is almost always prepared to mollify himself! and who exerted her influence on our behalf beforehand.

Simms, along with Bryan O'Neil, whom I knew at Oxford, has got the new Assistant Inspectorship under Peers and B.-F. at the Office of Works, so things have settled down very nicely. However, one knows what to expect of B.-F. He is largely Irish, and blows hot and cold a good deal, though underneath he is a very good sort, and not the man to let one down readily. The chief point about him is that he is the sort of man who manages in his life always to get other people to do his work for him. One knows that if one does it faithfully one will not fail of one's reward, but it means sticking to it pretty hard – in this case throughout the winter in writing up results – and then probably next year more work here: heaven knows how much longer I shall be committed to working in this place!

The weather is still more often bad than good, and the difficulties of liaison with the local people are still by no means negligible. . . .

Christopher was asked to go again to Portofino the following Easter, and it was there that he met the husband of Dr Ruth Bensusan-Butt. 'Bulger' Butt, as he was affectionately known, was on a business trip to Italy from Colchester, and in staying with his wife's old friend, Dr Stella Churchill, he was delighted to discover that Christopher was the young man who was doing the excavations just outside his home town. Always hospitable, he at once insisted that Christopher must stay with them, and not at The Peveril as he had expected to do. When he turned up at the Minories, however, he found that the family was away, and none of the servants had any idea that he was supposed to be coming. He wrote to his mother:

There is a queer position here: Bensusan-Butt has had a complete breakdown in health (bad heart) and has gone to South Africa. His wife, the doctor, and all offspring are also away – they never told me a word, and I was most perplexed – telephoning to maids who knew nothing of me etc. But her partner in practice, a very nice woman, Dr Hugh-Jones (cousin, I find, of my friend Maurice H.J.) stepped in, and now all is well. I now have a letter from Dr B.B., on her way to the Canaries, telling me to stay as long as I like. She returns – perhaps – in the middle of September – her boys perhaps sooner. Dr H.-J. is guaranteeing to safeguard convention when Betty arrives, and meanwhile I am alone with the servants, who do me very well. . . .

There were a lot more volunteers that season:

I have a very nice party. Hutchinson, a Cambridge man who works in Greece, as my chief assistant – an Oxford science don, Lattey, and a Bournemouth Prep-school master, Calkin (both here last year), Miss Jolliffe, a not very senior classical don at Reading University, and the charming Jacquetta Hopkins, daughter of Prof. Sir Gowland H., discoverer of vitamins, PRS and Trustee of the BM. She is such a nice girl, taking archaeology for her Tripos (one year more).

In the same letter Christopher wrote of his discovery that Rex Hull, the curator of the museum in Colchester, had been a subaltern at Boldon in the war: 'He remembers Daddy, of whom he was terrified, quite well, but never thought of connecting him and me.'

Camulodunum in 1931. Christopher shows a party round the site

Towards the end of August Bushe-Fox visited the site with Donald Atkinson, who was acting as his assistant in the excavations at Richborough. They arrived at lunch-time, while the workmen were in their hut: only Christopher and the foreman, a young man named Smith, were on site to greet them. The foreman very unwillingly took the planks away, and down he went with Christopher following uneasily after him. Almost immediately the trench gave way. They were completely buried. Had it not been for the fact that the fall of stones and sand came from behind they would almost certainly have been killed. As it was Christopher had a small space in front of him so that he could breathe; and fortunately he was able to get his hand free enough to clear Bushe-Fox's face as he had been buried more deeply, and was struggling for breath. Donald Atkinson, who had been much too cautious to go down with them, raised the alarm, and at once the men came running to dig them out. Christopher said that the sound of their approach was like a stampeding herd of elephants. Also very quickly there to help was the young student from Newnham College, Cambridge, Jacquetta Hopkins. Her tutor, Miles Burkitt, whom Christopher had met at the museum when he came in to see Reggie Smith, had asked him to take his promising pupil as an assistant, which Christopher had been delighted to do. She had found digs in the town, and she bicycled to and from the site every day. Jacquetta sent for an ambulance to take the injured Bushe-Fox to hospital. She still remembers the occasion very well, and wrote the following description in a letter to the author (dated 29 September 1989):

A leading discovery of the excavations, to be known as Sheepen Dyke, had been a massive rampart and ditch forming the innermost defence of the British city. The victorious Romans destroyed it by throwing the mass of the rampart back into the ditch, sealing beneath it the layer of sludgy silt accumulated since Cunobelin's day. Bushe-Fox was eager to examine this earliest deposit, datable by Belgic pottery and other pre-Roman artefacts. He therefore asked to be taken to the bottom of a three-foot-wide trench which Christopher had cut across the ditch-filling to reveal the successive strata. At this point the ditch was nearly twelve feet deep, and since the gravelly soil was unstable the trench had been shored up with planks and cross-struts. The Chief Inspector insisted that this framework should be removed. The story of the accident has been distorted through the years! My own part in it has been slightly reduced in one direction and magnified in another. When the workmen were thundering towards the trench 'like a herd of elephants' I was responsible for checking them before they got near enough to the edge to cause another landslide. On the other hand I did not have to go out onto the road to enlist a passing motor-cyclist . A young man called John Buxton [one of the East Anglian family, afterwards to be a lecturer in English Literature at Oxford] was one of the volunteers. He came to the site on his own motor-bicycle, so I only had to have the wit to send him without delay for the ambulance. . . .

Christopher at Portofino in 1932, with George Churchill

Bushe-Fox was taken away, seriously injured, to the Essex County Hospital in Lexden Road. Although they were both buried for at least a quarter of an hour, Christopher, astonishingly, was unharmed. Norah Jolliffe made him some strong, sweet tea in the site hut, and almost at once he fell asleep. His body's natural reaction provided all that he needed to recover from the shock.

Bushe-Fox remained in hospital for some time, where they all visited him, taking little gifts. He had a cracked shoulder-blade as well as other injuries, and never really recovered from the accident. When he was released from hospital he went into a convalescent home; not very long afterwards he married one of the nurses who had looked after him.

Christopher had moved to the flat in Gloucester Terrace on March quarter-day 1931. The flat was unfurnished, but he was able to collect most of the things he needed, with a little help from his parents. He had a knee-hole desk, which he bought in the Tottenham Court Road, plenty of bookshelves, and a couple of quite comfortable upholstered chairs. He also had the basket chair which he had had in his rooms at Oxford; and with the continuing generosity of Uncle Frank, who had paid for the hire of a piano throughout his time at Oxford, Christopher was able to buy a second-hand upright for the flat. He enjoyed entertaining; and with careful budgeting he was able to afford small drinks parties for his friends, as well as giving dinner to some occasionally. His dining-table could just about seat four, and he had a pressure-cooker, in which he could prepare all kinds of things very economically; but more often, when funds permitted, they dined out. He also quite often dined out alone, as it saved time, and there were several quite reasonable small restaurants not far away.

Jacquetta, shortly after her marriage

For his third and last season at Colchester Christopher persuaded his parents to take a house in the Avenue at Colchester, which would be large enough to accommodate the family and two guests. He invited Jacquetta and another girl, Thalassa Cruso, who was also working as an assistant on the site, to join them. He had in fact known Thalassa since childhood, when they had both attended Miss Woodward's Saturday gym class, near Notting Hill Gate, but it was not until Wheeler employed her to organize the costume collection at the London Museum, and had her made the Archaeological Institute's assistant secretary under Christopher, that he came to know her well; they became great friends. She married Hugh Hencken, and went to America in 1938, where she still lives, in Boston, as his widow.

The family holiday at Colchester, though on the whole successful, was not without its difficulties. C.P. was interested to meet Rex Hull, and they had an amusing conversation one evening about their memories of the Northumberland Fusiliers; but after a single site visit neither he nor Ellie took any interest in the excavation, preferring to go for walks in the town. Also by then the family had a car, which Penelope had learned to drive, and she was able to take her parents on trips into the surrounding countryside. But a growing chilliness between his mother and sister and Jacquetta made things increasingly awkward for Christopher. His mother was very fond of Thalassa, as indeed Christopher was, but she made no attempt to disguise her disapproval of Jacquetta, to whom her son was clearly becoming more and more deeply attached. As the daughter of a Cambridge scientist, Jacquetta had none of the obvious sophistication of Christopher's London friends. She wore no make-up, and though she had some nice clothes, and was always sensibly dressed on the site, she was unaffectedly not interested in her appearance. She was also passionately devoted to archaeology, and very intelligent indeed. She had heard something from her friends about this brilliant young archaeologist from the British Museum, whose academic achievements were no impediment to an energetic social life, and she had also been told of the glamorous girlfriends he had, and of his success with them; and that she would have little chance of being noticed by him. Not unnaturally this provided something of a challenge: 'It sent me to Colchester with a keen interest in my Director of Excavations.'[3] So her first encounter was not at all encouraging: 'I suppose I had assumed that this paragon, who had a Spanish grand-mother, would be dashingly handsome, so that when I found him to be rather short, and very short-sighted, I felt badly let down.' But she soon began to find him less disappointing: 'Of their very nature archaeological digs produce a fine tilth for love affairs, and Camulodunum was no exception. I soon found that I could have a choice of suitors, but Christopher Hawkes could not fail to eclipse the rest. There was his advance reputation, he was lively, clever, immensely energetic, a master of my beloved subject – and the boss.'

The following piece appeared in The Times in August 1932:

Mr Christopher Hawkes, who is acting as one of the national secretaries of the International Prehistoric Congress which opens in London today, belonged only a few years ago to the race of infant prodigies. While still at Winchester, his knowledge of pre-Roman roads in Hampshire brought him almost as much fame as his contemporary, Mr John Sparrow, now a promising young barrister, won by editing Donne at the age of 16.

At 27 Mr Hawkes is a Fellow of the Society of Antiquaries, and has taken charge of a first-class excavation at the Roman city of Colchester, where he has successfully proved that the splendours of the pre-Roman Chieftain Cymbeline were by no means exaggerated by Shakespeare.

This International Congress was an improvement on an earlier series promoted by Nowell's father, the future Sir John Myres. While Christopher was digging at Colchester in 1931 he was summoned to Oxford for a meeting to begin making plans for the event, which was to be held in London in the first week of August 1932. Sir Charles Peers was to be president, two of the four secretaries were Christopher and Vere Gordon Childe; the others were H.S. Kingsford and C.A. Ralegh Radford. Gordon Childe was then Abercromby Professor of Prehistoric

ABOVE AND OPPOSITE: Participants in the 1st International Congress for Pre- and Proto-historic Sciences, King's College, London, 1932

Archaeology at Edinburgh. Born in Sydney in 1892, he took his degree at the university there in 1913, with a scholarship which enabled him to continue his studies at Queen's College, Oxford.

He never in fact completed the requirements for the diploma in classical archaeology, though he spent a year under the tuition of J.D. Beazley (who later became Professor of Classical Archaeology at Oxford) and Professor Myres, whom he found an inspiring teacher. After three years at Oxford, having achieved a first in Greats, he returned to Australia, to teach Latin at the Maryborough Grammar School in Queensland. However, his Marxist beliefs, which had been strengthened by his time at Oxford, soon led him into conflict with the authorities, and he left the school at the end of the year. He was then offered the post of senior resident tutor at St Andrew's College, Sydney University. This post suited him well at first, though before long his unorthodox political views again led to trouble, and he was forced to resign, though he had many supporters among members of the staff, and it was felt that he had been very badly treated. Disillusioned with the academic world, he turned to politics, becoming the secretary of the newly-elected Premier of New South Wales, John Storey, in the spring of 1920. Storey recognized his great gifts, and wanted him to use them more fully; so he sent the young man to London with the job of research officer for the State of New South Wales. This post was very short-lived, however: Storey died, and his successor, James Dooley, was replaced in the election in December, when the Labour government fell to the Conservatives. The next four years were financially very insecure, though he continued both his archaeological research and his political involvement, while earning money as a translator. In spite of his shortage of money he travelled widely in Central and Eastern Europe; and in 1925 he was offered one of the very few archaeological jobs in Britain, as Librarian to the Royal Anthropological Institute – a body of which Professor Myres was an officer. Through this work Childe became friendly with O.G.S. Crawford, who was still working at the Ordnance Survey, and also with Tom Kendrick, whom he met at the British Museum.

He published his first great book, *The Dawn of European Civilization*, in 1925; and it was this work, which he read in the evenings while he was digging for Donald Atkinson at Wroxeter, which set Christopher firmly on the path of prehistory. Two years later Childe was offered the Abercromby Professorship at Edinburgh. The chair had first been offered to a number of people, including Miles Burkitt and Wheeler, but all had turned it down. Essentially a solitary man, Childe was almost always gentle and courteous. He never married; and he seems to have enjoyed few deeply emotional relationships. His extraordinary appearance must in some measure have contributed to this detachment. In her biography Sally Green gives a vivid description of him in middle life:

His appearance was strange enough to excite comment wherever he went, for his clothes served to accentuate his already odd looks. He always wore a large, black, wide-brimmed hat, reminiscent of Australian sheep-farmers, and commonly supposed to have been acquired in some outlandish East European country; though in fact it was purchased from a highly respectable Jermyn Street hatter. His shirt or tie was as often as not red, to emphasize his left-wing views, and clashed violently with his bright pink nose and rather carroty hair. In summer he frequently wore very short shorts, with socks, sock suspenders and great heavy boots. Extremely characteristic of the man was his shiny black mackintosh carried over his arm or flung carelessly over his shoulders like a cape. Childe was undoubtedly well aware of the sensation his appearance could cause, and on occasions enjoyed the discomfiture of the Establishment at his inappropriate dress.

He was extremely proud of his knowledge of languages, and took every opportunity of showing off his supposed skills. The problem was that, although his reading knowledge of several languages was adequate, his spoken renderings were usually unintelligible. He spoke them all in his own individual accent, rather on the Churchill principle.

The 1st International Congress for Pre- and Proto-historic Sciences opened on Monday 1 August 1932, with the plenary session attended by

Vere Gordon Childe with Maria Bersu and Alexander Keiller at Avebury

about four hundred members and associates, in the Great Hall of King's College, London. There were in fact 639 members in all, with fifteen vice-presidents, among whom were Sir Arthur Evans,[5] Sir Flinders Petrie and Sir George Macdonald.[6]

On the first evening a reception was held at the London Museum, Lancaster House, where the delegates were received by the First Commissioner of the Ministry of Works, the Rt. Hon. W. Ormsby-Gore. An exhibition of aerial photography and recent developments in archaeology had been arranged by Wheeler and Crawford, both of whom were members of the congress.

Reginald Smith was one of the vice-presidents, and when he realized that Christopher, as one of the national secretaries, was quite naturally expecting to attend the proceedings, he attempted to prevent him from taking time off from the museum. There had already been rumblings of dissent between him and Christopher. Smith was jealous of his young assistant keeper, as he had been of Kendrick when he had joined the department in 1921; and the fact that Christopher found it very difficult to get up in the mornings, and was often late in arriving, did little to improve matters: Smith was almost pathologically punctual.

Most of the time there was an uneasy peace in the department, but this business of the congress was too much for Christopher. He appealed to Peers, as president, who at once agreed that it was absurd, and, of course, he must be there. This unfortunate episode merely served to deepen Smith's resentment. However there was no further unpleasantness during the week.

Gerald Dunning spoke first, on Tuesday morning, on the excavations at Salmonsbury Camp, Bourton-on-the-Water, in Gloucestershire. Evans gave his paper on Knossos on Thursday, and Christopher followed Van Giffen later on in the day, and like him gave his paper in French: 'La vie du pays britannique a l'age du fer'. There were no formal sessions that evening, so as to allow members to give private parties; and as Christopher's parents were away for the week, at Canterbury, he was able, with their permission, to give a party himself at Campden Hill Square. It was Jacquetta's birthday. He wrote to his mother on 7 August:

> ... I must thank you for your splendid kindness to the Congress in general, and to myself and Jacquetta in particular, by giving, as you really did, this very happy and successful party on Thursday. It was a terrific success. The food and drink were admirable, the servants worked excellently, everyone was in marvellous form, and inter- national amity was given an enormous fillip! Freiherr von Richthoven, a tall, young German nobleman, the archaeologist brother of the famous flying ace, made a rousing and felicitous speech, of course in German, at the cutting of the cake. At the end, when many had left and only some thirty of the inner ring remained, there were superb charades. . . .

What he didn't say was that after the birthday-cake speech he was taken to one side by Gerhard Bersu and told very firmly that he should not have allowed himself to be too obviously friendly with Bolko von Richthoven: 'He is a dangerous man . . .'. He was, in fact, a Nazi, though he survived the war to end his days quietly at Garmisch-Partenkirchen. He wrote to Christopher in 1946, a pathetic letter asking if he remembered him. Christopher replied, and later, when he was passing through Garmisch after attending the Hamburg Congress in 1958, he made enquiries, but found that von Richthoven was already dead. His brother Manfred, who was known as 'the Red Baron' because of the colour of his plane, had shot down eighty Allied aircraft before being killed himself, in action, in 1918, at the age of twenty-six.

After the congress was over there were excursions to Oxford, Cambridge, Wiltshire and Ireland. Christopher went down to Winchester by train on 9 August, to meet a party at St Catharine's Hill. He gave them a brief lecture on the site, translated on the spot by Bersu.

Gerhard Bersu, who was made an honorary Fellow of the Society of Antiquaries the following year, was born in 1889 at Jauer in Silesia. He began his archaeological career in 1907 near Potsdam, and in the years following he worked in France, Switzerland, Italy, Greece and Romania. During the First World War he served in the Office of Protection of Monuments and Collections, and in 1924 he began his long association with the German Archaeological Institute in Frankfurt, becoming its second director in 1928, and three years later its first.

C.W. Phillips records one interesting fact about Bersu in his autobiography:

> Bersu had one unique distinction: he was the first German to fly in a heavier-than-air machine. As a conscript doing his military service he had been a member of a squad standing by to be generally useful while the Wright brothers demonstrated their machine to the German army High Command at Potsdam. After a successful demonstration the Wrights were asked if their machine could carry a passenger. They looked over the fatigue squad and picked out Bersu as the smallest of them; there was no proper accommodation on the machine but he was strapped to the undercarriage and was successfully carried through the air for several flights up and down the parade ground.[7]

By the time Christopher met him in 1929, when Bersu paid a visit to the museum, he had put on weight. With an impish twinkle in his dark brown eyes, and a pipe clamped firmly in his mouth, he was a most amusing and entertaining companion. The photograph of him which belongs to Professor Stuart Piggott, who has kindly allowed it to be reproduced here, is very characteristic.

After Jacquetta had graduated (she got a first) she was awarded a travelling scholarship, and she went to dig in Palestine with Dorothy Garrod. She already knew Christopher's intentions when she left England:

Gerhard Bersu in the 1930s. Photograph kindly lent by Professor Stuart Piggott

> ... When I went off to excavate Neanderthal men in the Mount
> Carmel caves, I took a framed photograph of Christopher with me.
> Every evening in camp I stood it up in my little cabin and gazed at it,
> trying to decide whether or not I should agree to marry him on my
> return. As time went by I became more and more inclined to say yes.[8]

She did so, while they were visiting the Neolithic flint mines in Norfolk
called Grimes Graves in the spring of 1933.

'From the moment of our engagement I was caught in a tide of alien
events,' she wrote.[9] Christopher very much wanted to be married in
church. Jacquetta, coming from a scientific background, had not been
baptized, and she felt that this would be wrong: 'There was a day at
Winchester College when he marched me, weeping, round and round
the cloisters until I surrendered and agreed to be wed in my father's
college Chapel.'[10] It was Christopher who worked out the order of
service, and chose the hymns and music, while Jacquetta was 'taken
over' by Ellie, who made arrangements for the wedding dress – a
beautiful satin-and-gold gown by Elspeth Fox Pitt. The bridesmaids
were dressed by the fashionable theatrical designers, Motley.

It must have been obvious to her mother that Jacquetta was not really in love with her husband-to-be. During the months of preparation Lady Hopkins asked her daughter several times 'if she really wanted to marry Christopher'. And Christopher was having problems of his own. His sister clearly disliked Jacquetta, and he was distressingly torn by an inevitable division of loyalties. He wrote to his mother in March 1933, with the wedding still seven months away:

> Thinking over our words the night before last, I feel you encouraged me much – morally, especially, by your advice – and I do fairly confidently hope Pen will feel and come to be all right with Jacquetta. But she has been worse than icy to her on past occasions, you know! That was the only 'rift in the lute at Colchester', for example, and she has made her own gulf bigger to bridge. Still, in that and in all things she must know her own difficulties far more keenly than we do. We must have been in many ways a difficult family to grow up in! I know I am critical, but three people must have three points of view, even if some do pop out explosively at times. I'm sorry I cannot manage to be always equable, but such a crucial time in one's life can't help being a strain, and I have not been able to keep free from anxiety, considering their so very different psychologies, lest my loves for the four people I love best in the world should fall to pulling different ways. . . . I *will* try not to be a hindrance to what we are all so anxious for together. . . .

The previous Christmas had been very unsettling. In writing after the holiday to his mother, Christopher tried hard to explain his feelings:

> I am glad you said what you wished to. But what makes me retort rather fiercely to these warnings about self-centredness (now of long standing) is they always spring from your accusing me of rudely appearing bored or impatient with conversation not my own – which is never, or scarcely ever just. Because I am always only too anxious to join in *any* conversation, whatever it's about: I have many interests, and am never too 'superior' to join in on anything – But the trouble is with you and Daddy that it is next to impossible to do so, so very often! I think you do not realise how maddening your unrestrained cutting in on what people try to say is! You do it without thinking, and it is death to any proper talk. In order to get one's word in, one inevitably shouts, which of course is silly, because it makes it worse, and usually an altercation sets in. Then one is always nervous and jumpy. If you are so keen on this business of guarding against 'self-centred moodiness' as you say, you *must* see that the only way to do it is to encourage talk on all subjects, not to bottle it up. Actually I often go home reflecting that whatever the theory may be, in practice home is the one place where I *cannot* find relief in general conversation for my long hours of solitary work. And that I know is the exact opposite of what you intend.
>
> The moral point you make is one I fully appreciate, and have for

years; but I really think you cannot see how your own impulsiveness, working as it does with the natural manifestation of Daddy's always having more to say (because he *has!*) than other people, defeats your own aim constantly. The occcasional explosiveness in the last few days (and when looked back on it was not much more) has been entirely due to that. Not moody self-absorption on my part, but the natural result of my being just the opposite – excited and expansive – and being unthinkingly checked and cut off and bottled up in what would otherwise be perfectly natural and friendly talk.

It is honestly absurd to make out that love and respect for parents are at stake, when all that is needed is the ordinary human give and take of civilized conversation. Anyone who naturally feels things warmly, as I do, and often has different opinions from yours, is bound to feel resentful when treated so; and though I always regret explosions, I truly don't blame myself for putting up some spirit to try and get this silly state of affairs remedied.

It is wretched that you should become upset and unhappy, and imagine all sorts of undesirable characters showing themselves in me, when really it's all nothing but a matter of how to conduct a conversation. If you will only try and help by being reasonable in small things, you need never in any case fear that anything is wrong in big things. Of course, when I am excited, as now, little things feel worse, as they do to you.

It is not selfish reluctance to be agreeable that makes me peevish when I am, but the thwarting of my natural eagerness to be so. So to make your very salutary advice have its full effect, do, I beg you, give it a chance in practice.

I think you will find Jacquetta changed from what you estimated her last summer, after her sojourn in the wilderness. Her letters show it, and the reaction in returning will enhance it. But it is not a change that has altered the bond between us as it was when she left: it has quite plainly made it immensely firmer. I truly believe it is very, very strong, and have myself every hope, and every intention of going ahead. . . .

10 London, 1933–9

While Christopher was at Oxford he had been introduced by Nowell to a friend of his sister Rosalie's who was staying with the family. Julia Webber was tall and dark: unconventionally handsome rather than pretty, with vividly sparkling brown eyes, and she was full of laughter. Christopher was drawn to her at once, for she provided the easy companionship of a sister. She lived in Cambridge in a house next to Newnham College. Her mother had been a great beauty, the daughter of Professor J.W. Clark (who wrote, with Robert Willis, *The Architectural History of the University and Colleges of Cambridge* in 1886), but her marriage ended with the desertion of her husband, who went off to South Africa and left her to bring up their two daughters. Julia was the younger, still living at home when her sister married.

When Christopher was in a state of great anxiety after his brief engagement to Daphne, Julia sustained him. She seemed to know exactly how to comfort him. She asked him to go with her to watch the boat-race trials, and as Christopher's friend Vyvyan Stopford was cox that year, he eagerly accepted her invitation. She talked merrily on every topic she could think of, diverting him from the sting of humiliation without embarrassment. At the very end of the afternoon she leant towards him and whispered 'courage . . .'.

Christopher was helped again by her tactful affection as the day of his wedding approached. Realizing his extreme innocence, she gave him a little booklet explaining what would be expected of him in bed. His father's dutiful enquiry into his knowledge of sexual matters, which was woefully inadequate, had merely extracted a breezy assurance that he knew all about it. Greatly relieved, C.P. never referred to the subject again, except to make a pointed remark about the importance of reading Marie Stopes, in view of his precarious financial position.[1] In spite of her scientific background, Jacquetta's knowledge was not much more worldly than Christopher's, although on her own initiative she had been fitted with a birth-control device, and had had her hymen pierced.

It is perhaps difficult to understand such emotional and physical innocence now, when young people are barely allowed a year or two of real childhood before the awareness of the implications of their sexuality begins to dominate. But in the 20s and 30s there was very little sex education beyond the statutory warning on the perils of 'indulgence' in preparatory schools for boys, and often there was no information at

Jacquetta and Christopher after their wedding

all given for girls. Children were more or less left to find out for themselves, often with disastrous consequences.

Christopher stayed with the Webbers on the night before the wedding, which took place on Saturday 7 October 1933. There was a civil ceremony at the registry office in Cambridge before the service in the chapel of Trinity College – Jacquetta's father's college, and also that of Christopher's best man, Serge Orloff. Something of the bride's state of mind may be judged from the following passage from her book:

I recall a sense of bewildered incredulity as I went up the chapel on my father's arm, my long train supported by bridesmaids in their elegant gowns. I saw through my veil that Christopher was wearing spats. The knot was tied and we processed out into the glorious pale autumn sunshine in Trinity Great Court. The reception in the college hall was crowded and well supplied with champagne. I believe that A.E. Housman was among the notables present; I floated through it all, lost in unreality.

That this expensive and conventional wedding had only a slender chance of lasting success will be obvious if I confess to a final incident. I recollect it only too clearly. When Count Orloff, the dashing Russian emigré whom Christopher had chosen as his Best

Man, saw us off from Cambridge Station, I leant out of the window and said, 'I wish you were coming with us.' I may have been light-headed from excitement and champagne, but I spoke quite unaffectedly. My words did not then strike me as ill-timed.[2]

Christopher's memories of the wedding were equally vivid. He hugely enjoyed the music, which he had chosen, and he sang lustily, with Serge's fine Russian bass below him, all through the service. He also enjoyed the reception, though there was a moment of slight awkwardness when Sir Frederick's intense shyness made him refuse to make the speech before the cutting of the cake, and he prevailed upon C.P. to do it for him. In a wave of champagne and merriment, with glowing pride in his son, C.P. ended up by stressing how fortunate the bride was to be marrying such a man, instead of the other way round. More laughter; then his words were acknowledged with the usual good humoured applause.

After the speeches and toasts the bride and bridegroom were led away to separate rooms to change. Christopher's stiff wing collar was signed by all those closest to him, including his father and Serge, and Michael Zvegintzov; he has kept it, carefully wrapped in tissue ever since (see the illustration below).

Alone at last they set off on the long journey by boat and train to Majorca, where they were to spend their honeymoon, at what was then the small fishing village of Cala Ratjada. They called on their way through Barcelona on don Pedro Bosch Gimpera, whom Christopher had known ever since the preparatory meeting for the London Congress, in Paris towards the end of 1931. When they arrived at the university and asked for don Pedro, they were told that he was invigilating at an examination. Fully expecting a long wait, they were astonished when the beaming rotund figure appeared to greet them almost at once. He took them to a little café near the university, where he entertained them, congratulating them on their marriage – eager to hear all their news. Before they left he gave them one of his books, written in the Catalan dialect, on the prehistory of the Iberian peninsula, which he inscribed

Signatures on Christopher's wing collar

for them. They finally took the boat for Majorca late in the evening, and arrived on the island in time for breakfast.

Cala Ratjada lies on the east coast of Majorca. In 1933 it had not yet become a popular resort, but there was one nice small hotel. Writing of her honeymoon many years later Jacquetta recalled an incident which might well have caused acute embarrassment to any young bride:

> Christopher made ambitious preparations for our union, insisting that our twin beds should be changed for a huge *cama matrimoniale*. The small hotel was shaken by the tramping and banging of the removal and installation. . . .

After the excitement of the wedding and the long exhausting journey, it is scarcely surprising that Jacquetta should have found her new state rather less blissfully happy than she might have hoped. But, 'We quite enjoyed our honeymoon,' she wrote, 'it was neither a joy nor a disaster.' They enjoyed the bathing, the sun, and visiting antiquities. There was dancing in the evenings in the hotel, and they met some amusing English people who were also staying on the island. One afternoon, a few days after their arrival, Christopher was alarmed to discover that his wife had disappeared. His enquiries merely established that the *Señora* had 'gone off on her own for a walk'. It was some hours before she returned, by which time Christopher had become extremely anxious. She had suddenly panicked, overwhelmed with feelings of uncertainty. Had she made a terrible mistake? A long solitary walk had calmed her sufficiently to face her husband's natural anxiety, and Christopher had the sense not to refer to it again once he had made sure that she was alright.

On 14 October came the dramatic announcement by the Nazi government in Berlin that, because of the humiliating and dishonouring demands of the other powers, Germany would take no further part in the Geneva Disarmament Conference, and, in addition, would withdraw from the League of Nations. That night Hitler made a long speech on the wireless in which he reiterated Germany's peaceful intentions. 'Equality, not arms' was his aim. This news sent shivers of unease across the airwaves of Europe. Fears were reinforced a month later when it was reported that the Nazi party had been given massive popular support in a plebiscite on the issue: 95 per cent of the voters supported their move. In the voting for the one-party Reichstag, which was to have no women and no Jews, the Nazis received 92 per cent of the votes, with spoiled papers accounting for the rest.

This was not Christopher's first glimpse of the rising menace of the Nazis. In the early spring of 1933, when Adolf Hitler had been in power for only a matter of weeks (the flamboyant leader of the National Socialists had been appointed Chancellor by President von Hindenburg on 30 January), Christopher was invited by Bersu to take part in a joint meeting under the Dutch professor van Giffen, at Groningen, in the north-eastern part of the Netherlands, not far from the German border. Christopher was the only Englishman in the party. The university authorities at Groningen had been asked to arrange accommodation for the delegates, and among those who offered hospitality to the visiting Germans was a Jewish professor. They were much relieved to find an Englishman in their midst. Christopher stayed with Professor Benjamins and his daughter, who were very hospitable and kind, and he was grieved to hear afterwards that they had suffered under the occupation.

After the meeting, Christopher went on up the Rhine to Haltern and Münster and then to Frankfurt, where he was put up by Bersu and his wife Maria. Not long after this Bersu was removed from his post as director of the *Romisch-Germanische Kommission* of the *Deutsches Archaeologisches Institut*, because of his partly Jewish descent.

The newly-weds took up residence in their first home, a two-storey flat in Cleveland Gardens, not far from Paddington station. Christopher had found the place shortly before their marriage, and they were to remain there until the early summer of 1938. Although they had comparatively little money, with Jacquetta's allowance of £250 a year from her parents, they were able to do quite a bit of entertaining. But they were more often entertained 'by prosperous friends of the Hawkeses so that the laundry bills for Christopher's white waistcoats and ties were quite a serious burden'.[3] And Jacquetta did have help in the house, so she could get on with her academic work. At weekends they often went to Cambridge to stay with her parents at their house in Grange Road. Christopher enjoyed these visits, and he grew very fond of Sir Frederick.

Born in 1861 in Eastbourne, his family came originally from Wales. His father was a first cousin of the Jesuit poet Gerard Manley Hopkins. As a young man Frederick had had raven-dark hair, but it had turned white by the time Christopher knew him; and his moustache, though matching his hair, was tinged with yellow from a lifetime's addiction to nicotine: 'my poison', as he used to call it. Owing to his Uncle James's violent disapproval of science, he spent several years in an insurance office, then, after public analyst's work, partly at a big railway company, a small legacy enabled him to study chemistry at University College. Here his performance in the examination brought him to the attention of Sir Thomas Stevenson, who was a Home Office analyst and a lecturer at Guy's Hospital on forensic medicine. Stevenson offered him a job as his assistant, which he eagerly accepted. While he was working with Stevenson, he was able to read for his B.Sc., and he entered Guy's Hospital as a medical student in 1888, graduating in 1894. Four years later he went to Cambridge to become a lecturer in chemical physiology. At the beginning of the First War he was elected Professor of Biochemistry, and afterwards Sir William Dunn Professor, a post which he held until his retirement in 1943.

Portrait of Sir Frederick Gowland Hopkins, presented to the Royal Society in 1983

Sir Frederick's most notable achievement was the research he carried out into the isolation of what he called 'auxiliary food factors' – vitamins, as they came to be known. This brilliant research won him a knighthood in 1925; and four years later he shared a Nobel prize with the Dutch physician, Christiaan Eijkman, who had originated the concept of dietary deficiency disease after his work as a doctor in the East Indies. In 1930 Sir Frederick was elected President of the Royal Society and at the end of his five years' service to that august body, he received the highest honour bestowed by his sovereign – the Order of Merit.

Such a reputation could have made him an intimidating father-in-law. In fact Christopher found him gentle and sympathetic; and as so often with the really great, he was unassuming, unaffected and approachable.

These weekend visits to Cambridge had started before Christopher and Jacquetta were married. While Jacquetta spent time with her family, Christopher was taken out into the Fens by Charles Phillips and Grahame Clark, both members of the newly formed Fenland Research Committee. Some time in 1932 Major Gordon Fowler, who was the traffic manager of the great Anglo-Dutch sugar-beet processing factory at Ely, and was responsible for organizing transport of the harvested beet, began to notice meandering banks standing up above the level of the peat. His curiosity was aroused, and he cut a section through one of them. Unlike their surroundings, these raised banks, or 'roddons' as they were called locally, were silt. They were the remains of ancient watercourses. When the Fens were drained in the 1630s by Dutch engineers the waterlogged peat became drier and drier, leaving the old watercourses standing proud above it. In his section through one of these roddons, Major Fowler found some pottery. Realizing that it must be ancient, he took it to the Museum of Archaeology and Ethnology in Downing Street, Cambridge, where he was introduced to Charles Phillips, a fellow of Selwyn College, who was then working in the museum. This discovery of what proved to be large quantities of Roman pottery caused a great deal of interest, and because of it the Fenland Research Committee was set up, with Professor Sir Albert Seward as its president,[4] Phillips as treasurer, and Major Gordon Fowler as vice-president. There were about forty members of the committee in all, including Miles Burkitt, O.G.S. Crawford, Stuart Piggott, Sir Cyril Fox (who was then Director of the National Museum of Wales) and Professor Ellis Minns, Disney Professor of Archaeology at Cambridge. Christopher was brought in to deal with the Roman material, while the work of analysing the pollen samples from the silt was done by Harry Godwin and his wife Margaret, from the Botany School. The shrinkage of the peat had produced curious round patches of sand. Clark, with brilliant insight, was able to see what these patches were: the tops of natural sand which had been the surface of the land before the peat had formed.

On Sundays, immediately after lunch at Grange Road, Christopher would be collected by Phillips and Clark, and they would spend the afternoon driving round the Fens in Phillips's car, while Jacquetta was able to talk to her family, though she went with them on more than one occasion.

The summer of 1934 saw the clouds of oppression gather over Europe. President Hindenburg died on 2 August and three hours later Hitler abolished the title of president, naming himself as Führer and Reich Chancellor. As Supreme Commander of the Armed Forces he exacted a sacred oath from both officers and men of unconditional obedience – not to Germany, but to himself personally. By the middle of October the German army was reported to be three times the size allowed by the Treaty of Versailles. In a speech on 28 November Winston Churchill warned that Britain's weak defences could lead to 'absolute subjection' in a war with Germany, whose factories were already working under war conditions. Within three years, he said, the German air force would be twice the strength of Britain's. But in the years up until 1939 many people believed that there could never be another war. The 1914–18 war had been 'a war to end all wars'.

Christopher felt deeply uneasy, watching the rise of both Mussolini and Hitler with a sickening awareness of the fragility of the life that he was then enjoying. He and Jacquetta nevertheless found that summer a happy one. They set off on a long summer vacation in France, first digging with Olwen and Denis Brogan on the bleak plateau hill of Gergovia, some eight miles south of Cleremont-Ferrand. Denis Brogan (who was later knighted) had been modern history tutor at Corpus Christi College, Oxford, before becoming Professor of Modern History at Cambridge. They had their meals at a tourist place called 'La Hutte', where Christopher and Jacquetta also slept.

Christopher was given a section to cut through the main rampart and ditch from which the defenders had repulsed the Romans, and in it he found fragments of amphora which enabled the rampart to be closely dated to the early part of the first century BC.

In 52 BC the town had been besieged by Caesar. Having failed to shift the plucky inhabitants, he then tried to take it by assault. One centurion got up on to the rampart, and hauled up another, but it was too exposed and the sides of the hill too steep, and they were very quickly despatched. The Gauls hurled their spears and stones on to the heavily armoured troops, and Caesar was forced to withdraw having lost forty-six centurions and seven hundred men. The charismatic Gallic leader, Vercingetorix, whose native town it was, provided the model for the extremely witty and literate French cartoon series which first appeared in the 1950s, in which the hero, Asterix, always succeeds in outwitting the Romans.

After the dig Christopher and Jacquetta did some sightseeing. They went down the Rhône to Arles and Nîmes, accompanied by John Ward Perkins, who had also been digging with the Brogans, and then on through Montpellier and Toulouse into the Dordogne. They had been invited to stay at the Château de Bity by its owner, an Englishman named Noel Lucas Shadwell, who had lived there for many years with his French wife. He was a keen amateur archaeologist and had visited Gergovia while they were digging. Having a small excavation of his own near Bity he was eager for Christopher and Jacquetta to visit him. Shadwell was a delightful character – very tall and thin and gangling – and despite his years in France, and his French wife, he had never progressed beyond an hilarious schoolboy accent, though his command of the language itself was perfectly adequate. As Jacquetta recalls, the most surprising thing about this château-dwelling aristocrat was his strong left-wing sympathies. He had worked as an election agent for a Labour candidate in at least one election. Christopher wrote a long descriptive letter to his parents from the château:

> Our wanderings, of which I now sit down to give you some small account in advance of our homecoming, have not been really very sensational, but we do feel now at the end that we have had a well-balanced and satisfying holiday, and both are in the very best of health.
>   We reach Victoria at 6.05 a.m. on Friday [5 October] and you should get this the night before. I must be at the Museum at 10! So we are staying out till the very last!
>   When I left you the night before sailing I did not – could not – finish my book. I further decided that my last chapter would have to be put off and done afresh when I returned. Methuen have accepted this reasonably well, and so I have a week or ten days' work still before I can get my money. However, having come to the decision I was relieved, and with great turmoil 'finishing off' at the museum and packing, I had not many minutes to spare in catching the boat train in the evening.

The book was the second in a series called London the Treasurehouse. The first volume, on the collections in the Victoria and Albert Museum had already been published, and Christopher was asked to write up the British Museum's prehistoric collections for the second volume. It was Sir George Hill who had suggested that he write the book, which provided yet more fuel for the already dangerously overheated atmosphere in the department. Reggie Smith was bitterly jealous, and he sniped at Christopher quite mercilessly: 'Neglecting your duties to write that book of yours . . .' There was worse to come. Meanwhile, however, the holiday gave him a much needed break:

> The journey was tiring but uneventful. I duly picked up Jacquetta at the Empereurs (which we didn't much like, but which gave me a hot bath), and we travelled comfortably to Clermont, where the diggers awaited us at about 2.30. Then passed a restful and invigorating fortnight of very simple living and almost complete forgetfulness of

the world. We made it clear that we were only amateur attachés to the dig, and it gave just enough occupation and interest without being a burden – though once or twice Jacquetta had to come to the rescue and extricate me from undertaking (in spite of myself) too much.

We scarcely ever left the plateau (about one and a half miles round) except for evening walks, though we made one attempt to climb the Puy de Dôme – frustrated by cloud and mist! The weather, though, as a whole, was wonderful, and the views over mountains and plains, with changing clouds, was always lovely. We got on well with the Brogans; and though we didn't take much to M. Desforges, it was really because he was too energetic, and just that.

The second Sunday the Académie de Clermont held a *Congrès* on the Plateau – a lunch, and many speeches, of which I had to make two. When the time came to go we were full of fresh air and health (but in fact on the last day I was bad with a tummy pain, due, we later found, to eating something not quite fresh) – and ready for a bout of travelling, which we started on by train to Orange by way of Lyon, and then to Vaison (never visited by me when in Provence before); Avignon, Arles and Nîmes again, and then Montpellier, Narbonne, Carcassone and Toulouse. Up to Nîmes John Ward Perkins was with us. We weren't only in towns – Vaison is a lovely country place in the mountains.

We made the acquaintance of local archaeological savants, and took notes in museums, but never interrupted the holiday spirit. Finally after a week full of sun and colour and changing scenes – ending with the wonderful medieval ramparts and towers of Carcassonne, and the Romanesque towers of Toulouse – we reached this charming spot [the Château de Bity] on Saturday afternoon. The country is lovely. Wild hills, exquisite little valleys with brawling streams, tiny farms and villages, and all clothed in perfectly blending autumn tints.

The Château (a real one, XVI–early XVII century) is delightful, and our host and hostess kindness itself. We have been for lovely drives and also had ample time to ramble on our own. Thus in perfect country rest and refreshing calm our holiday has ended, and we leave by the night train tonight. . . .

On his return there was more trouble awaiting him at the British Museum. His first book for Methuen had been published in 1932, written jointly with Tom Kendrick. *Archaeology in England and Wales 1914–1931* (which became known simply as 'Kendrick and Hawkes') was an enlarged version of the article in German that had been published for the International Congress in London that year by the *Romisch-Germanische Kommission*. As Kendrick says in his preface, they added the chapters on Roman and Anglo-Saxon antiquities. The following paragraph shows a great deal about the character of this lovable man:

I have written chapters I–VIII and XII of this work, and Mr Hawkes chapters IX, X, XI. We do not pretend that we have collaborated throughout, and indeed, so far as collective responsibility is concerned, I think it will be easily understood that the most we can do is to say that we endorse vaguely (and in my case admiringly) each other's contributions. But we are prepared to be judged separately on our respective parts.

Christopher's chapters on the Late Bronze Age, the Early Iron Age and Roman Britain, run from pages 119 to 302, followed by a further forty-eight pages of Kendrick on the Anglo-Saxon period. The book had been very well received, and because of it he had been invited to write another by a different publisher. His keeper's view of such activities became increasingly sour. One afternoon at precisely 4 p.m. Smith came into the department to put his keys in the safe before going home. 'Hawkes,' he snapped, 'that book of yours is off. It's all over.' Christopher was stunned. He had heard nothing from the publishers, and he was already working on the final chapter. What had happened was that the first volume in the series had been a failure, and they had decided to abandon it altogether. Smith had somehow got to hear of this, and lost no time in using the information to maximum effect. Tom Kendrick was appalled when he heard what had happened, and hastened to console Christopher. He was also able to give practical help. He suggested that Methuen should commission another work, this time on prehistoric Europe. This was arranged, though in fact it was almost a year before Christopher was able to begin work on it.

The tension between him and Reginald Smith which had been exacerbated by a number of minor incidents, especially since the congress two years earlier, exploded at the beginning of February 1935. The combination of fatigue and emotional pressure finally drove Christopher beyond the limits of his self-control. Not surprisingly he now has no memory of the actual row, but it was mainly over his duty to keep up the accessions register. By that time he had let it slip quite seriously, as he had so much other work to do, and with his undoubted success in so many fields both within and outside the museum, this was the one area in which Smith could find serious fault. It is more than likely that there was also some reference to Christopher's perpetual struggle to arrive on time in the mornings. These attempts to creep in without being detected, sometimes as late as 10.15 a.m., caused great amusement, and there were hugely exaggerated stories about this which survived long after he had left the museum. There was no question of his failing to do enough work. As Charles Stevens remarked to him in a letter in February, he was 'doing a good deal more than three persons' work'.

What he said to Smith that morning, though he now has absolutely no recollection of the scene itself, was sufficiently impertinent to send Smith in a cold rage straight to the director, Sir George Hill. Christopher was sent for at once and given the inevitable carpeting for insubordination, at which point something snapped. He offered his resignation and went home at once in a state of collapse. His doctor wrote the following letter to Hill:

> I beg to certify that Mr Christopher Hawkes is under my medical care. I find him suffering from the effects of overwork. I have questioned him carefully about the nature of his work, and I understand that he is engaged in a considerable amount of special work in addition to his routine duties, and that this necessitates regular work at night and at the weekend. He finds moreover that he is compelled to work even in his vacations in order to keep up with the progress of his subjects.
>
> I have come to the conclusion that Mr Hawkes's breakdown is not due to any inherent nervous instability, but that it is the direct result of overwork.
>
> I have advised Mr Hawkes that he should have a month's complete rest; and I have further advised him that in the interests of his health he should resign his appointment unless the conditions of his service can be materially altered.
>
> A. Bevan MD

He slept round the clock for three or four days. Then the letters began to arrive. The first from his father was brief and sensible:

> Dear old chap,
> A line of wishes and enquiries from us all about your condition and your quarters. Do force yourself to an *absolute rest*.
> This interlude, I am convinced, is providential, and will affect your intellectual efficiency for years to come. . . . All well here,
> much love to you both . . .
> 'Peace, perfect peace,
> All B.M. thoughts transcending – !

The letter was sent to him at a cottage near Petersfield which was owned by Dr Carr, in the beautiful village of Steep – the White House, on Bell's Hill. Here he and Jacquetta were not far from Uncle Frank and Aunt Helen, whom they visited once or twice, but apart from them they saw no one. Christopher only remembers sitting huddled over a log fire. It was very cold. The next letter came on 7 February, from Sir George Hill:

> I am very sorry to receive a medical certificate to the effect that you are suffering from overwork. Although I hesitate to worry you in your present state, something in the very unusual tenor (to say no more) of the certificate seems to make it necessary for me to write to you.
> The gist of it is that the work of your department as at present established and your own ideals and ambitions are incompatible. Now I am the last person to wish to choke the ambitions of individual

C.P. Hawkes in 1933

members of my staff, nor do I wish you to think that I suppose your ambition to be entirely personal. I mean to say that I fully recognize your aim as being to give the Department a leading position in the subject in which you are specially interested.

At the same time it is not possible for more than one reason, for a junior man to run the Department, or even his part of it, as he pleases. There may be many faults in the regime, but discipline and good team-work are essential if the Museum is to go on at all.

I am sorry that the wording of the medical certificate, which is rather in the form of an ultimatum to the Trustees than a certificate of your illness, makes it necessary for me to write like this. In such a conflict it is not the Department that must yield.

To be quite frank, I doubt whether you will ever be in your element here, even when the change anticipated a few years hence takes place. I think it is pretty clear that you are better suited to working by yourself, or at any rate, not in a subordinate position. If, therefore, your circumstances make it possible for you to change your position, I think you should seriously consider your doctor's advice; for it is quite clear that the conditions of your service here cannot be materially altered. You have, as you know, already had considerably more freedom than your colleagues.

Let me assure you once more how sorry I am to write to you in these terms, when you are anything but well; also that though your subject is one on which I am not competent to judge, I know your high reputation has been justly earned, and that your departure would mean a great loss to the Museum.

But I really think that for your own sake, if you will make a decision now, it will probably be better than later on; for I see no likelihood of a more palatable solution, and a sour draught is not sweetened by keeping.

By the same post was a letter from Kendrick:

Hill's letter was not meant to be all that acid. He explained to me that as Director he was bound to write formally pointing out what view he has got to hold and sustain in his official capacity. He said that Wheeler had already warned you that in the event of a crisis you would always be in the wrong, even if you were in the right (just like 'the customer is always right' and other injustices), and he, Hill, felt that you would understand that he has really conceded a point in writing to you privately to let you know his official views. Actually, of course, he really does view the affair with gravest concern, and he has insisted on Smith sending down a full statement, to be debated at the sub-committee's meeting. He said you had many friends in it, and proceeded to tick off Smith so soundly that the poor man was completely flabbergasted. When he returned to consciousness he performed the ritual of tearing down the anti-Klaxon notice with squeals of rage. He then asked me if I wanted to give a lecture in the Albert Hall as he understood his staff had ambitions which he was opposing; asked Tonnochy if he called himself a genius, as he would like the geniuses in his department to be *plainly labelled* in case he failed to recognize them; and asked us if we wanted sofas to lie down on when tired!

You must forgive Hill for writing when you were away ill. He asked me if I thought you would rather hear nothing, and I said I expected you would be glad to hear.

You will have to think things over with the now certain knowledge that there is no immediate prospect of improvement in conditions or pay, and not even a limited prospect of material improvement in pay in the immediately post-Smith period. Unless I die or retire.

In spite of this it is quite certain that the Director and a number of the Trustees 'appreciate all you have done, my boy' and have no doubt whatever that the fault lies elsewhere. I would adore to listen in to their discussion!! But I fear the real truth is that the position is exactly as outlined by you on the sofa the other night. I cannot draw a picture of the Department's future here because there is no Indian ink on the table, and this stuff is not black enough. But it would be pretty murky.

The purpose of this letter is to beg you to avoid giving the impression you are searching after jobs while on sick-leave. Don't take Wheeler's Institute business without consulting friends here. Discuss what you like with Collingwood and that sort of person, but don't canvas the London group, at least until you hear from me how the meeting goes off.

Nearly everyone is on your side; but go on being 'really very seedy, though we expect him to come back thoroughly fit'.

About resigning: I do not honestly know what I think you ought to do, and will not worry you further with quite useless burbles. Get well; and love to Jacquetta. Sorry to write such a ragged letter, but am tired out.

The letter Kendrick referred to from Wheeler arrived on the same day, marked, 'VERY PRIVATE':

Here's a practical suggestion that may help. *Don't* bother to reply at present, but bite on it.

The Assistant Keepership here is likely to become vacant in the autumn. Salary £337 rising by £30 annually to £738. We could probably arrange for your transfer at you present actual salary on to this scale.

This is *not a promise*, but is a possibility – contingent, of course, upon your staying at the B.M. till the vacancy occurs. You will then be second in command here, and I shan't make old bones.

Anyway, consider it.

Rik

One of the trustees, Sir Charles Peers, who was also a friend of Christopher's, wrote on the same day:

> I am more sorry that I can say to hear of this breakdown. But if, as I hope, good is to come out of it, you must for the present strictly avoid work (which ought to be possible), and what is even more important and more difficult, avoid worry.
>
> You are young, and have time; and this pause in your work may well be a blessing in disguise. What is to be your next step mustn't worry you now; but nothing that has happened so far need give your friends any anxiety about the brilliant future which must await you.
>
> I shall see Hill this week, both at the Trustees' meeting, and otherwise, and for the moment will say no more than that I should regard your possible resignation from the Museum as a calamity in every sense. . . .

Finally in this bundle of letters came one from Reginald Smith:

> I was sorry but not surprised to hear of your collapse and can only wait for better news. Even youth cannot defy nature, but your case is interesting in another way, as I have never heard of a civil servant being overworked as such: it is against the Union rules.
>
> I presume that your resignation will not take effect however anxious you may be to take up more interesting work, till your special and ordinary leave as well as the month ordered by your doctor, have run their course.
>
> The report for the special committee has to be in by Saturday [9 February] and will contain nothing unfavourable to yourself.

Whether the letter was meant to be humorous in a heavy-handed way or was simply sarcastic, has to be viewed in the light of Kendrick's description of Smith's behaviour after he had been reprimanded for being 'a petty tyrant'.

Christopher and Jacquetta went on to Devon after their stay in Hampshire, for the remainder of his enforced rest. They spent several weeks at the home of Jacquetta's friend, Humphrey House (who was an expert on Jacquetta's kinsman, Gerard Manley Hopkins) and his wife, at Silverton, near Exeter; and at the end of February Nowell Myres wrote the following letter, full of wisdom and and genuine concern:

> I was glad to hear from you: I had not written any thoughts on your affairs, which have been much in my mind, because I felt that you ought to be left to vegetate for a bit. It was odd that your letter should have come the morning after I had dined at Chiselhampton with Sir Charles, and found Sir George there too. You may like to know the impression I got of their views on the situation. They seemed to be in

a state of rather irritated equanimity, taking the line that if you did not feel up to the work, you had better go: they were definitely irritated by the tone of your doctor's letter: Sir George observing with some pain that he was not used to being told how to run his Museum by the medical advisors of his subordinates. I hope I did well in emphasizing (a) that in a normal atmosphere there was no reason why you should have got into the state you did, and (b) that from the two days which I spent in the department last month I felt that unless something was done to ease matters it would not only be you, but T.D.K., who would have a nervous breakdown.

The thing which alarmed me about the situation is their determination if you leave to appoint a Medievalist in your room, which would mean of course that the whole prehistoric side would be left to R.A.S., and would in fact lapse altogether for the next two years: at the end of which a reasonably experienced prehistorian would be brought in from outside to start it again *ab ovo*. I said I thought this would certainly mean a breakdown for T.D.K., but how far that impressed them, I don't know.

From all of which I draw the moral that the public interest necessitates your remaining in the Museum unless you are positively kicked out by the doctor. It would be lamentable if prehistoric studies were allowed to collapse in that way, but if you go there is no doubt they will. On the other hand you must most carefully refrain from conveying the impression that you are making any sacrifice by remaining; for nothing would be more calculated to heat the furnace in your department 7 times more than it is wont to be heated. In other words I am certain you should do exactly what I advised you to do before you went away.

I frankly can't see what will come if you go out. If you apply for jobs teaching ancient history, (a) are there any? (b) you face the competition of the bright young things fresh from the Schools, Rome, Athens etc., (c) everyone will know that you are in fact only waiting for something better, and may for that reason prefer a humble two [second-class degree]. If you go away and write a book, how will you be subsidized? Leverhulme? I think they only appoint people who are in jobs and can get a year off. But you might get something from them. I should doubt very much if Oxford could help: there are such masses of the deserving young beings turned out every year, who must necessarily be a first charge on such funds as there are for research.

I put all this bluntly because I see year after year the ceaseless struggle to keep first-class academic persons from selling rubber or mending motor cars, to make both ends meet.

Meantime I hope you are really better, and will forgive me for this bald and unconvincing lecture. Nothing would induce me to write it if I did not profoundly sympathise with your point of view: and did not regard your present and future welfare as a matter of great moment ... which it is, isn't it, Jacquetta?

Kendrick wrote again from Vienna, where he was staying at the Hotel Fuchs. He had no new information except that Smith was convinced Christopher would stay away for several months: 'He doesn't seem to be in the least bitter, but quite obviously he intends to hoard up the registration for you.' He ended by assuring Christopher that 'outside the Department several senior B.M. people have expressed their astonishment and anger at the affair. You can be sure no one thinks you mutinous or insubordinate, you have merely to struggle against the official tendency to back the higher placed man whatever happens.'

When Christopher returned to the museum he took up the threads again without too much difficulty. The registration had indeed been 'kept for him', and it actually took him two years to catch up, often working on after 5 p.m. By the time Smith retired in 1937, Christopher was able to tell him that he had successfully brought the register up to date. When he announced this there was a long pause. Smith was unable at first to find words. An awkwardly mumbled 'Very good' was all he could muster, before he turned on his squeaking heels and escaped, determined not to reveal the slightest glimmer of emotion. Under the crusty, small-minded civil servant there must still have been traces of the old Smith, whom Bersu had remembered in Germany before the war – chatting merrily in a jaunty straw boater – before jealousy and dyspepsia overtook him. The end of his life was not as bleak as might have been expected. He was already friendly with a widow, Mrs Pat Green, who was quite a local 'character' in Colchester, where she had succeeded her husband on his death as a borough councillor. She also grew roses. Reggie sometimes stayed with her at weekends, returning to the museum in an almost jovial mood, with one of her blooms in his lapel. Though he remained a bachelor to the end, he was at least spared the loneliness of old age. When he died it was she who settled his affairs and arranged his burial near Colchester. Tom Kendrick replaced him as keeper, and Christopher's hours in the museum were thereafter immeasurably lightened.

Christopher had sufficiently recovered by the summer of 1935 to undertake another excavation. He was invited by the President of the Hampshire Field Club, Sir Charles Close, to dig for three weeks in the hill-fort at Buckland Rings, near Lymington, in the New Forest.

Christopher and Jacquetta had a room in a local pub, and Jacquetta's parents came down for a few days to visit them. One of the diggers, a pupil of Norah Jolliffe's (who was also digging with them), a bubblingly enthusiastic girl named Ursula Wratislaw, remembered playing darts with 'Hoppie' (as Jacquetta's father, Sir Frederick, was affectionately known) in the pub one evening.

The site had been surveyed in advance by members of the staff of the Ordnance Survey, under the direction of O.G.S. Crawford; and in 1934 a small preliminary excavation was carried out by J.P. Preston, a cousin of Stuart Piggott's wife.

Digging began on 14 July. Buckland Rings is a triple-ramparted fortification lying a mile to the north of Lymington between the roads leading to Brockenhurst and Sway, and a mile south from the boundary of the New Forest. It occupies a flat-topped hill at the end of a dry, gravelly ridge, 90 ft above sea-level, overlooking the trough of the Lymington River about a mile from its entry into the Solent. Where undisturbed, the earthworks are composed of three ramparts and two ditches which are thickly wooded, covering an area of about seven acres.

It was clear from the nature and form of the Rings themselves that the site was Early Iron Age: the excavation was carried out to establish a more precise date, and to find out if there was a possible connection with the Belgic invasion of peoples from Northern Gaul who were believed to have landed on the Wessex coast some time around 50 BC. On the evidence they found (four sherds of coarse and uneven but wheel-made pottery) Christopher was able to confirm the Early Iron Age date of around 50 BC for the earthwork, with earlier occupation in the centre: they found two flint implements, two flint cores and half a stone hammer, which were probably Neolithic or Bronze Age (around 1500 BC).

In contrast to Maiden Castle, which was more of a fortified hill-town, Buckland Rings was a true hill-fort, built as a refuge in conditions of war, and not as a permanent fortified capital. Its defences were deliberately dismantled, and Christopher said in his report: 'it is by no means impossible that this was done by command of the conquering power of Rome'. He also noted that a division of the army of King Henry V had encamped on or near the site before embarking for the campaign of Agincourt in October 1415.

In the summer of 1936 there was another congress, this time in Oslo, which enabled Christopher and Jacquetta to take their last European holiday before the war. Once again his letter home gives a vivid picture. It was written from Visby on the island of Gotland on 27 August:

We started on a Saturday night – I can hardly remember it – with Nowell. Hamburg was crowded and noisy but cheerful (all Deutschland then garlanded and placarded *Wilkommen* for the Olympics). Kiel was most interesting – a wonderful museum with the great Nydam ship, a complete ship 75 ft long, found in peat-moss, with a huge treasure inside: it belongs to the Angles (about AD 400) before they crossed over. In fact in such a ship must our forefathers have raided the Saxon shore, and later flocked across to settle the land.

Afterwards we went the length of the Kieler Hafen, but it poured with rain. Then a not very comfortable night journey by train to Copenhagen. My clearest memory is emerging into glorious early sunshine about 5.30 a.m. on the deck of a wonderful train-ferry streamer across the Great Belt as smooth as glass. Copenhagen was simply delightful – a really charming, human, civilized, easy-to-enjoy, happy, carefree sort of city. The museum is marvellous and its staff most friendly.

Director Brøndsted took us to lunch at the Yacht Club. We went one afternoon to Roskilde with its lovely cathedral, and another to Elsinore and the 'Hamlet' castle of Kronborg. That night we crossed to Oslo. The Sunday we spent settling in and on Monday the Congress began. Crowded days of note-taking, archaeology talking in three languages at once, and being entertained to countless enormous Norwegian meals. Jacquetta's paper was extremely good – clear, controlled and assured. Mine was less good in that I had rather too much to say and exceeded my time! Tom Brown read a fine paper of early agriculture.

The Norwegian collections, especially of course their Viking ships and other such treasures, are fine, but everything (including the Royal Palace where we had an afternoon reception) is on a very small scale, which they rather strained themselves by almost excessive hospitality to off-set.

The only black spot was the announcement of Bersu's enforced resignation from the Council; and the eventual acceptance after an anxious and rather mismanaged discussion, of the worthless and wicked Nazi proposed by the German government in his stead. [This was a Professor Schultz from Halle.] This will certainly bear evil fruit. I voted against it, but considerations of diplomacy (short-sighted I'm convinced) got him in by 19 to 17. Anyway, there it is, and we were soon off on our week of excursion. By train to the Valdres valley in the central Norwegian mountains, through which we motored all day, to Laerdal on its deep fjord, where we slept – a tiny wood-built place, only an hour or so from high snow-covered mountains and glaciers, among which we halted for tea, watched by real Lapps and a herd of reindeer!!

Next day we went by steamer along a series of fjords visiting another wonderful *stavkirke* (wooden church) at Urnes; and after more mountain motoring and a final train journey, we reached Bergen at night. Quite unlike Oslo, which is mostly new, Bergen is a marvellous old Hanseatic town. Everything smelt of fish.

More huge Norwegian hospitality, and the Congress then broke up into smaller parties. We went by boat to Stavanger and spent a delightful day there, seeing town and museum, and the sites of excavations on the hills behind; winding up with a bathe and a final farewell dinner. We had previously got good bathing in Oslo fjord, and near Bergen, too. It hardly rained at all – I think only two wet days and a few showers all the time we were in Norway – but it's distinctly expensive – e.g. laundry: 1/6 for a shirt!

We were tired when we got to Stockholm, but had long enough there to recover, and see the main sites, and work through the Museum, winding up with a supper-dance evening.

Brøndsted also took them on a 'mystery tour' one night, which turned out to be a visit to see the department store where Greta Garbo had once worked.

Christopher and Jacquetta ended up at Visby for a short holiday:

This is the perfect situation for writing a holiday letter home. I am sprawling on the sandy beach, under the slanting rays of a warm afternoon sun, with sky of cloudless blue in which white gulls wheel; healthy and refreshed by two bathes in the placid Baltic Sea. Actually the Baltic Sea today is freezing cold and we couldn't stay in for more than a minute each time! This is because the night before last a chill north-westerly gale blew up, straight from the Norwegian glaciers we visited a fortnight ago; and yesterday was gloriously sunny, but with a cutting wind. Today the wind has dropped and the air is calm and beautifully warm, but the water has not yet had time to cook up to a nice bathing temperature again yet. Two days ago it was warm, and will be again, though of course this sea isn't the Mediterranean.

Meanwhile it's lovely here on the beach, sunbathing in shorts. The beach is called 'Snakgardsbaden', and is a couple of miles north of Visby, facing – like it – full west across to the Swedish mainland. Buses ply between it and the town, and there is a smallish but luxurious pleasure hotel on the cliff above, under the same management as ours in the town; so that pension clients like us can lunch at it free by getting coupons from our head waiter in the morning. Unhappily Snakgardsbaden closes on August 31st, so for our last few days here next week we plan to do a walk round the island. It is some 75 miles long and quite narrow, and there are said to be many comfortable villages and inns. [In the end they hired bicycles, which enabled them to explore further.]

Visby itself has a practically complete circuit of 13th century stone walls, almost perfectly preserved; eight or ten fine churches of the same period or earlier, mostly complete but for roofs; and a beautiful cathedral. In those days it was a rich Hanseatic merchant town, the centre of the Baltic trade; but from the 14th to the 19th century it seems to have been in decay. Its chief industry now is tourism. It has steep, narrow cobbled streets and wooden houses, a little harbour, and two cinemas – at one of which we went to see the same Mozart film as you wrote that you had seen in London.

Our hotel is comfortable and not dear. It has a terrace dining-room and dancing four nights a week (a very modest effort at 'Life' – the band is comically miserable). We have a Swedish paper daily, and *The Times* three days late to tell us of the dreadful doings in other parts of Europe. Actually, since the Non-Intervention agreement the German press has been much fuller of Moscow, and seems already to envisage war in eastern Europe. These Scandinavian countries seem the only ones where life goes on more or less as usual, with expectations of a normal tomorrow. . . .

Two months after their return from Visby those expectations became even more poignantly real. Jacquetta's pregnancy came as the signal voices of war grew more and more explicit. Seventeen years later she wrote the following passage:

> . . . a female knows that relentlessly, inside a body which hitherto she has regarded as being in a sense herself, cells are going to divide, proliferate, and specialize to a pattern determined half a million years ago. She knows this will happen quite apart from her wishes: whether she delights in it or resists it. She may busy herself knitting woolly bootees or hemming nappies, she may go to the most aggressively ordinary department store for her expanding maternity gowns, but still she is aware that this is no tame domestic affair which has caught her by the hair. She is forced to see that this body with whose idiosyncrasies of form and colour she is so familiar from her looking glass, this physical self, is now the slave of some great and marvellous and absolutely tyrannical purpose of which neither she nor he who launched the sperm has been vouchsafed any understanding.[6]

Everywhere the signs of anxiety and discontent were ripening. The Jarrow March began on 5 October; and six days later London's East End was thronged by a crowd of a hundred thousand, ranged in furious opposition to the black-shirted supporters of Sir Oswald Mosley. On 27 November the Foreign Secretary, Anthony Eden, warned Germany that Britain would fight to protect Belgium, thus laying another stone of the inevitable road to war. The only story that succeeded in diverting both press and public was the affair of the king and Mrs Simpson. George V had died in January, and in the months that followed the accession of his son Edward, the gossip columns had seethed with speculation. On 11 December, when the unhappy monarch finally gave up his throne for the woman he loved, public opinion was split. But there was little doubt that the plight of those two most public persons did much to entertain amid the gradual disintegration of order all over Europe.

By the following February idealists from all over the world were making their way to Spain to fight in the Civil War. The International Brigade, though run by Communists, included many who were quite simply opposed to Fascism. On 26 April bombers of the German air force were sent by Hitler to destroy the Basque town of Guernica. Although there were military targets in the town, the German bombers never went for them. They simply unloaded their bombs indescriminately, and then set the whole town alight with incendiary devices. The carnage was indescribable.

The new king, George VI, was crowned in May, and Neville Chamberlain took over from Baldwin as prime minister. In this atmosphere of tension and instability Christopher and Jacquetta retreated to Cornwall for a short holiday. He wrote once to his mother on 20 May, enclosing a letter of condolence:

I have been very distressed to hear of poor Stella's death. [His pretty young cousin had died tragically in childbirth.] Will you please forward the enclosed to poor Cousin B., whose address I don't know?

Thank you for sending the various things you have sent, and for your nice letters. We have heard also from Diana Zvegintzov who is in a nursing home in Cheniston Gardens – 9½ lbs, since you seem so keen on weights! [Michael had married Diana Lucas, whom Christopher had known slightly while they were both at Oxford.]

Our ten continuous days of fine weather rather broke last night, and today is showery, but we've been wonderfully lucky, and expect to arrive home on Saturday evening [22May] refreshed and well. May we come to Sunday supper? . . .

On 9 August shortly after 6.30 a.m. their son was born. Christopher wrote to his father that evening:

I visited Jacquetta and the baby again this evening and found both doing very well. He is said to be like you! But I should wait to believe this until you have seen for yourself. Jacquetta has had a peaceful day, sleeping and resting and looks very well, which indeed she did this morning, though it was only two and a half hours after what was evidently a pretty tough business. As you heard she had gone into the home – I am glad it was so close to us! – after tea yesterday; the doctor then said she had better come back to supper, and so she went in finally at ten. Lady H. stayed with her until soon after 12, and I'm afraid she had none too good a time until the hour came for the doctor to arrive at four. They telephoned us at 5.30, when the anaesthetist came, and Lady H. went over to the waiting room while I hung on here (for practical purposes no further off). The trouble was he was the wrong way up, and this 'posterior presentation' as they call it, naturally took a bit of dealing with. The result has involved two or three stitches in her, and temporary marks on the baby's temples (now already nearly vanished); but though Dr Crosby [acting for Dr Bourne, the specialist, who had had the 'watching brief' for the case) was warned to stand by if necessary, the two women (our Dr Adams and her anaesthetist) managed it with perfect success, finishing about a quarter to seven.

Everyone has been enormously pleased with her, and at 8¼ lbs the baby is generally admired. He has quite a lot of hair, greyish eyes, and not too raw a colour. Jacquetta, as I say, is quite wonderful after it, and though rather stiff and smarting, is cheerful and alert and smiling – I left her eagerly starting quite a good broth and chicken-wing supper.

The nursing home people seem extremely nice, and she is clearly going to be very well looked after. Lady H. is naturally very relieved, as from J.'s shape her training had suggested to her how it would turn out; and we were both very glad to be able to sit down and toast the family in early morning tea. She has been so nice here with us these

Jacquetta and Nicolas in 1937

tedious and hot weeks. She is staying till Sunday morning, and will end up her string of good works by securing and presenting us with a pram.

By telephone, telegram, or letter, I think I have passed the news to all uncles, aunts and principal friends. Though we should both like a daughter too, we are very glad it is a boy, as I am sure you all are. I hope Mummy has not felt the strain of such a terrible long wait too badly. I look forward to hearing from her and you all in the morning, and will then write to her further myself tomorrow.

I had to spend the late morning and all the afternoon at the Museum, where in my colleague's holiday time I can't very well be spared, so I am a bit sleepy now. His first name is definitely to be Charles, and if it seems to suit his style I don't see why he shouldn't be called this in practice. . . .

Two days later he wrote to his mother:

I meant to write to you last night but was tired in a restless sort of way. I could only settle myself with soporific reading to get ready for sleep. Tonight I am simply drowsy and heavy and haven't energy to write much. Simply the reaction.

Jacquetta is said to have been a little tired looking this afternoon, but she rests and sleeps well, and this evening was very fresh and cheerful as usual, and quite herself. She has begun to breast-feed the baby with great success. His head, which was a little pinched-looking at first, is now filling out nicely, and is a good shape – long, but well proportioned – with nice eyes and nice ears, and neatly formed face and features.

The flowers are banked up everywhere! All kinds and sizes from mignonette to the Ivor Thomas's magnificent sprays of Madonna lilies. There were many telegrams, and letters continue to pour in. Lady H. has today secured a beautiful pram – by speeding off to Golders Green in answer to an advertisement in this morning's *Nursery World* – a twenty guinea affair, second-hand, for 5 guineas, she says, in perfect condition but for the hood, which she is having replaced by a new one. It will nicely fit the little garage we have been lent by the girl opposite.

Sir F. is coming up to pay his visit tomorrow, and they will both go back together. It seems he has felt sadly lonely all this long time, quite by himself.

J. is having her stitches out on Friday (this is good progress), and I will see what the Sister says about visiting on Monday – hitherto she has had only one at a time, of course. I really like my son very much; he looks a thoroughly agreeable and friendly sort of baby, and has nice little hands and feet. But we can't call him 'Davison' – your father was called that after his mother's family, and if he had a similar name it should come from the Hopkins side. This is the Spanish in you coming out, subconsciously wanting 'Hawkes y Hopkins y Cobb y Davison'! There's ample time to decide, but anyhow at present both Charles and Nicolas look like staying in (quite possibly these two alone will do best). . . .

Jacquetta pencilled a card the next day to Ellie and C.P., thanking them for the roses they sent:

> . . . We are both getting on very well in our respective ways, although as you can imagine, the heat is rather exhausting. Its effect on Nicolas is merely soporific. He is still *very* plain, but admirably sound in wind and limb: I hope that by the time you come he will be more handsome.
> Pencil doesn't indicate invalidishness, but merely that I haven't any ink. . . .

Towards the end of August they took the baby down to Winchester for a short holiday. Through the kind offices of Cyril Robinson, Christopher had been able to rent a house in Kingsgate Street while its owner, Mr Phipps, who was a master at Winchester, was away on holiday. It was a very nice house, looking directly on to the college's playing fields. They stayed there for a couple of weeks, with a monthly nurse to help look after Nicolas:

> The weather here continues fine and warm, with only some hazy cloud, and we have settled down very comfortably. Jacquetta can now take a daily quiet stroll in Meads, and Nicolas is getting quite a healthy out-of-doors look from his slumbers on the lawn. He is on the whole very good and peaceful.
> I have two dogs – lovely ladies, golden retrievers – to help exercise (the man who feeds them only comes morning and evening) and we had a good run round Hills this afternoon. . . .

And they had a visit from Uncle Frank and Aunt Helen:

> I am glad you liked the photograph! N. was taken again yesterday, in the arms of his beaming great-uncle, a very amusing occasion: Aunt Helen and I stood by in fits, and even the infant seemed to realize that something funny was up. They went off after tea in high good-humour. . . .

On their return to Cleveland Gardens Jacquetta engaged a very cheerful and good-natured Welsh girl, 'Nurse Polly', to look after Nicolas, and she was able to return to her academic work, although some of her time was still taken up with the baby, and other domestic activities. Christopher was by then deeply engrossed in the book on prehistoric Europe which he had begun writing soon after they returned from the Oslo congress the previous autumn. Forty-three years later

Jacquetta wrote that even before Nicolas was born she had begun to feel dissatisfied with her life:

> The arrival of a son during the fourth year of our marriage gave me natural satisfactions and perhaps took me one more step on my way towards maturity, but could do little to revivify our marriage. Christopher was by now staying up every night into the small hours working fanatically at a book, bringing our social and companionable life almost to a stop. We never quarelled but were by now, so far as I can recall, for the first time becoming positively unhappy.[7]

But there were still excavations to be shared, and Christopher at least had moments of great happiness with his wife and child, and Jacquetta's life was as full as her husband's. She was working on a book called *The Archaeology of Jersey*, for which Tom Kendrick had done much of the work soon after the First World War; but his interests had gradually taken him further and further away from the subject, and he had asked Jacquetta to take it over. She was able to get a grant to spend some months in Jersey to complete the necessary research, and the book was published in 1939.

At the end of August 1938 Jacquetta and Christopher did an excavation, again for the Hampshire Field Club, at Quarley Hill, seven miles from Andover and two miles from the Wiltshire border at Cholderton. The hill itself is the most conspicuous site in north-west Hampshire, rising 560 ft above sea level, a mile from the village of Grateley.

They had rented a small farmhouse on the way to Grateley station, from where the excavating party, which consisted of the two senior Hawkeses, Nurse Polly, and a pram containing the junior Hawkes (who was then almost exactly one year old), had to walk to the farmhouse. They were met on their way from the station by Frank Warren, the secretary of the Field Club, who apologized for being too late to meet them off the train. Warren was a very nice man. He was director of the printing firm which did all the work for Winchester College through the college bookshop, P. & G. Wells. Very quiet and unassuming, he had a small, narrow face with a little brown moustache and ruddy cheeks. He had joined the firm around the time Christopher left Winchester, so their acquaintance was mainly through the Hampshire Field Club, which paid them an official visit while they were digging.

The line of a Roman road between Silchester and Old Sarum, known as the Port Way, runs a quarter of a mile from the southern slope of the hill, which is oval in shape and has a clump of trees – mostly beeches and conifers – on the top of it, rather like St Catharine's Hill. They found the slopes overgrown with juniper, and the whole site overrun with rabbits.

The hill-fort itself encloses an area of $8\frac{1}{2}$ acres, with a single rampart which stands about 16 ft above the silted-up ditch. The hill was first used by man for the passage of a boundary ditch which was cut along the watershed of the Avon river system in the Late Bronze Age – during the first half of the first millennium BC. These boundaries were between separate farms, and would have been used as 'cattle-ways' or roads between the establishments. A single flint axe and a few flakes and cores were the only artefacts found from that period.

In the fourth century BC a palisade-enclosure was built on the summit, while the ditches were still in use for traffic. The occupation of this enclosure was intermittent and probably confined to emergency use, as the nearest running water was two miles away. A century later a bank and ditch were dug on the line of the old palisade ditch, thus converting the enclosure into a hill-fort, with entrances to the north-east and south-west. During this period the inhabitants lived on domestic animals, cooked on fires made from local wood, and meal ground in sarsen querns. Between forty and fifty cooking pots were found, of varying degrees of coarseness, as well as burnt scraps of flint and stone, and a lot of charcoal. There were bones and teeth, mostly animal, though they did find a few human bones mixed up with them, but no implements or metal objects. One or two stray scraps of Roman material were also found on the north-east slope of the hill.

Among others they were assisted by the young John Brailsford, who was later to take over from Christopher at the British Museum when he left it to return to Oxford after the war; and with the financial support of the Hampshire Field Club, they were able to employ eight labourers. Jacquetta drew the pottery and flints, and she also took the photographs, while Christopher did the plans and sections for the report, which was published the following year.[8]

That winter Jacquetta's restlessness was to some extent absorbed in the finding of a new and larger home. C.P.'s generosity enabled them to secure the lease of 39 Fitzroy Road:

> . . . I am sure you will like the house; though it is true that the remoter end of the same road goes socially a bit down-hill, close to Primrose Hill and with a clear view over Regent's Park (and the Mappin Terraces) southward at the back. . . .

The rent on the property was £110 a year, with the rates £35, for a five-year lease. They spent a modest amount on carpets, curtains and decorations, and Jacquetta herself did some of the distempering. As Christopher's promotion to assistant keeper (first class) at the museum took place in May (the tenth anniversary of his actual appointment) and his salary increased to £600 a year, he very properly explained to his father that he wanted to consider the money he had given them as a loan and not a gift.

They moved in on Friday 6 May. Ellie had very thoughtfully given Jacquetta a sewing machine, and she was able to make some of the curtains herself; as well as a 'much needed blue silk dressing gown' for Christopher. Nine days later he wrote to his mother:

This evening we are really approaching feeling 'straight' and I can sit down and write in a study fairly well in order, with the rest of the house well on the way to proper arrangement. All the books are dusted and arranged, a good many pictures hung, and most of the painting and that sort of thing finished. We have been very grateful for what you have bought – not least for the fine sewing-machine, with which Jacquetta has been busy. 'Uncle' Crawford's books are beautiful, and I'm sure Nicolas will be delighted in due time with many of the old nursery ones awaiting him. . . . Lastly I should simply love an armchair for my birthday present! It is a most happy suggestion. . . .

With this chair, however, came rather more than they wished for:

Thank you for orderering the chair. I cannot understand why you are 'disappointed' that I want it to go in the drawing room and not in the study. I cannot see that this makes any difference! We decided some time ago to have the sofa in the study, where it suits both of us; and when you kindly offered to give me a comfortable chair I at once said that I would like one very much as it was just what was needed for the drawing room. I understood that this was what you would do, but I gather that instead of having it covered with the same stuff as the other ones in the room, which you find too expensive, you are leaving us to supply that. This is quite all right, as I never remember you undertaking to supply a cover for it at all! But when you write to me like this of Jacquetta's 'extravagance' it is really time I stepped in and begged you to be more careful of your language. I mean this – your fatal passion for controlling others will lead to serious, irreparable harm if you do not check it where we are concerned. Your being 'horrified' and saying and writing these disagreeable things is really extremely painful. And to go on and complain that Jacquetta is 'slow' in making our home comfortable and finished 'as a whole' is simply thoughtless impatience. Surely you know what delays shops make, and how long it often takes to make up one's mind about furnishings? We are both determined not to spend the money that Daddy has given us rashly and without thought. We are being extremely careful precisely because he has been so generous; and for you to cut in with these ill-conceived carpings and complainings is enough to spoil all the feelings of gratitude one naturally has at an additional gift on your part like this chair.

More than that, coming as it does on the top of a great deal of previous exhibition of the same kind, and accompanied with language to Jacquetta on the telephone and whenever you have come here by yourself to see things, which has upset her and me more than I can say, it is helping to pile up a state of feeling which has already done serious harm, and if you go on like this, is going to prove disastrous. Jacquetta is happily not easy to rouse, and we are both resolved to be as easy and sympathetic as we can, for the sake of everyone concerned. But I warn you that your behaviour since Nicolas was born has been making me very uneasy.

Though you may restrain yourself nine times, what you say or do on the tenth will cancel anything. I do not expect you ever to be fond of Jacquetta – that hope you killed a long while ago – but I do expect that you should keep a proper hold on yourself and treat both of us with the good manners and considerateness which Daddy and you yourself set before me as a rule of life when I was young. I do most earnestly beg you to listen to this appeal, for it is really that, from your only son. Years are going by, and are you gradually antagonizing me from you by your ill-nature against my wife? You'll say no: but are you so sure? You know we are both devoted to Daddy, and he is to you; serious trouble between us would tear him in two. And as for Nicolas, it might well mean that he would never come to know his grandparents. You see we simply mustn't let it come to our facing that. But it is I who would have to decide, and a man's own wife and family come inevitably first.

You may be horrified at my talking like this, and say that it can have no relation to the present situation, but it is the little things that matter. And to the little things I fear you may be growing more and more insensitive as you allow yourself to give way to the jealousy in you. So this isn't only an appeal: it is a warning. I won't apologise for using you with frankness – if a son cannot, who can? You will say there are faults on both sides. Yes, and while we look to our own, do you look to yours. Stop and think. Stop and make yourself think. Each time. Think how much depends on it – for us all. . . .

On 30 September Chamberlain went to Munich; and following a twelve hour meeting between himself and Hitler, Daladier and Mussolini, he signed an agreement with Hitler. The Sudeten region of Czechoslovakia, which was inhabited by a German-speaking minority, was to be handed over to Germany. This pact did little to help the Czechs, in spite of the guarantee that the rest of their country was to be protected from aggression; but it gave the British government a little time in which to build up its pitifully inadequate resources. While Chamberlain spoke of 'peace for our time', he authorized the mobilization of the fleet.

On 28 March the following year the Civil War in Spain came to an end with a victory for the Nationalist forces; and two months later, on 11 May, Chamberlain warned Hitler that the use of force in Danzig would mean war. But the main preoccupation in the streets of London at that time was the threat of bombing by the Irish Republican Army. Forty houses in north London were raided in July in the hunt for bombers, and five IRA men were sentenced to twenty years in jail. By the middle of August, with the continuing threat of hostility, the major museums and galleries in London began packing up their treasures. This, of course, involved Christopher, but not until after he had carried out one more excavation in Hampshire.

Bury Hill in the parish of Upper Clatford lies about a mile and a half south-west of Andover. It rises abruptly with a 300 ft contour line around the brow of its flattened, plateau-like top. There are in fact two forts on the hill: the later one a reduction of the former – smaller, but more strongly defended. The first fort, which is oval in form, roughly follows the natural contour of the hill, 'now tree-clad and bitten into by a chalk pit'.[9] The circuit of the second fort only touches the brow-line at the head of a shallow gulley on the north-east. The entrance to both camps is on the south-east, facing the Clatford–Redrice road. The soil is chalk with a layer of clay-with-flints which was exceedingly hard to dig.

As with the excavations at Quarley Hill the previous summer, Christopher had been invited to carry out the excavation by the Hampshire Field Club, and their support enabled him to employ between five and seven workmen. While Christopher was digging Bury Hill, Jacquetta carried out a small-scale investigation half a mile to the north-east, at Balksbury. The object of the excavation was to try and find out what the relationship was between the two sites. Christopher commented in the excavation report:

In area Balksbury is a very large camp, covering as much as 45 acres on a rounded plateau between the two valleys; at its highest point it

Christopher and Nicolas at Quarley Hill, Dorset, in October 1939

reaches only 265 feet, and is thus dominated, overshadowed almost, by the 310 feet of Bury Hill. The plan is roughly triangular, the southern side standing above the River Anna and facing Bury Hill, while the eastern overlooks the trout-filled Anton.[10]

The trout-filled Anton provided Christopher and Jacquetta with two excellent meals. C.P.'s old Cambridge friend, Cecil Lupton, who was by then a widower, had left his big house at Upton upon Severn, and was living not far from Bury Hill. His earlier passion for hunting had been replaced by the more tranquil but no less absorbing pastime of fishing. He had been able to by an old mill-house, called Rooksbury Mill, with fishing rights on the Anton, which, being a tributary of the River Test, was likewise bountifully stocked with trout. He invited Christopher and Jacquetta to spend an evening with him while they were digging; and they went away with another delicious meal, carefully wrapped up to be grilled the following day.

Phillips and Crawford both visited the site during the excavation, as did Gerhard Bersu, from his own dig at Little Woodbury, near Salisbury. The previous year Bersu had made it known to his friends in England (among them Phillips and Gordon Childe) that he was very anxious to be given something to do in England. His position at that time in Berlin was becoming increasingly perilous, and he and Maria were eager to escape; although he carefully returned to Germany after each digging season was over to keep up his permit. Indeed, they made every effort to protect themselves: after the second season at Little Woodbury, in early September, the Bersus made a spectacular dash by car to King's Lynn, supposedly attempting to catch the last boat back to Germany, having first made quite sure that they would miss it, and that as many people as possible were aware of their attempt. Thus, in the event of Hitler's winning the war, they would at least be able to say that they had tried to return, but had missed the boat by a matter of hours.

It had been decided the previous year at a meeting of the Prehistoric Society, that Bersu should be offered Little Woodbury. Crawford, of course, had air photographs of the site, which covered an area of some four and a half acres on the brow of a hill looking towards the River Avon at Britford, on the southern outskirts of Salisbury. The Bersus stayed at the Mill Race Hotel in Salisbury, with Phillips, who drove them to and from the site every day. Phillips 'acted as guardian of the interests of the Society, quarter-master, general provider and often pit-excavator.'[11] He also dug a deep section, single-handed, right across the ditch at Great Woodbury (the hill-fort which lies just a few hundred yards from the enclosed farmstead of Little Woodbury), to find out if the two sites were contemporary. They were. Bersu's first season, which had taken place in the summer of 1938, while Christopher and Jacquetta were at Quarley Hill, had lasted for three months. The second one ended with the outbreak of war in September the following year. Apart from Phillips, Bersu's helpers during both seasons included the Piggotts, and

John Brailsford. Christopher remembered the Piggotts hilariously imitating the Bersus when they were out of earshot, but it was always done affectionately. With Phillips, however, there were undercurrents of jealousy beneath his recognition of Bersu's genius as an excavator. When Christopher visited the site, which he did several times, he would be taken to one side first by Bersu and then by Phillips, to be told by both that they had 'had a terrible time' with each other. Phillips was undoubtedly resentful of his German colleague's success; and sadly he allowed this to show in his autobiography, which was published after his death in 1985. But Phillips was soon to be given one of the richest and most celebrated sites of the century to excavate, while poor Bersu had to face internment on the Isle of Man.

In the summer of 1938 Mrs Edith May Pretty decided to investigate a group of eleven mounds on her estate at Sutton Hoo, near Woodbridge in Suffolk. Assisted by Guy Maynard, the Director of the Ipswich Museum, and Basil Brown, she opened three of the lesser barrows in the group. In one of them they found what was then presumed to be the remains of a boat, some 18 ft long; and in the others there were cremation burials and objects which were recognized as being of sixth or seventh century date. Recent excavations by Professor Martin Carver have shown that what was found in 1938 were in fact not the remains of a boat at all, but of a timber burial chamber. The finds were taken to the Ipswich Museum. One of the other barrows was much larger, and the following May Mrs Pretty decided to examine it. Very soon it became clear that this was no ordinary barrow, and the Office of Works was informed. Paul Baillie-Reynolds, as Inspector for England, was called in, and, realizing that the British Museum would undoubtedly be involved, he telephoned Christopher, and arranged to pick him up at Camden Town tube station and drive him down to Woodbridge to see the excavation. Both Maynard and Brown had realized that they were not sufficiently experienced to cope with what proved to be a great ship burial. Bushe-Fox, as Chief Inspector, detailed his Inspector for England to find out exactly what was going on, and to give him a full report. Having established the importance of the site, the Office of Works had then to find someone to take over the excavation. Baillie- Reynolds asked Christopher's opinion. At once he suggested Phillips. Apart from his work at Little (and Great) Woodbury, Phillips had done a masterly excavation of a Neolithic long barrow at Skendlebury, in the Lincolnshire Wolds, some five or six years before. Christopher had seen it and had been greatly impressed. Bushe-Fox took some convincing, and it took Christopher a little while to persuade him that there really was no one else. Eventually it was agreed, and Phillips began work on 3 July, with Brown, clearing material from the area where they expected the burial to be. Mrs Pretty's two gardeners had already cut back the turf, and they were very soon able to put a trench through the central mass of the barrow. Phillips was assisted by the Piggotts and W.F. Grimes, who did much of the painstaking work of uncovering the delicate golden

Jacquetta and Nicolas at Seatown, Dorset, October 1939

objects. In view of the undoubted value of these artefacts, they were taken to the British Museum under police escort, and a coroner's inquest was ordered to determine their ownership. This was held on 14 August in a hall in Sutton parish before the Coroner for West Suffolk, Mr L.H. Vulliamy. The inquest should in fact have been handled by the Coroner for East Suffolk, but, as he was the Pretty family's solicitor, he could not of course be officially recognized as being impartial, in view of the immense value of the treasure.

All the objects were brought back from the British Museum and were on display during the hearing. Piggott described the burial, and it was made abundantly clear that there had been no intention to recover the material. The verdict, that it was not Treasure Trove, gave the ownership to Mrs Pretty, who at once handed it over to the British Museum by deed of gift. It was the largest gift ever made to the museum in the lifetime of the donor. Mrs Pretty was later offered the honour of Dame of the British Empire, but she declined it.

Phillips published an account of the excavation in the *Antiquaries Journal* (XX, ii (1940)); and the whole volume of the quarterly review *Antiquity* for March 1940 was given over to a series of articles on the ship burial and its artefacts. The last of these, by H. Munro Chadwick, was entitled 'Who Was He?'. Chadwick believed it to be Redwald, who died about 624/5; there was some dispute about this, but Chadwick was proved to be right.

It was almost thirty years before a fully illustrated handbook was published by the British Museum. It was written by R.L.S. Bruce-Mitford, who was then Keeper of British and Medieval Antiquities, having entered the department on the retirement of Reginald Smith, in the early months of 1938.

Towards the end of August Christopher and Jacquetta returned to London, and Christopher and Tom Kendrick were almost immediately plunged into the immense task of selecting and packing up as many of the objects from the department as could reasonably be transported to a safe place. The inevitability of war had become increasingly clear over the summer months, and the authorities prudently began to expedite the plans which had been made to protect the nation's treasures. The objects were carefully packed with kapok and placed in large, green, coffin-sized boxes. Jacquetta helped with this packing and she remembers it vividly because the conditions were so awful. The fluff from the kapok filled the air, and though they covered their faces they were still half choked. For almost two weeks a couple of elderly horse-drawn carts covered with tarpaulins plied their stately way between the Museum and the empty tube station at Aldwych, bearing their priceless cargo to safety. The reason for this somewhat eccentric means of transport was not as absurd as it may seem. In view of the

Christopher and Nicolas at Seatown, October 1939

activities of the IRA in London, it was felt that an expensive-looking and heavily-guarded vehicle loaded with boxes would undoubtedly excite attention, and might provide a target for the bombers.

Christopher was detailed to act as 'officer in charge' at the tube station end, with a list of all the boxes he was to receive; and a chute was made down one of the unused escalators, with a pile of sawdust filled sacks at the bottom to ensure a tolerably easy ride for the swaddled objects. The boxes were carefully labelled and stacked against the walls, and the museum's conservation officer was sent to check the humidity, which proved to be acceptable. On one occasion Jacquetta went down to see how they were getting on, and she noticed a large white chalked square on the platform. It was clearly marked 'FOR SUTTON HOO'.

At midday on 3 September Chamberlain's expected announcement brought with it the immediate danger of air raids on London. Jacquetta and Christopher reinforced one of the basements of the house in Fitzroy Road with planks, and Jacquetta prepared to take Nicolas to Cambridge to stay with her parents; but before this the family had a brief holiday together. The packing up at the museum was completed by the end of September, and, as Christopher still had two weeks' leave owing to him, he asked if he might take it.

They spent the time at Seatown, on the Dorset coast, not far from

Three generations of Hawkeses in the garden of Campden Hill Square beside 'the little stupid'

Beaminster, walking in the glorious late autumn sunshine, or on the beach. Nicolas was able to build castles in the sand, or play with the lovely rounded pebbles which flanked it. They once climbed almost to the top of the Golden Cap, the famous high cliff headland, with its top stratum of a yellowish colour.

Not long after this holiday Jacquetta and Nicolas returned to Dorset to stay with friends. Christopher had come down from London to join them for a weekend, and there was an air-raid warning. In that tranquil countryside the reality of war seemed bewilderingly far away, and they wondered what in the world they could do that would be of any use. Then, peering out, they noticed their bicycles leaning against the hedge outside the garden gate. Christopher went out, and with feigned solemnity wheeled them into the garden, shutting the gate firmly behind him.

POSTSCRIPT

Monday 26 September 1989

Naturally, Di my dear, you've known ever since you resolved on, and wrote to explain to me, your reasons for wanting the book to be ended in Autumn '39 – though when we talked of it last Tuesday you did agree to have a tailpiece added on. I have thought and thought about all you wrote, and I agree with nearly everything. Nearly, but I have to say not quite.

The book's subtitle, saying what its subject is will be (I think I'm right) 'The Early Life of Christopher Hawkes'. But who IS this person Christopher Hawkes? Is he really so renowned that his name alone will be recognized at once, letting people immediately say, 'Oh yes, this must be that old Professor Hawkes, the archaeologist'? For other archaeologists, or Oxford people, fair enough! but aren't we expecting readers from a wider circle than those? To count on it as enough by itself for recognition would make me feel immodest; and your book doesn't picture me as that. An interesting figure, perhaps, or a figure with an interesting past; but really not a cocky one; I'm not – or at least don't mean to be.

So what I'm putting to you is just this: leave the subtitle as it stands, but end the book by placing me where my identification is easy – at Oxford, where I've lived since 1946.

What I want you to tell, very briefly, are the actual happenings that ended in my placing here as a Prof. And they begin already before, though not very long before, the Autumn of 1939. It's not a long story.

Our Department at the British Museum shared its tea-break with that of Ethnography. Its Assistant Keeper, one Adrian Digby, had been acting as External Examiner for the last three years (from 1935) to the Pitt-Rivers based Oxford Department of Anthropology, which included Prehistory. They were feeling that the next External Examiner ought, for a change, to be Prehistorian. So Digby came back, and just afterwards, at tea, asked me it I'd care to take the job for the next years, 1937–9. I said I would. The Examiners were Tom Penniman, the Pitt-Rivers Curator (an Ethnologist) and Prof. W.E. le Gros Clark (a Physical Anthropologist), and me for the Prehistory. The two of them felt so strongly that Oxford should have a permanent post created, to take care of Prehistoric Archaeology, that our final Examiner's Report contained an outright plea for just this.

It went to the Faculty Board, then up to the General Board. On the way it attracted the attention of E.T. Leeds, who had known me first as an undergraduate, and often visited our B.M. Department. He was the Ashmolean's Keeper of Antiquities by then and so quite a power in the land. He talked about this to Nowell Myres, whose war-work in the Ministry of Food was at Oxford, so that he never left home there; also to J.D. Beazley, soon to be Sir John, the Professor of Classical Archaeology.

In the war years, just as before them, I was able to make occasional visits to Oxford; and had another friendship there, with Colin Hardie and his wife: a tutor at Magdalen, he also took part in Classical Archaeology (he had been Director of the British School at Rome), and also had his war-work in Oxford.

As soon as the course of the war allowed post-war planning to be embarked on, the General Board appointed a Committee to discuss and report on the idea of a new archaeology post. I was privately asked by Myres what I thought should be its title, and answered 'something (lecturer, Reader?) in European Archaeology' – rejecting Prehistoric as too narrow, as there was still no post in Roman, nor in Anglo-Saxon Archaeology. As for its grading: Hardie on one of my visits took me to tea with the Beazleys, J.D.B. walked up and down his lawn with me innumerable times, insisting that if there were to be any such post, it MUST be a Professorship – nothing lower – to stand any chance of University approval. I remember that afternoon very well. There was an overhanging branch in the direct line of Beazley's concentrated pacing; and as he walked me up and down, intent upon his subject, he pushed that branch out of his way each time he passed it rather than altering his course, as most people would have done.

Not long after this Hardie bid me to dinner at the Magdalen High Table. Its President, Sir Henry Tizard, was at the time University Vice-Chancellor. His personal fame was in science and practical engineering – pretty remote from archaeology – but in the Common Room after dinner he sat me beside him, appeared to know everything about me, and put me through a genial but extremely thorough grilling, mostly about what my business in archaeology was all about.

The next thing was, in 1945, the inclusion in the official list of Professorships chosen to be created (and in due course advertised), of a Chair of European Archaeology. At the news, quite early in 1946 (I'd returned to the Museum on 1 January), I of course consulted Tom Kendrick. He said at once that I must put in for it, and so did the Director, Sir John Forsdyke, who let me name him as one of my referees. So I made my applications, C.V. and all. But right up till nearly the end of July I heard nothing. Penniman afterwards explained to me what had happened. They didn't want Gordon Childe to put in for it, which would mean their having to elect him, which they didn't at all want to do. But he was known to be applying for the new Prehistoric Chair in London, and not till he got it did they make their choice of me. Right at the end of the month, going to hang up my house-key in the hall of the

Museum, I found, impaled upon its hook, the telegram from Myres that told me I was elected.

With the Chair came a Fellowship at Keble. I called on the Bursar, C.V. Davidge, in August. He wasn't very keen on professors, but when I told him I wanted to reside, he fixed me rooms, which I entered on the evening of 30 September, after saying goodbye to the Museum that same afternoon.

Now my setting out the story in full like that, is meant to do no more than give you the facts, but vividly enough for you to catch some of the flavour of it. And you can see from it how, down there on the beach at Seatown, I knew already that – granted the war would be won – there was a hopeable prospect of a post-war post at Oxford. Not indeed a professorship, though I had in fact put in for the Chair at Cambridge which went to Dorothy Garrod (with whom Jacquetta had gone to excavate in that cave on Mount Carmel). I was, so to speak, flexing a muscle by applying, encouraged by Jacquetta.

So I plead with you to see how, on that brief sunny holiday at Seatown, I was dreaming even then, because of the Examiner's Report that I had signed, of a future, however remote, which in fact was to turn out better than the dreams. Altogether, how lucky I was!

Chesterton
Thursday 4 October 1989

You're quite right, of course! One shouldn't simply launch a character on to the market without his proper placing and identity. But I have to confess that I didn't (and still cannot) see it as being either cocky or immodest to do so in this way. But I take your point about the need for some sort of conclusion; and as your letter places you at Oxford far more vividly than I could possibly have done, the idea came to me that we might continue this exchange a little further. What about that trip you made to Paris at the end of the war . . .

Walton Street
Friday 12 October 1989

Yes, yes, but you must first hear what happened before that!

For a time that winter I was bidden by my mother (herself away at Farnham) to keep my father company at Campden Hill Square, as Jacquetta was also away. I did the index there for my Prehistoric Europe book, with the piano-top for sorting all the paper slips. My father, working daily as a Registrar at Somerset House, was then Chief Air Raid Warden for the Campden Hill district (only weekending with my mother at Farnham); and onwards from the summer when the bombing began, he was out on the streets at every raid. He was well into his sixties by then, and had only his cook to look after him. It must have been a terrible strain. In fact I was told just last week by my cousin Joan (who was staying here to visit a granddaughter at New College), that one weekend during the war my father appeared as expected at Farnham on the Saturday morning, but looking even more white-faced and exhausted than usual. When asked what had happened, he explained that he had sat up all night holding the hand of a woman who had been trapped in the wreckage of a bombed house. We never found out what happened to the poor woman, but that kindness and concern was typical of him.

Anyway, at last I was ordered to the Ministry of Aircraft Production (I was Secretary to the Air Supply Board from '41 till '43), and I was appointed to serve Sir Eric Bowater as a member of the Ministry's Council. What came of this, early in the summer of '45, was an unexpected visit with him to Paris. Despite Montgomery's armistice with the Germans, Mussolini was expected to go on fighting. Sir Eric was to arrange with the French what planes should be built at their only aircraft factory down in the south-west, near Toulouse.

Sir Eric was very, very grand, and rather pompous. I amused the girls in the office one day by observing that he wore stays – it was quite obvious, actually, that his impressive figure was neatly corsetted. He never appeared at the Ministry on Saturdays, as he needed to devote some time to the paper-making firm of which he was one of the Directors; and for this concession he received no salary from the Ministry.

Well, the Wing Co. and I were invited to Sir Eric's posh mansion somewhere in Surrey, in the general direction of Leatherhead, on the Sunday before our departure for France on Monday morning. He took us for a leisurely stroll round his estate, before the other guests arrived about 6 o'clock – a huge crowd of equally gilded people from other Surrey mansions. It was a very jolly occasion, with plenty of liquid refreshment. In fact it was exceedingly difficult not to get drunk. In fact I had to retreat rather hastily from the dining table. I staggered upstairs to my bedroom, which was luckily furnished with a fine porcelain basin. I was very sick indeed. But this saved me, for I was as right as rain by the next morning. I've no idea how long the party went on, but they must all have been pretty hardened drinkers, as none of them appeared to be any the worse for the excesses of the evening.

After breakfast (bacon and eggs! Great luxury after the privations of rationing) we were driven to Wisley airfield, where there was a small private plane awaiting us. Our first sight of Paris bathed in early sunlight was, for me at any rate, a tear-jerking experience. It was the first time I had been abroad since well before the war. We came down at a little airfield south of Versailles, and were taken to the branch of the M.A.P. where we spent that night. I had to borrow a cake of soap from

Sir Eric. He had two, you see, and soap was very short – so he was able to be generous. He liked that.

The following day we called on the French Minister. I had to remain outside in the outer office. There was a long colloquy, and when he came out Sir Eric announced that he was to be flown next day from Paris to Toulouse, to inspect the aircraft factory. I was to have the day off. They said to me: 'We had set aside a service car for you, with a WRAF driver; as Sir Eric won't be needing transport, would you like the car?' I said I would very much like the car, and could I possibly use the telephone? I got the number of the Musée de St Germain, and asked to speak to M Lantier. All the other officers in the room seemed highly amused that I was speaking French, with a French accent!

I explained to my old friend M Lantier that I had the opportunity to take him and his wife out for a drive in the forest next day, if they would care to come with me.

That night, before Sir Eric left for Toulouse, an Air Commodore friend of his took us, with two fair ladies, to the *Folies Bergère*. That was great fun!

Next morning the car was waiting for me with a very pretty young WRAF driver. We drove all the way to St Germain on its cliff above the Seine, and picked up the Lantiers, who were overjoyed at being taken for a drive. It was the first time they'd been allowed in a car since the collapse of France in the summer of 1940. We went to a beauty spot where the Oise and the Seine join together. Lantier remembered the pretty girl driver and that day out for years afterwards.

When we returned, I was told that I wasn't needed any more, and packed off with a lot of other people who were going on leave, in one of those bombers that had been converted to carry passengers. No portholes. We had to sit in the dark . . .

Chesterton
1 November 1989

Oh dear, that was rather a come-down after the flight out! But it was nice of them to let you have the car.

You must have a lot of wartime memories – what happened to Bersu, by the way? While I was sorting through some of the old files the other day, I came across a bundle of his letters. Many of them were sent from the Internment Camp, somewhat incongruously named Southlands, at Port St Mary. They were censored, of course, and he seems to have been limited to just 25 lines at a time, but he doesn't seem to have suffered unduly; though having said that, it can't have been easy for him. What happened to Maria? He mentions her helping him with the measuring on one of his excavations. Was she in another camp there, on the island, or was she allowed to be with him?

Walton Street
11 November 1989

It was curious reading those letters again after such a long time, and I have to admit that while my memory tends to enhance the good points of my friends who are long dead, it also fades the recollection of their faults. I think I was a little over kind about him, for he could be unpleasant, especially when his sense of humour failed him. Then he was bitter, cynical, and sometimes downright unfair. Phillips thought he was over-fussy, and certainly at Woodbury there were tensions. I've told you about that already. But I can tell you a little more about them both, for I continued to see Maria after Gerhard's death.

Having made their dash to King's Lynn, at the outbreak of the war, they were rescued by Gordon Childe, who brought them to Scotland, where his good friend Thorneycroft had a place, in a Perthshire glen. Police supervision was mild; and it was there that Gerhard finished his Woodbury report.

The summer of 1940, which left Britain facing Germany alone, swept the Bersus (and yes, Maria was with him throughout), into the round-up of German and also Italian refugees for interning in the Isle of Man. His experiences there, as described in Gerhard's letters to me and others, and by word of mouth later on, were not without amusing sides. The Italians, for instance, hoarded their rations of watery jam, and distilled it into a kind of vermouth.

And then there came the time, in the middle years of the war, when the authorities were prevailed upon to recognize, by the Manx Museum and the Society of Antiquaries' President, Sir Alfred Clapham (who spoke for himself, but also for others), that the island had archaeological sites. Moreover, it was realized that excavation of some of these sites by internees would give them suitable employment; and that luckily one of them was eminently fit to conduct it – Bersu himself.

There was a parade at the camp, where volunteers were lined up for marching into town to visit the Museum. The officer in charge, a grey-haired veteran, clearly a stranger to any museum, eyed the ranks (among whom there were learned academics), called them to 'attention', and addressed them with the words, 'I understand that some of you chaps are interested in museums . . .'

'Imagine!' he exclaimed to me afterwards, telling me the story, 'The FACES!' All were struggling with their feelings, especially one of them, the great Paul Jacobsthal.

'That was a PICTURE!' he said.

The renowned professor from Marburg, of Classical Art and Archaeology, interpreter also of Celtic Art, was soon to be one of the many academics who were released. He was allowed to return to the place he had been previously given at Oxford, where in 1944 he was to publish his monumental *Early Celtic Art* – and remained there until his death, a firm friend of my own.

I last saw Bersu in Spain, at Zaragoza. Our host, Professor Antonio Beltran, took us out to a hill-fort, quickly marked by him as resembling one he explored in Switzerland. Next year, invited specially to visit East Germany, he was inspecting the still bombed-out expanses of the old town of Magdeburg, when his fatal stroke fell upon him. Maria lived on, very bravely bearing up, and I continued to keep in touch with her. We met for the last time in Frankfurt. I stayed in a small hotel with one or two other people: we were attending a small conference, I think; and when it was over I went to see Maria. When I left her (I'd ordered a taxi to take me to my train), she turned away to hide her tears, but I had had just a glimpse of them. Getting into the taxi I said to the driver who had watched her turning away, '*Eine Witwe ist immer traurig.*' ['A widow is always sad.'] Driving off he prompty turned his cab wireless to playing doleful music; but as soon as we reached the next street he switched it to a cheerful tune to cheer me up.

Chesterton
25 November 1989

You know, one of the most frustrating things about writing a book like this, which depends so much on the vividness of living memory, is the essential capriciousness of the human power of recall. Just when one is all eagerness for a description of some character or scene, the memory fails. Where there are letters, things can be remedied. And there are, of course, other people's views to draw on. But unlike the early years, when your ability to conjure up a breathtaking pageant carried us along like a small craft on a homing current, the later years are misted over in places; and I feel that it isn't for me to peer too closely through that mist.

I'd have liked to ask you to tell me about your *Prehistoric Foundations*. Not about the book itself, for it is there to be read; but about the actual writing of it. The influences upon you at the time, the pressures and the problems. So when you told me that you could remember almost nothing about the writing of it, except that you wrote most evenings, far into the night, in long-hand first, and then on your father's old typewriter, I was very disappointed. Oh yes, and that it took about two years, and the book was published in the Spring of 1940 on the very day that Holland was invaded!

I realise that much of the book is now out of date, and that it is impertinent, to say the very least, for me to make any comments at all about it. But I have to say that as I read it, knowing little about its subject, what struck me most powerfully was not the content, which I am ill-equipped to judge, but the use of language. It is uncommon to find beautiful writing in a work of scholarship; and I can think of no more appropriate way of ending this book than with these words:

There is no true cleavage between history and prehistory: the verbal distinction between them rests simply on the presence or absence of written material in our equipment for their pursuit. It is indeed often said that 'there are peoples which have no history'. But all peoples have culture which can be assessed and accounted for, and beyond the scope of history this is the business of archaeology, which thus carries out for the peoples of the past the work which anthropology does for those who have remained 'without history' until the present, in its critical sifting of not only diffusion among them, but functional inter-locking within them, of living elements of culture. And the further archaeology can go towards fixing events of the human past in definite order of time, the greater will be its contribution to the anthropologist's, no less than the historian's, knowledge of humanity.

Ultimately prehistory has its natural place in the understanding of the evolution of life as a whole, the scientific appreciation of the adaptiveness which, as its surroundings change, alone offers opportunity for its survival. The sensitive vitality which can so respond supplies the momentum of evolution, by gradual increase of control over environment and its changes, from dependence towards dominance. And the biological climax of evolution has been in man.

The faculty of even the simplest speech could substitute precept for mere example in the training of the singly born children whose slow-passing infancy kept them so long in need of it.

To the hunter vitally dependent upon his hunting, the magic of life and death concerned not his own kind alone, but above all the animal quarry whereon his own kind subsisted. The same inspiration of primary want had impelled his predecessors in Western Europe to what was an animal art essentially, the hunter's spontaneous imagery of the beasts it was his life to kill. The portrayal of the heart, the weapon shown mortally piercing the beast's flank, the outline of the trap around his body, are occasional features which leave no doubt of the reality of this tremendous hunting magic.

The pathetic mystery of death might call for the magical replacement of the departed life-force, which had seemed to reside in the warm vitality of the blood, and in the covering of the bones of the dead with red ochre we may see a rite created to assure them life and warmth renewed, as unseen but still no less powerful members of their tribe.

Thus the collective experience of the human group could become an inheritance handed down the generations by means of that human peculiarity, a spoken language. So the capacity to create and transmit the elements of culture is the direct outcome of man's organic evolution, and thereby that evolution in humanity has been exchanged for cultural progress. It is in this progress that the adaptive vitality of mankind is manifest, and the history of human culture will be its record of achievement.

Primitive man, like the young child in all ages, knows but one all-embracing world: sense and imagination are for him on the same plane of reality. In all things he will see bodies endowed with forces answering to his own, able if it so be to outdo his own, but also perhaps to assist him in his needs and desires. From the remote past of human antiquity this heritage will have accumulated, and in the beliefs and practices therefrom engendered emerges the raw material of the study of primitive religion. That study is here not our direct concern, but it behoves the prehistorian never to forget the deep-seated inner inheritances, which in the long childhood of the mind were interwoven with the whole fabric of humanity's material existance.

And the Europeans, who from their Paleolithic past made a Mesolithic background ready for civilization, and thereon fashioned civilization into a thing of their own, have throughout our story kept that adaptiveness alive, and so have built on foundations whose instability of balance has been the measure of their success under the law of all life.

Christopher Hawkes
Mid-summer 1939

CHRONOLOGY

1905	Charles Francis Christopher Hawkes born on 5 June at 35 de Vere Gardens Kensington.
1906	Spring: the family moves to 17 Campden Hill Square, Kensington.
1907	August: family holiday at Berneval-sur-Mer, near Dieppe, with Mlle Danton (Maddie).
1908	Summer holiday at Alnmouth.
1909	Eleanor Frances Penelope Hawkes born on 1 October.
1910	Summer holiday at Lee, in North Devon.
1911	Summer holiday at Pedlinge, near Hythe in Kent. Autumn: begins at the Norland Place School in Holland Park Avenue.
1912	Summer holiday at Château d'Oex, Vaud, Switzerland.
1913	Summer holiday at Étretat, in Normandy.
1914	War declared on 4 August. Father joins his battalion, the 3rd (Special Reserve) Battalion, Northumberland Fusiliers, at Newcastle. Mother takes the two children to stay with Uncle Frank and Aunt Helen at Backwell, near Bristol. Began first term as boarder at Sandroyd School, Cobham, in Surrey. By Christmas the family had moved to Stratford House, East Boldon, Co. Durham, where father's battalion had by then been stationed.
1915	Moved to Hill Lodge, East Boldon, and afterwards to Lawn Cottage, then the Fairfield, East Boldon.
1916	Visited Durham with his mother, met Canon Greenwell; also cycling holiday with her, visiting places on Hadrian's Wall from Hexham.
1918	Summer: won first scholarship to Winchester College. Autumn: first term at Winchester. Armistice on 11 November. Last Christmas at East Boldon.
1919	Early spring: father's battalion moved to Larkhill Camp on Salisbury Plain. Home moved to Bournemouth. Easter holiday there. Then moved to Redworth House, Amesbury. Late autumn: father demobilized. Family returns to 17 Campden Hill Square.
1920	Summer holiday at Haslemere, Surrey.
1923	December: won Scholarship to New College, Oxford.
1924	First term as freshman at New College.
1925	July: dug with Wheeler at Brecon Gaer.

August: first season digging at St Catharine's Hill, Winchester, with Nowell Myres, Charles Stevens, and others.

1926   April: holiday with his father in Portugal. News of first in Classical Hon. Mods.

July: Dug for Donald Atkinson for two weeks at Wroxeter, Shropshire; then second season at St Catharine's Hill.

September: dug at Alchester near Oxford.

1927   February: played the part of the Earl of Kent in *King Lear* with the OUDS.

Easter holiday in Greece with Emrys Lloyd. Third season at St Catharine's Hill (hillfort begun).

1928   February: death of Maddie.

April: interview for British Museum.

Took Greats in June. Fell in love with Daphne Lambart, while she was visiting Oxford with her sister for the OUDS Ball. Short holiday in N. France immediately after leaving Oxford. Dug with Paul Baillie Reynolds at Caerhūn in N. Wales. Announcement of first in Greats. Final season digging at St Catharine's Hill.

1 September: began work as assistant in the Dept. of British and Medieval Antiquities at the British Museum.

November: became member of Royal Archaeological Institute.

1929   January: engagement to Daphne Lambart announced, but soon broken off.

April: trip to France with Gerald Dunning collecting material for paper on the Belgae.

Summer: excavation at Caerleon at invitation of Tessa Wheeler. Finished his part of St Catharine's Hill report while Myres and Stevens were in South Africa.

Autumn: Title of post at British Museum changed to assistant keeper (second class).

1930   Summer: first season, digging at Colchester (Camulodunum). 'St Catharine's Hill' published by the Hampshire Field Club. 'Belgae of Gaul and Britain' published jointly with Gerald Dunning in *Archaeological Journal* for 1930.

1931   Second summer season digging at Colchester. Met Jacquetta Hopkins, sent to dig for him by her tutor at Cambridge, Miles Burkitt. Buried in trench with visiting Director of Excavations, J.P. Bushe-Fox. Unharmed, but Bushe-Fox seriously injured.

December: trip to Paris for executive committee meeting to prepare for International Congress.

1932   January: elected FSA, proposed by R.G. Collingwood.

April: trip to Berne for final preparatory meeting for Congress. 1st International Congress for Pre- and Proto-historic Sciences, held at King's College, London, in first week of August.

1933   April: invited to a meeting of a German archaeological body at Groningen, hosted by A.E. Van Giffen. Travelled afterwards to visit museums in West Germany and Belgium.

October: marriage to Jacquetta Hopkins in Trinity College, Cambridge. Honeymoon in Majorca.

December: Country Life book on Winchester College published.

1934   Summer: with Jacquetta dug for Olwen Brogan at Gergovia, followed by touring holiday in France.

1935   Summer: excavated with Jacquetta at Buckland Rings, near Lymington in the New Forest, for the Hampshire Field Club.

1936   2nd International Congress at Oslo. Afterwards, holiday with Jacquetta on Gotland.

1937   Son Nicolas born in London on 9 August. Family holiday at Winchester.

1938   Promoted assistant keeper (first class) at British Museum.

Summer: excavation for the Hampshire Field Club at Quarley Hill, with Jacquetta.

1939   Summer: excavation at Bury Hill, near Andover, for the Hampshire Field Club.

3 September: War declared. Supervised storage of material from British Museum in empty tube station at Aldwych. Afterwards brief holiday on Dorset coast with Jacquetta and Nicolas.

1940   April: *Prehistoric Foundations of Europe* published by Methuen.

August: transferred to Ministry of Aircraft Production.

1945   31 December: left Ministry of Aircraft Production

1946   1 January: returned to British Museum.

Late July: elected Professor of European Archaeology at Oxford, with a Fellowship of Keble College. Took up post on 1 October, living in rooms in college.

1947   *Camulodunum* published by the Society of Antiquaries.

1948   July: made a Fellow of the British Academy, recommended by Gordon Childe.

1950   April: 1st Congress of Mediterranean Archaeology in Florence. President of Council for British Archaeology (till 1954, when gave the presidential address).

Summer: 3rd International Congress at Zurich. Balearic Summer School. Contracted paratyphoid; in Isolation Hospital in Oxford for two months.

1951   February: Presidential Address to the Prehistoric Society.

Summer: Meeting of Prehistoric Society in Dublin, after holiday with Jacquetta and Nicolas in Co. Kerry.

1952   Last holiday with Jacquetta and Nicolas, cycling in New Forest.

1953   June: Marriage dissolved.

September till following February: first George Grant McCurdy Lecturer at Harvard.

1954   16 March: elected to Honorary Membership of Royal Irish

Academy in Dublin, in the section of Polite Literature and Antiquities.

Summer: 4th International Congress in Madrid.

1955   Leverhulme Research Fellow. Travelled in Europe while still teaching at Oxford during term.

Summer: Research Laboratory for Archaeology and History of Art set up at Keble Road. Secretary of this (ex officio as Professor of European Archaeology).

1956   Death of father, C.P. Hawkes, in London in his eightieth year.

1957   Presidential address to Section H of the British Association in Dublin.

1958   5th International Congress at Hamburg. Travelled in East Germany, Italy and France.

December: with Sonia Chadwick, curator of the Scunthorpe Musuem, at a conference at the London Institute of Archaeology (they had previously met on two occasions in London).

1959   30 January: married Sonia Chadwick in Oxford.

1961   Became a Visitor at the Ashmolean Museum, Oxford (till 1967). Moved to the Priory, Dorchester-on-Thames.

1962   6th International Congress in Rome.

1966   7th International Congress in Prague. Death of mother, E.V. Hawkes, in her 93rd year.

1969   Moved to 19 Walton Street, Oxford.

1971   23 July: French Honorary Doctorate conferred at 4th International Congress of Celtic Studies at Rennes.

1972   March: Irish Hon. D. Litt. conferred at Dublin.

April: British Council Visiting Professor in Budapest.

30 September: retired from Oxford University and subsequently made Professor Emeritus.

1973   *Prehistoric Foundations of Europe* reprinted.

1974   Summer: Guest Professor at University of Munich.

1976   Summer: 9th International Congress at Nice.

1981   April: received Society of Antiquaries of London gold medal.

1989   Contributed to *The Pastmasters, Eleven Modern Pioneers of Archaeology*, edited by Glyn Daniel and Christopher Chippindale (Thames and Hudson), pp. 46–60.

NOTES

1 Prologue

1. C.F.C. Hawkes, 'Archaeological Retrospects 3', *Antiquity*, LVI (1982). With acknowledgement to Paul Morgan of the Bodleian Library, Oxford, where he had come upon Holyoake's own autobiography.
2. Matthew Holbeche Bloxham, FSA, wrote *Antiquities of Warwickshire* (1875). He published a number of other volumes.
3. I, iii, issued in 1843; then in the whole volume of 1848, with Pl. XIV an engraving of the finds. Also *Victoria County History: Warwickshire* (1904), p. 202. See also Gerloff (1975), p. 172 and Pl. 27, No. 332.
4. Letter from Charles Samuel Hawkes to Frances Richards shortly after their marriage in 1868.
5. Letter from J.P. Richards dated 19 June 1868.
6. Charles Langbridge Morgan (1894–1958), novelist, critic and dramatist, was the author of *Portrait in a Mirror* (1929), *The Fountain* (1932), *Sparkenbroke* (1936), *A Voyage* (1940), *The Empty Room* (1941), *The Judge's Story* (1947), and *The River Line* (1949, adapted as a play in 1952).
7. Richard Thomas Church (1893–1972), poet, novelist and critic, and Vice-President of the Royal Society of Literature. Born in London, he was three times married, and was made a CBE in 1957.
8. *Over the Bridge: an Essay in Autobiography* (William Heinemann, 1955).
9. *Over the Bridge*, p. 195.
10. Ibid.
11. Ibid., p. 196.
12. *Heydays: A Salad of Memories and Impressions* (Methuen, 1933), p. 1. The book bears a dedication to Rudyard Kipling, with whom the author had a brief but very cordial correspondence, and whom he knew at the Garrick Club.
13. Ibid., p. 2.
14. Ibid.
15. Sir Bernard Partridge (1861–1945), *Punch* artist and cartoonist. He was knighted in 1925.
16. George Louis Lapmella Busson Du Maurier (1834–96), writer and illustrator, born in Paris, creator of the character, Svengali.

17. Sir John Tenniel (1820–1914), artist and cartoonist, who joined the staff of *Punch* in 1850, and drew over 2,000 cartoons; illustrated Lewis Carroll's *Alice in Wonderland* (1865) and *Alice Through the Looking-Glass* (1872). He was knighted in 1893.

18. Oscar Browning (1837–1923), a pupil of W.J. Cory at Eton, then assistant master there from 1860 to 1875, and later President of the British Academy of Arts in Rome. He was the author of *A History of the Modern World 1815–1910* (1912), *A General History of the World* (1913), and *A Short History of Italy* (1917).

19. Arthur Woolgar Verrall (1851–1912), Professor of English Literature and Fellow of Trinity College, Cambridge. He edited several Classical Greek plays.

20. Sir John Emerich Edward d'Alberg Acton, 8th Baronet and 1st Baron Acton (1834–1902), historian. Born at Naples of a Catholic family from Shropshire, he was Regius Professor of Modern History and Fellow of Trinity College, Cambridge, from 1895 until his death. His library of 59,000 volumes was purchased from the family and presented to Cambridge University in 1903.

21. C.P. Hawkes, *Heydays*, p. 32.

22. Ibid., p. 23.

23. Ibid., p. 34.

24. Ibid., p. 201.

25. Ibid. p. 205.

26. Edward Tennyson Reed (1860–1933), caricaturist on the staff of *Punch* from 1890 to 1912.

27. C.P. Hawkes, *Heydays*, p. 206.

28. James Kenneth Stephen (1859–92), always called 'J.K.S.', was the author of some brilliant light verse collected in *Lapsus Calami* and *Quo Musa Tendis*, published in 1896.

29. Advice given to C.P. by Sir Edward Parry. See *Heydays*, p. 128.

30. C.P. Hawkes, *The London Comedy* (Medici Society, 1925), p. 183.

31. C.P. Hawkes, 'Trusty and Well Beloved' in *Heydays*, pp. 68–72.

32. Richard Burdon, Viscount Haldane (1856–1928), FRS (1906), FBA (1914), statesman, lawyer and philosopher. He was created Lord Chancellor in the Labour administration in 1924.

33. The Downs are the waters between the Goodwin Sands and the east coast of Kent.

34. Frederick Cobb was born on 6 February 1796 and he died on 2 September 1883. He was one of the few doctors who remained in London, at the London Hospital, during the cholera epidemic in the autumn of 1832.

35. Their first child Cicely was born in 1878; Harry the following year; Audrey in 1880; Stanley in 1881; Madge (who lived to within a year of her 100th birthday) in 1883; Frederick in 1885; and finally Hester in 1888.

36. Each of the two girls received a sum of around £30,000, which gave them an assured income of £1,000 a year.

2   Childhood, 1905–12

1.   C.P. Hawkes, *The London Comedy*, p. 227.
2.   The next village to their home at Barrow Gurney.
3.   John and Amy Brooke-Little often visited Backwell. These entries were made on 5 and 24 August.
4.   C.P. Hawkes, *The London Comedy*, p. 199.
5.   C.P. Hawkes, 'Requiem', in *The London Comedy*, p. 227.
6.   Giles St Aubyn, *Edward VII: Prince and King* (Collins, 1979), pp. 472–81.
7.   C.P. Hawkes, *Heydays*, p. 82. However, O.G.S Crawford spent that day walking the Roman road from Dibden Purlieu to Stone on the Solent, and he writes in his autobiography, *Said and Done* (Weidenfeld & Nicolson, 1955) that it was a wet day: 'we arrived at the farm drenched to the skin'(pp. 76–7). This walk with Williams Freeman ultimately led to the Ordnance Survey map of Roman Britain.
8.   Norland Place School was established in 1876 in the existing buildings, 162–6 Holland Park Avenue, which it still occupies.

3   Childhood, 1912–14

1.   Sir James Matthew Barrie (1860–1937), novelist and playwright. He was made a baronet in 1913 and an OM in 1922. He was also Lord Rector of St Andrews (1919), and the author of many novels and plays besides *Peter Pan* (1904), including *The Admirable Crichton* (1902), *What Every Woman Knows* (1908), *Dear Brutus* (1917), and *Mary Rose* (1920).
2.   The friendship between Barrie and his wife Mary, who later divorced him to marry Gilbert Cannan, and Arthur Llewellyn-Davies and his beautiful wife Sylvia, was of such complexity that it is impossible to describe in a few words. It is most sensitively and fully documented by Janet Dunbar in her biography of the playwright, *J.M. Barrie: The Man Behind the Image* (Collins, 1970). The two youngest Llewellyn-Davies boys, Michael and Nicholas, went to the Norland Place School. Michael was eleven years older than Christopher, though, and it was only Nico, who was two years older, who took part in these cricket matches in the Square.
3.   The royalties from *Peter Pan* and all related books were left in perpetuity to the Great Ormond Street Hospital for Children.
4.   Cynthia Asquith, *Portrait of Barrie* (James Barrie, 1954), p. 10.
5.   Ibid., p. 2.
6.   Ibid.
7.   Ibid., p. 7.
8.   Ibid., p. 137.
9.   Ibid., p. 19.

10. Charles Robert Owen Medley, painter and theatrical designer, was born on 19 December 1905 and made a CBE in 1982. At Greshams School he was a contemporary of W.H. Auden; and it was he who suggested that Auden should write poetry, in 1922. Auden later wrote:

> Kicking a little stone, he turned to me
> And said, 'Tell me, do you write poetry?'
> I never had, and said so, but I knew
> That very moment what I wished to do.

Quoted by Humphrey Carpenter in *W.H. Auden: A Biography* (George Allen & Unwin, 1981), p. 28.

11. From C.P. Hawkes, 'Trusty and Well-Beloved', an essay in *Heydays*. The exercise was headed by General Allenby, and many well-known figures took part, including Winston Churchill and F.E. Smith. C.P. published drawings of these great men in the volume, which was received very well by both press and public.

12. Prince Louis Alexander of Battenberg (1854–1921), cousin of King George V. He became a British subject in 1868, and was First Sea Lord from 1912 to 1914. At the king's request he assumed the name of Mountbatten in 1917, and was created Marquess of Milford Haven that same year.

13. On 12 August 1915, a year after the event, Churchill wrote a letter to the prince stating that he had specifically asked him not to allow the fleet to disperse. Prince Louis replied at once, by letter, denying this. (See Martin Gilbert, *Winston Churchill*, vol. 3, p. 5.)

14. An attempt was made by Christopher's mother and aunts to use the nickname 'Kit' which he hated. Aunt Madge persisted with the awful abbreviation to the end of her life, but Christopher did manage to prevent its wider use, and has always been known by his full name.

15. From C.P. Hawkes, 'Trusty and Well-Beloved', *Heydays*.

16. 'Neil Johnson-Ferguson is a very sensible chap, with a slight turn for engineering. He has red hair and spectacles. He cannot sing a note but is good at mathematics. He gets a rotten time here – everybody rags him. Why, I can't think, he's such a nice chap. . . .' So wrote Christopher in a letter to his mother dated 8 July 1917.

17. A break in the end of the ulna and radius, the bones in the forearm, near the wrist. Named after the Irish surgeon Abraham Colles (1773–1843).

4   Sandroyd, 1914–18

1. Charles Harry St John Hornby (1867–1946), also educated at Harrow and New College, Oxford, founded the Ashendene Press (1895–1935), which published forty major works. He collected

medieval and Renaissance manuscripts and books. In later years he was the devoted admirer of Mavis de Vere Cole, who became Sir Mortimer Wheeler's second wife in 1939.

2. Some time after his retirement Mr Shortt did, in fact, marry very happily.

3. Arthur Michael Ramsay (1904–88), bishop and archbishop, was created Baron of Canterbury (Life Peer) in 1974, and an Honorary Fellow of the British Academy in 1983. He was a trustee of the British Museum from 1963 to 1969.

4. Rt. Revd Roger Plumpton Wilson, born on 3 August 1905, went on to study at Winchester and Keble College, Oxford. He was ordained in 1936, and was Bishop of Wakefield from 1949 to 1958 and Bishop of Chichester from 1958 to 1974.

5. Katie and Lola both met their husbands on a trip to India in about 1910. Graham Snow was already in his fifties when war broke out.

6. From an unpublished memoir of G.L. Cheesman by P.J. Campbell, who was taught by Cheesman at New College, and whose family were his closest friends. Campbell was later Headmaster of Westminster School. The Cheesman papers are in the Bodleian Library.

7. Frederic Cobb was the fifth child of Charles Davison Cobb by his second wife, Clara. Ellie was especially close to him.

8. John Masefield, *Gallipoli* (William Heinemann, 1916), p. 5.

9. Ibid., p. 84.

10. John North, *Gallipoli, The Fading Vision* (1936, reprinted 1966), p. 71.

11. Ibid., p. 43.

12. Kenneth Guy Jack Charles Knowles (1908–88), after a spell in schoolmastering, went to University College, Nottingham, where he lectured in social history and economics in the Extramural Department. He was bursar of the newly established St Cross College at Oxford from 1965 to 1972. On his retirement he devoted his considerable energies and artistic ability to glass engraving, producing many beautiful commemorative pieces, as well as several church windows. He was four times married, and had six children.

13. J. Collingwood Bruce, *Handbook to the Roman Wall* (13th edition, edited and enlarged by Charles M. Daniels, 1978), p. 109.

14. Ibid., p. 105. The turret (26a) was examined in 1959 and produced two levels of occupation, but no finds later than the second century.

15. Sir Charles Leonard Woolley (1880–1960), archaeologist, dug at: Carchemish (1912–14, and 1919); Sinai (1914); Tel el Amarna (1921–2); Ur (1922–34). He is the author of *The Sumerians* (1929), *Digging up the Past* (1930) and *Ur of the Chaldees* (1934).

16. Francis John Haverfield (1860–1919), Roman historian and archaeologist, scholar of Winchester and New College, Oxford, and

Camden Professor of Ancient History and Fellow of Brasenose (1907–19). He created the scientific study of Roman Britain. His works include *The Romanization of Roman Britain* (1905) and *The Roman Occupation of Britain* (posthumously edited by Sir George Macdonald, 1924).

17. G.L.(Leonard) Cheesman (1884–1915) was born at Hove, Sussex. He won a scholarship to Winchester, where he was taught by M.J. Rendall, who complained that he spent too much time reading books not required for his school work. He went up to New College in 1903, and afterwards became fellow and tutor there in ancient history. He is the author of *The Auxilia of the Roman Army* (OUP, 1914). On the outbreak of war he was commissioned in the Hampshire Regiment and posted to Gallipoli, where he was killed on 10 August 1915. His death was said to have hastened Haverfield's death, as he was devoted to Cheesman, whom he was grooming to take his place.

18. Jocelyn Plunket Bushe-Fox (1880–1954) dug at Wroxeter (1912–14), Hengistbury Head (1911–12), Swarling (1921) and Richborough (1922–39). He became an Inspector of Ancient Monuments in 1920, and was Chief Inspector from 1933 until 1945. He was made a CBE in 1945.

19. C.F.C. Hawkes, 'Archaeological Retrospects 3', *Antiquity* LVI (1982), p. 94. The article is reprinted in Glyn Daniel and Christopher Chippindale, ed., *The Pastmasters, Eleven Modern Pioneers of Archaeology* (Thames and Hudson, 1989).

20. William Greenwell (1820–1918), Canon of Durham, was Librarian to the Dean and Chapter from 1862 until 1907, and rector of St Mary the Less in Durham from 1865 until his death. He was made a Fellow of the Royal Society in 1878.

21. William George Armstrong, Baron Armstrong of Cragside (1810–1900), born in Newcastle, was the inventor of the improved hydraulic engine in 1842, which generated electricity from steam.

22. See below, p. 68.

5 Winchester, 1918–24

1. J.d'E. Firth, *Rendall of Winchester: The Life and Witness of a Teacher* (OUP, 1954), p. 88. The quotation is from Rendall's own autobiography, which he was writing at the time of his death.

2. Montague John Rendall (1852–1950), born at Great Rollright in Oxfordshire, was the fourth of the nine sons of Revd Henry Rendall and his wife, Ellen Harriette, née Davey. A scholar of Harrow and Trinity College, Cambridge, he joined the staff of Winchester College in 1887, and was second master from 1903 to 1911 and headmaster from 1911 to 1924. He was Governor of the BBC from 1927 to 1932, and was made a CMG in 1931.

3. Kenneth Clark, *Another Part of the Wood* (John Murray, 1974), p. 61.

4. Ibid., p. 61.

5. C.F.C. Hawkes, *Winchester College* (Country Life, 1933), p. 16.

6. Hubert Murray Burge (1862–1925), born at Kingston, Jamaica, was headmaster of Repton College from 1900 to 1901, and of Winchester from 1901 to 1911. He was Bishop of Southwark from 1911 to 1919 and Bishop of Oxford from 1919 to 1925.

7. Firth, *Rendall of Winchester*, p. 103.

8. Ibid., p. 76.

9. Ibid., p. 104.

10. Ibid.

11. Ibid. The headmaster received £3,500 a year.

12. Ibid., p. 91.

13. Ibid., p. 239.

14. Ibid., p. 250.

15. Clark, *Another Part of the Wood*, p. 60.

16. J.d'E. Firth, *Winchester* (Blackie & Son, 1936), p. 81.

17. A game peculiar to the school which is played on a long, narrow strip of ground 80 yd long, 30 yd wide. Each side is framed with iron posts with netting to keep the ball in. There is a row of posts at 10 ft intervals, with a rope through holes at the top. The whole of the end of the pitch is the 'goal'. Although played with a round ball it is more like rugby than soccer. The players are divided into the Hot and the Hot-watchers, and the Hot are the scrum. There are two forms of the game, fifteen-a-side and six-a-side.

18. By the mid-thirties both terms were used indiscriminately in accordance with modern practice. In the eighteenth century boys were officially referred to as 'the children'. Firth, *Winchester*, p. 145.

19. Rex Herdman, *Winchester During and After the First World War 1916–1921* (privately printed, 1970), p. 61.

20. Cloisters were also a place of burial.

21. Lester Simpson-Gray later joined the colonial service, and perished, as did Uncle Fred, at the hands of the Japanese, after the fall of Singapore in 1941.

22. There were also separate colours for those in College and for 'Commoners'.

23. From Christopher's first letter to his father from Winchester, dated 10 October 1918, 10 p.m.

24. Firth, *Winchester*, p. 144.

25. There were also four War Scholars: one named Howell, and three White Russian refugees, Zvegintzov, Orloff-Davidoff and Volkoff.

26. C.F.C. Hawkes, *Winchester College*, p. 19.

27. Firth, *Winchester*, p. 149.

28. Alexei Brusilov (1856–1926), Russian Commander-in-Chief from June to August 1917. His troops mutinied, and Kornilov took his place.

29. Alexander Kerensky (born in 1881), a Russian revolutionary born at Simbirsk, studied law in Leningrad and took a leading part in the Revolution in 1917, becoming Minister of Justice first, and then Premier in July. He crushed Kornilov's revolt in September, but was deposed two months later by the Bolsheviks, and fled to France. He went to Australia in 1940, and to America in 1946.

30. Sir William Searle Holdsworth (1871–1944), lawyer, was educated at Dulwich and New College, Oxford, and was called to the Bar in 1896. He was a Fellow of St John's College, Oxford (1897), All Souls Reader in English Law (1910), and Vinerian Professor (1922–44). He became a Fellow of the British Academy in 1922, was knighted in 1929, and was awarded the OM in 1943.

31. Firth, *Rendall of Winchester*, p. 169.

32. Nicholas I (1796–1855), son of Paul I, married the daughter of Frederick William III of Prussia. He succeeded to the throne on the death of his brother Alexander I in 1825. He died during the Crimean War, his reign being marked by cruelty and despotism.

33. The famous novel by Thomas Hughes (1822–96) which was published in 1857. It is the story of an ordinary schoolboy at Rugby under the headmastership of Dr Arnold (who was himself a Wykehamist). The story shows the cruelty of the loyalties that were so much a part of the public school way of life. The book had considerable influence. Hughes had been educated at Rugby, and at Oriel College, Oxford.

34. Courtenay Edward Stevens (1905–76). He took a first in Greats at New College, Oxford, and in 1933 he was appointed a research fellow of Magdalen. One of his notable achievements during the war was the suggestion of the use of the first four notes of Beethoven's Fifth symphony – 'V' in Morse code – to introduce the BBC Radio transmissions to occupied Europe. After the war he returned to Magdalen as official Fellow and Tutor in Ancient History, and Vice-President (1950–1).

35. A letter from Christopher to his mother dated 15 December 1918.

36. D.C. Somervell, *The Reign of George V* (Faber and Faber, 1935), p. 199.
    Winston Churchill, who was newly appointed to the War Office 'scrapped his predecessor's scheme and set to work demobilizing at a rate of 50,000 a day – priority being given to length of service and number of wounds. It was estimated that 900,000 should be retained' (Ibid., p. 207).

37. Humphrey Carpenter, *J.R.R. Tolkien* (George Allen and Unwin, 1977), p. 247.

38. Somervell, *The Reign of George V*, p. 199.

39. The 46,000 ton British liner of the White Star Line. Thought to be unsinkable, she carried only enough lifeboats for half of the 2,224 passengers she carried on her maiden voyage. On the night of 14/15 April 1912 she struck an iceberg near Newfoundland. She sank,

with the loss of 1,513 lives. The wreck was located and photographed by divers in 1985.

40. On 1 September 1915 the monument was sold, along with thirty acres of surrounding downland, as lot 15 of the Amesbury Abbey estate, formerly owned by Sir Edmund Antrobus. It was sold for £6,600, to a Mr C.H. Chubb.
41. Grace, the wife of the second master A.T.P. Williams, presumably extended a friendly invitation, with the suggestion of some extra pupils, which Maddie rather ungraciously seems to have refused.
42. Osbert Guy Stanhope Crawford (1886–1957).
43. *Said and Done* (Weidenfeld & Nicolson, 1955), p. 12.
44. Ibid., p. 103.
45. Ibid., p. 306.
46. Ibid., p. 307.
47. Letter dated 9 May 1922 from the Ordnance Survey office in Southampton.
48. A letter from Christopher to his mother dated 19 October 1918.
49. A letter from Christopher to his mother dated 7 May 1921.
50. Old Wykehamists were allowed to stand on their chairs for the singing of 'Domum', the school song. Others had to stand in front of their seats.
51. A letter from Christopher to his mother dated 28 July 1921.
52. A letter from Christopher to his mother dated 6 December 1921.
53. An organization for Christian fellowship, founded at Poperinghe in Belgium (eight miles west of Ypres) in 1915, by the Revd P.T.B. (Tubby) Clayton, as a military chapel and club. It was named Talbot House after Gilbert Talbot (1891–1915), the youngest son of the Bishop of Winchester, who was killed in action. Toc H is the army signaller's designation of the initials T.H.
54. Revd Philip Thomas Byard Clayton (1885–1972), educated at St Paul's School and Exeter College, Oxford, became chaplain to King George V and to George VI, and extra chaplain to Queen Elizabeth. He was created a Companion of Honour in 1933.
55. R.L.A. Du Pontet, a French-speaking Swiss, Latin scholar; and the son of an abbé, taught the upper school composition, prose and verse.
56. Maurice Platnauer, who became a tutor and finally Principal of Brasenose College, Oxford.
57. Frank Carter taught classics to the Junior VI. He had formerly been Professor of Classics at a Canadian university. Appointed by Burge at the beginning of the century, he retired during Christopher's time at Winchester.
58. Malcolm Robertson, nicknamed the 'Bobber', was a major in command of the OTC.
59. Horace Jackson, captain of C Company. He collected Orientalia.
60. Adam Carse, who taught music to the lower school, under Dr Sweeting.

61. Mr Humby, a physics teacher who served in the OTC as a captain.
62. Mr Quirk, a housemaster who had formerly been captain of boats at Eton. He had a large, domed, bald head.
63. The letter, to C.P., bears only the date of 21 July but it was almost certainly written in 1923.
64. Herbert Albert Laurens Fisher (1865–1940), historian, statesman, and Warden of New College, Oxford (1915–40), was Vice-Chancellor of Sheffield University (1912–16) and President of the Board of Education (1916–22), MP for the Hallam district of Sheffield (1916–18) and for the Combined English Universities (1918–26). He was made an FBA in 1907, an FRS in 1920, and an OM in 1937.
65. A letter from Christopher to his father, written on 27 November 1923.
66. J.d'E. Firth, 'Budge' as he was always known, had been prefect of hall in the summer of 1918, and he returned to Winchester some years later to become a chaplain. His two works, *Rendall of Winchester: The Life and Times of a Teacher* (OUP, 1954) and *Winchester* (Blackie & Son) have already been quoted from earlier in this chapter.
67. Richard Howard Stafford Crossman (1907–74) gained a first class degree in Mods and Greats at New College, Oxford. He was Fellow and Tutor at New College (1930–7), lecturer for Oxford University Delegacy of Extramural Studies, and for the WEA (1938–40), assistant editor of the *New Statesman* (1938–55), Minister of Housing and Local Government in the Labour government (1964–6), and Leader of the House (1966–8).
68. William Empson (1906–84), poet, born in Yorkshire. After Winchester he went to Magdalen College, Cambridge. He became Professor of English Literature at Bunrika Daigaku, Tokyo (1931–34), Professor of English Literature at Peking National University (1937–9), BBC Chinese Editor (1941–6), and Professor of English Literature at Sheffield University from 1953.
69. John Hanbury Angus Sparrow, born in 1906, was a scholar at Winchester, and at Oxford gained a first class honours degree in Mods (1927) and in Lit. Hum. (1929). He was a Fellow of All Souls, Oxford (1929, re-elected 1937 and 1946), was called to the Bar at Middle Temple (1931), and practised in Chancery Division (1931–9). He was commissioned in the Coldstream Guards in 1940, having enlisted in 1939 in the Oxford and Buckinghamshire Light Infantry, and worked in the War Office from 1942–5. He was awarded the OBE in 1946 and made Warden of All Souls College, Oxford, in 1952.
70. Edward Stuart Talbot (1844–1934), educated at Charterhouse and Christ Church, Oxford, became Bishop, successively, of Rochester, Southwark and Winchester. He was the first Warden of Keble, from 1869 to 1888.

6 Oxford, 1924–5

1. University College was founded in 1249, Merton in 1264, Balliol between 1263 and 1268, Gloucester College (which became Worcester in 1714) in 1298, Exeter in 1314, Oriel in 1326, and Queen's in 1340.
2. James Wyatt (1747–1813) also rose to fame on account of his design for the Pantheon in London (now destroyed), which was based on Hagia Sophia in Istanbul. He also restored both Salisbury and Durham Cathedrals.
3. William Beckford (1760–1844) He inherited a vast fortune at the age of eleven, on the death of his father, and he spent his life collecting art, travelling in Europe and writing. He published a number of travel books, and a classic 'Gothic' novel, 'Vathek' in 1782. He had a good eye for pictures, and it was he who bought Gibbon's library after the historian's death in 1794.
4. Sir George Gilbert Scott (1811–78) restored many churches and cathedrals including Westminster Abbey. Among his original buildings are the Government Offices in Whitehall (1861), the Albert Memorial (1864), and St Pancras Station (1865).
5. Sir Giles Gilbert Scott (1880–1960), famous for his design of the Anglican cathedral in Liverpool.
6. The New Bodleian was built on the north-east corner of Broad Street. When King George VI came to open it, the presentation key he was given to use for the ceremony snapped in the lock. At which he remarked, 'Britain can make it, but I can break it.' The key was forcibly turned from within by the porter.
7. Jennifer Sherwood and Nikolaus Pevsner, *The Buildings of England: Oxfordshire* (Penguin Books, 1974), p. 168.
8. He was Warden of New College from 1903 till early February 1925, having been Dean of New College from 1867 till 1889. He was ordained in 1872. He retired to north Oxford, where he died in 1930.
9. Julian Huxley, *Memories* (George Allen & Unwin, 1970), p. 136.
10. Ibid.
11. A.H. Smith, *New College Oxford and its Buildings* (OUP, 1952), p. 140.
12. Ibid., p. 141.
13. Julian Huxley, *Memories*, p. 136.
14. Smith, *New College Oxford and its Buildings*, p. 143.
15. The terms at Oxford are Michaelmas (autumn) after the feast of St Michael and All Saints at the end of October; Hilary (spring) after the fourth-century saint, Hilary of Poitiers, whose feast-day is in mid-January: and Trinity (summer) after Trinity Sunday, the first Sunday after Whitsun.
16. Emlyn Williams, *George, an Early Autobiography* (Hamish Hamilton, 1961), p. 302.
17. Sir Hugh Percy Allen (1869–1946), organist and Fellow of New

College from 1901 to 1918, then Fellow and Heather Professor of Music (the chair was founded by William Heather in 1626) from 1918 until his death and Director of the Royal College of Music in London from 1918 until 1937. He was knighted in 1920, made a KCVO in 1928 and a GCVO in 1935.

18. Bowra, *Memories*, p. 109.

19. Sir George Gilbert Aimé Murray (1866–1957), who made brilliant verse translations of the plays of Aeschylus, Sophocles, Euripides and Aristophanes. He stood for parliament several times, and from 1923 to 1938 he was Chairman of the League of Nations Union. He was a Fellow of the British Academy, and the Royal Society of Literature and was awarded the OM in 1941. He is buried in Westminster Abbey.

20. William Schwenk Gilbert (1836–1911), who met Arthur Sullivan in 1870, forwhom he wrote the libretti of fourteen popular operettas. He built and owned the Garrick Theatre and was knighted in 1907.

21. J. Huxley, *Memories*, p. 139.

22. Sir Adrian Cedric Boult (1889–1983), conductor, was a pupil of Arthur Nikisch. He was conductor of the BBC Symphony Orchestra from 1930 to 1949, and the London Philharmonic from 1949 to 1957. He was knighted in 1937.

23. Jenkyn was the butler in a well-known cigarette advertisement.

24. Named after Edward Bouverie Pusey (1800–82), leader of the Oxford Movement after Newman's conversion to Roman Catholicism. A Fellow of Oriel College, he was ordained in 1828, in the same year that he was made Regius Professor of Hebrew at Oxford.

25. Sir Jack Allan Westrup (1904–75), educated at Dulwich College and Balliol, was director of the Oxford Music Club, and of the Opera Club (in 1927). He returned to Dulwich to teach classics (1928–34), and was assistant music critic on the *Daily Telegraph* till 1940. He was Barber Professor of Music at Birmingham University (1942–6) and Heather Professor of Music at Oxford from 1947 till his death. He was knighted in 1961.

26. Sir John Linton Myres (1870–1954). Educated at Winchester and New College. After travels in Greece and the Near East settled in Oxford as a don at Christ Church. He then became lecturer in Ancient Geography, and afterwards Gladstone Professor of Greek, at Liverpool University. Elected Wykeham Professor of Ancient History at Oxford (1910–39). He was knighted in 1943.

27. J. Collingwood Bruce, *The Handbook to the Roman Wall* (7th edition, edited by Robert Blair), p. 179.

28. Michael Ivanovitch Rostovtzeff (1872–1953) was born and educated at Kiev. In 1903 he became Professor of Ancient History at St Petersburg Imperial University. He left Russia in 1918, never to return. After two years at Oxford he went to America, where he

remained for the rest of his life, becoming Professor of Ancient History, first at Wisconsin, and then, in 1925, at Yale. He published many books, among them *The Social and Economic History of the Roman Empire* (1926), a *History of the Ancient World* (1926–7) and *The Social and Economic History of the Hellenistic World*.

29. Sir Mortimer Wheeler, *Still Digging* (Michael Joseph, 1955), p. 73.
30. *Antiquaries Journal* VI (1926), pp. 45–53.
31. Wheeler, *Still Digging*, p. 73.
32. A letter from Christopher to his mother, 18 February 1925.
33. A letter from Christopher to his mother dated 11 December 1925.
34. Sir William Henry Harris (born in 1883), organ scholar at the Royal College of Music in 1899, organist at New College (1919–28), conductor of the Oxford Bach Choir (1926–33), organist at St George's Chapel, Windsor (1933–61), and Director of Musical Studies at the Royal School of Church Music (1956–61). He was knighted in 1954.
35. A letter from Christopher to his mother dated 15 May 1925.
36. Jacquetta Hawkes, *Mortimer Wheeler, An Adventurer in Archaeology* (Weidenfeld & Nicolson, 1982), p. 90.
37. Ibid.
38. Ibid., p. 91.
39. R.E.M. Wheeler, 'The Roman Fort Near Brecon', published in *Y Cymmrodor* (the magazine of the Honourable Society of Cymmrodorion), XXXVII (1926).
40. Sir William Matthew Flinders Petrie (1853–1942) discovered the early royal tombs at Abydos, Pre-Dynastic cultures, the Hyksos, and the Sinaitic monuments. He introduced sequence dating to Egyptian pottery, and revolutionized excavation methods. He was knighted in 1923.
41. His earlier plans to go to Egypt had to be shelved because of hostilities between the British under Sir Garnet Wolseley, and the rebel general, Arabi Pasha, which ended on 13 September 1882 with the battle of Tel-el-Kebir. Arabi Pasha fled towards Cairo, and his army was broken up. Thousands were killed or taken prisoner. The British entered Cairo on the following day.
42. Margaret S. Drower, *Flinders Petrie, A Life in Archaeology* (Victor Gollancz, 1985).

7 St Catharine's Hill Excavation

1. C.F.C. Hawkes, J.N.L. Myres, C. Stevens, 'St Catharine's Hill, Winchester', *Proceedings of the Hampshire Field Club and Archaeological Society*, XI (The Wykeham Press, 1930), p. 193.
2. John Leland, *Itinerary* (2nd edn), pp. 3, 87; *V.C.H. Hampshire*, vol. 3, p. 315.

3. 'St Catharine's Hill', p. 196.
4. *Liber Monesterii de Hyde*, Rolls Series, Introduction, p. lxxiii.
5. 'St Catharine's Hill', p. 197.
6. 'St Catharine's Hill', p. 249.
7. Houghton-on-Hill (Leicestershire), Little Bardfield (Essex) and Ringshall (Suffolk).
8. Archibald Gordon Macdonell (1895–1941), novelist, was born in Aberdeen. Other publications included *Lords and Masters*, *The Autobiography of a Cad*, *A Visit to America* and detective stories written under the pseudonym of Neil Gordon. He was killed in an air raid.

8   Oxford, 1926–8

1. Montague Rhodes James (1862–1936) was born at Goodnestone, in Kent, where his father was curate. Educated at Eton and Cambridge, where he became Director of the Fitzwilliam Museum (1893–1908), in 1908 he was elected Provost of King's, his old college, and from 1913 to 1915 he was Vice-Chancellor of Cambridge University. He became Provost of Eton in 1918. He was made an FBA 1903, and an OM in 1930. Between 1895 and 1932 he catalogued the manuscripts of every Cambridge College, as well as those of Eton, Lambeth and Westminster Abbey.
2. Michael Cox, *M.R. James: An Informal Portrait* (OUP, 1983).
3. Sir William Goodenough Hayter (born in 1906), diplomat, was Warden of New College, Oxford (1958–76). He was educated at Winchester and New College, where he was only one year junior to Christopher. He entered the Diplomatic Service in 1930, and served in Vienna (1931), Moscow (1934), China (1938) and Washington (1941). He joined the Foreign Office as Assistant Under-Secretary of State in 1948. He was a Trustee of the British Museum (1960–70) and was awarded the CMG in 1948 and the KCMG in 1953. He published a biography of Warden Spooner (1977) and an autobiography, *A Double Life* (1974).
4. Donald Atkinson, *The Birmingham Archaeological Society Report on the Excavations at Wroxeter (1923–27)* (OUP, 1942).
5. *Archaeologia Oxoniensis* (1892–5), p. 267. This short-lived journal only lasted for three years.
6. 'Beef and beer' was a quotation from a delightfully funny poem by A.P. Herbert called 'Bacon and Eggs', which had been used in a review entitled *King and Castle*, in which it was sung by the producer, Nigel Playfair. Christopher had seen it at the Lyric Theatre, Hammersmith, with his parents.
7. *Antiquaries Journal* VII (1927), pp. 147–184.
8. *Proceedings of the British Academy*, XXIX (1943).
9. *Proceedings of the British Academy*, XXIX (1943), published as a separate paper, 'Obituary of R.G. Collingwood', p. 7.

10. Humphrey Carpenter, *OUDS: A Centenary History of the Oxford University Dramatic Society* (OUP, 1985), p. 78.
11. Ibid.
12. Ibid., p. 105.
13. Rt. Hon. Sir Denys Burton Buckley, born in 1906, was the fourth son of the 1st Baron Wrenbury. Educated at Eton and Trinity College, Oxford, he was called to the Bar in 1928. He became Lord Justice of Appeal from 1970 to 1981. He was knighted in 1960.
14. Robert Peter Fleming (1907–71), writer and traveller, was the brother of Ian Fleming, the creator of the character James Bond. He was a special correspondent for *The Times*, and wrote a number of travel books. In 1935 he married the actress Celia Johnson.
15. Published by Oxfoird University Press in 1987.
16. Carpenter, *OUDS*, p. 54.
17. Ibid., p. 107, quoting from Osbert Lancaster's own autobiography, *With an Eye to the Future* (1967).
18. Sir John Betjeman (1906–84), poet and author, was educated at Marlborough and Magdalen College, Oxford, though he failed to get a degree. His numerous books include the famous verse autobiography, *Summoned by Bells* (1960). He married Penelope, the daughter of Field Marshal Lord Chetwode in 1933. He succeeded Cecil Day Lewis as Poet Laureate in 1972. He was awarded the CBE in 1960, and was knighted in 1969.
19. John Bailey Fernald (born in 1905), educated at Marlborough and Trinity College, Oxford. He taught at RADA from 1934 to 1940, and was its principal from 1950 to 1965.
20. Carpenter, *OUDS*, p. 106.

9 London, 1928–33

1. According to the *Archaeological Journal* I, p. 146; quoted in C.F.C. Hawkes and M.R. Hull, *Camulodunum, First Report on the Excavations at Colchester, 1930–39* (1947), p. 21.
2. Aileen Henderson was to marry Sir Cyril Fox, Director of the National Museum of Wales.
3. Jacquetta Hawkes, *A Quest of Love* (Chatto and Windus, 1980), p. 210.
4. Sally Green, *Prehistorian: A Biography of V. Gordon Childe* (Moonraker Press, 1981) pp. 75–6.
5. Sir Arthur John Evans (1851–1941), son of the numismatist, Sir John Evans, was educated at Harrow and Brasenose College, Oxford, where he received a first class degree in modern history in 1874. After travels in the Balkans (1876–82) he began collecting vases and coins from Italy and Sicily, and prehistoric seal-stones from Crete. He was Keeper of the Ashmolean Museum from 1884 to 1908. In 1894 he acquired a share of an estate near Knossos, and

he excavated there from 1899 till 1907. He published his findings in *The Palace of Minos at Knossos* (four volumes, 1921–35). He was made a Fellow of the Royal Society in 1901. A founder of the British Academy in 1902, and President of the British Association (1916–19), he was knighted in 1911.

6.   Sir George Macdonald (1862–1940), numismatist, classical scholar and archaeologist, was also a civil servant. He received a first class degree in Lit. Hum. at Balliol College, Oxford (1887), and was a lecturer in Greek at Glasgow University from 1892 till 1904. He was assistant secretary (1904–21) and then secretary (1922–8) of the Scottish education department. He catalogued the Greek and Roman coins in the Hunterian Collection, Glasgow, and was a leading authority on Roman Britain. He was made a Fellow of the British Academy in 1913 and was knighted in 1927.

7.   Charles W. Phillips, *My Life in Archaeology* (Alan Sutton, 1987), p. 68.

8.   Jacquetta Hawkes, *A Quest of Love*, p. 210.

9.   Ibid., p. 211.

10.   Ibid.

10   London, 1933–9

1.   Marie Charlotte Carmichael Stopes (1880–1958), who was trained as a botanist, opened the first birth-control clinic in London in 1921. She published a number of books including *Married Love* (1918), *Wise Parenthood* (1918) and *Contraception: Its Theory, History and Practice* (1923).

2.   Jacquetta Hawkes, *A Quest of Love*, pp. 211–12.

3.   Letter to the author, 12 September 1989.

4.   Sir Albert Charles Seward (1863–1941), botanist and geologist, was educated at Lancaster Grammar School and St John's College, Cambridge. Fellow and tutor of Emmanuel College (1899–1906), lecturer in botany (1890), and professor from 1906 to 1936, he became Vice-Chancellor of the University of Cambridge (1924–?) and Foreign Secretary (1934–41). He became a Fellow of the Royal Society in 1898, and was knighted in 1936. He was general editor of the *Cambridge Botanical Handbooks* series.

5.   *Proceedings of the Hampshire Field Club XIII, ii* (1936).

6.   Jacquetta Hawkes, *Man on Earth* (Cresset Press, 1954), p. 18.

7.   Jacquetta Hawkes, *A Quest of Love*, p. 213.

8.   *Proceedings of the Hampshire Field Club XIV, ii* (1939), p. 188.

9.   *Proceedings of the Hampshire Field Club XIV, iii* (1939), p. 29.

10.   Ibid., p. 339.

11.   Phillips, *My Life in Archaeology*, p. 66.

12.   In his autobiography, *My Life in Archaeology* (p. 76), Phillips says that the inquest was held on Monday 18 August. The date was in fact Monday 14.

INDEX

In this index, CH stands for Christopher Hawkes, CP for Charles Pascoe Hawkes (Christopher's father) and BM for the British Museum. Alphabetical arrangement is word-by-word. Page numbers in italics refer to illustrations.